Sonja Schüler (Ed.)

Exchange, Dialogue, New Divisions?

Freiburger Sozialanthropologische Studien
Fribourg Studies in Social Anthropology
Etudes d'Anthropologie Sociale de l'Université de Fribourg

Band 45

LIT

Exchange, Dialogue, New Divisions?

Ethnic Groups and Political Cultures in Eastern Europe

edited by

Sonja Schüler

LIT

Cover image: Graffiti on a transformer station in Berlin-Charlottenburg.
Copyright: Thorsten Schneider, vielbauch.de.

Bibliographic information published by the Deutsche Nationalbibliothek
The Deutsche Nationalbibliothek lists this publication in the Deutsche Nationalbibliografie; detailed bibliographic data are available on the Internet at http://dnb.d-nb.de.

ISBN 978-3-643-80209-5

A catalogue record for this book is available from the British Library

Klosbachstr. 107
CH-8032 Zürich
Tel. +41 (0) 44-251 75 05 Fax +41 (0) 44-251 75 06
E-Mail: zuerich@lit-verlag.ch http://www.lit-verlag.ch
Distribution:
In the UK: Global Book Marketing, e-mail: mo@centralbooks.com
In North America: International Specialized Book Services, e-mail: orders@isbs.com
In Germany: LIT Verlag Fresnostr. 2, D-48159 Münster
Tel. +49 (0) 2 51-620 32 22, Fax +49 (0) 2 51-922 60 99, e-mail: vertrieb@lit-verlag.de
In Austria: Medienlogistik Pichler-ÖBZ, e-mail: mlo@medien-logistik.at
e-books are available at www.litwebshop.de

Contents

Acknowledgements

My special thanks go to Professor Christian Giordano and Professor Francois Ruegg for writing the preface and the postface of this volume. I also wish to thank Sylvia Naumann for revising the articles and Tomislav Helebrant for the layout design.

Introduction:
The Pervasiveness of Public Mistrust in Eastern Europe

Christian Giordano

Prelude: the problem of widespread public mistrust

This volume comprises two different and apparently unrelated thematic lines. On the one hand, it discusses interethnic relations, i. e. the question of the recognition of so-called minorities, and on the other, the existence of specific political cultures based on extensive clientelistic and corruptive networks, which protest movements have been challenging, especially over the past three years, thus possibly strengthening the impression of a more or less radical change in the citizens' behaviour.

In this introduction I aim to show that these two thematic lines, though significantly distinct, are indeed comparable and to some extent analogous, albeit highly dissimilar in terms of structure and function.

In fact, the interethnic relations, notoriously precarious at all times, the informal networks and the social movements that are currently characterizing the political life of Eastern Europe's societies political life are rooted in the phenomenon of widespread public mistrust present in the social relations between groups and towards public institutions. Yet, we need to draw attention to a seemingly minor, but actually significant difference. In the first case, in fact, the mistrust is "between", whereas in the second case the mistrust is "towards", better yet "in". This will be a recurring theme in my introduction.

National States and structural public mistrust between titular nation and minorities

In Eastern Europe, modern national States were a rather belated acquisition since for the most part they were established only after the gradual and inexorable breakdown of the three multinational empires: namely, the Ottoman Empire in Southeast Europe, the Austro-Hungarian Empire and the Russian Empire. The legacy of these three empires to all the national States of this region was a remarkable ethnocultural diversity that spawned major problems.

When we talk about national States in terms of ethnocultural diversity, of interethnic relations, thus of the question of minorities, we have to consider how these political communities typical of modernity are capable of developing a *politics of recognition*.

Accordingly, we have to consider that in Europe there are two ideal models of national States: one of these may be defined the *German* model, whereas the other is often styled the *French* model.

The German model

The national state based on the German model is often described as *ethnic*, in this context mainly with a negative connotation. The use of this adjective expresses, rightly or not, the fact that the German model of national State is based on genealogy, i. e., on the shared origin of its citizens.

In my opinion, linking the German model with the notion of *Volk,* which not always has an ethnicizing overtone, would be more appropriate from an historical viewpoint. It is common knowledge that Gottfried Herder, together with the Grimm brothers, popularized the idea of *Volk* and its derivatives such as *Volkgeist*, *Volkseele* etc. Therefore, viewing Herder as the first zealous advocate of the ethnic variant of the concept of *Volk*, thus stigmatizing him as the inventor of *the most dangerous explosive of modern times* (Talmon 1967: 22, Finkielkraut 1987: 56 ff.), would be both misleading and somewhat incorrect. In fact, Herder believed that the genuine expressions of *Volkgeist*, thus also of the *Volk*, were principally the language and its literary evidence, such as fairy tales, poems, proverbs, phraseology etc. This author was rather a representative of Germanic *cultural patriotism* and one of the creators of the concept of *Kulturnation* (Pierré-Caps 1995: 79 ff.).

Undeniably, however, during the 19th century several intellectuals, including renowned politicians, artists, jurists, philosophers, historians and, last but not least, folklorists *(Volkskundler)* increasingly defined the culturalistic notion of *Volk* in ethnicizing terms. Descent and origin, no longer regarded symbolically but strictly physiologically, became the inherent characteristics of the *Volk*, by then understood to be *my people* (the German one, clearly). Yet, for a long time this ethnicization of the idea of people and nation in Germany would circulate solely in intellectual circles and would not have juridical consequences on the right to citizenship. As pointed up by historian Rudolf von Thadden, a definitive shift towards the institutional birth of a German ethnic nation only took place in 1913 with the introduction of a restrictive variant of the *jus sanguinis* principle in the *Reich*'s juridical system (Pierré-Caps 1995: 112, Gosewinkel 2001). Accordingly, what became known as the German model of the national State, determined by the formula *the people as an ethnic entity is the essence of fully entitled citizens,* became a reality only at this time (Grawert 1973: 166). Thus, descent and origin become the two fundamental criteria to define who belonged to the nation and who was excluded.

The escalation of nationalism over the next years led to a gradual ethnicization of the German model, which, via National Socialism and its infamous

Nuremberg Laws, inevitably led to the racialization of the notion of *Volk* and of the national State. After the abominable aberrations of the Nazi period, post-war Germany, though never a strictly ethnic State, renewed its links with the previous model of national State in which ethnicity overrides culture. To corroborate this last statement we need only mention the notion of citizenship in the Federal Republic at the time of the two Germanys (1945–1990). As constitutionalist Böckenförde aptly noted, the Federal Republic recognized one citizenship only, i.e. the German one, regardless of all the changes that occurred after 1945 with the division of Germany into two separate States (Böckenförde 1968: 424). Before the reunification, therefore, neither a specific citizenship of the BRD (Federal Republic of Germany) nor one of the DDR (German Democratic Republic) was recognized. Instead, only one German citizenship was juridically regarded as such, i. e., the expression of both the unchangeable ethnic unity of the *Volk* and of the continuity of the national State born in 1866.

The power of ethnicity in the German model was noticeable also after the Fall of the Berlin Wall and the country's subsequent reunification, especially by comparing the situation of the *Aussiedler*, re-immigrants of German origin that wished to settle permanently in Germany, to that of immigrants mainly from eastern Europe, Turkey and other African and Asian countries. In fact, by virtue of the ethnic notion of *Volk* and of the *jus sanguinis* principle, the *Aussiedler* could acquire German citizenship nearly automatically, i. e., by proving to have had even remote ancestors from Germany in the past centuries. Until the red-green coalition headed by Chancellor Gerhard Schröder passed new laws, nationality was granted solely on the grounds of descent, regardless of potential links to the German culture. The other immigrants, instead, despite their lengthy residency and even their birth in Germany, including their acculturation and integration process in German society, still had to go through complex *naturalization* procedures to be granted nationality.

To remedy this paradox, on June 23, 1999 the German parliament led by a red-green majority ratified a new law on nationality that in essence sought to partially de-ethnicize the German model. The reaction of the opposition's centre-left parties (CDU, CSU and FDP) and most of the population was very negative. Yet, despite their initial opposition, the centre-right governments that replaced the red-green coalition did not repeal the law. German citizenship is currently based on the idea of belonging to a cultural collectivity and not a genealogical one. Under this aspect, the German model has been somewhat Gallicized.

The French model

It has often been remarked that the French model of national State is based on the idea of *political nation*. According to this widespread opinion, the national State would be the outcome of a *political agreement* or, better yet, of a *pact*, i. e., a *contract* between its citizens. On the subject, Jules Renan has spoken, somewhat rhetorically, about the nation, thus about its political organization, as *un plebi-*

scite de tous les jours. This well-known formula highlights that the *political nation* of French derivation is an elective community, implying the existence of a *patrie ouverte* in which religious and/or ethnic-related differences are irrelevant (Dumont 1991: 25). Under this aspect, the national State represents the outcome of a declaredly voluntary act of each citizen that mirrors the viewpoint expressed by baron Charles de Montesquieu in his *pensées,* for whom *Je suis nécessairement homme ... et je ne suis français que par hazard* (Montesquieu 1949: 10).

Nowadays we are aware that the non-ethnic concept of nation that stemmed from the French Revolution was markedly modified and relativized rather soon, since it was merged with ideas that were not utterly devoid of ethnicizing tendencies. The French experts who have delved into this matter point up that, according to the 1791 and 1793 constitutions, any foreigner living in France could be granted citizenship without having to prove that he had acquired a French identity. In plain words, this meant that obtaining citizenship came before obtaining nationality, i. e., before acquiring that sum of cultural stances and social rules regarded as typically French (Weil 1988: 192, Lochak 1988: 78, Weil 2002, Weil and Hansen 1999). The sequence *citizenship-nationality* was all but reversed in the course of the 19th century. This fundamental shift occurred together with and was justified by the introduction of further ethnicizing concepts by which the prerequisites to belong to the elective nation and its State were increasingly defined by ethnocultural criteria, such as knowledge of the French language and the acquisition of the way of life specific to the country.

Though weakened, the original idea of *citoyenneté* was never totally set aside. In particular, the *subjective,* thus individualistic vision of the nation (Sundhaussen 1997: 79), by which any foreigner living in France can take advantage of the apparently trouble-free mechanism of assimilation to become a citizen, remained unchanged. According to this scenario, any ethnocultural differences, identities and boundaries are never inescapable and insurmountable. Each human being, if he deems it worthwhile, is intrinsically able to adapt and consequently become a full-fledged member of the *cité* wherein all relationships between individuals, as well as all relations between people and public institutions, are regulated by a social contract, which, in theory at least, has no room for ethnicity and culture.

Whether ethnic, cultural or national, for the French model any type of belonging is never definitively set; on the contrary, it can be modified through acculturation processes that lead to integration via the assimilation of those who are not regarded as foreigners. The assimilation process, which clearly entails significant changes in the individual's cultural identity, legitimizes welcoming the *xenos* to the bosom of the community and the national State.

This brief presentation already highlights that the French type of national State is associated with the concept of a more *open* society than other models of political-administrative organization. This fact is further substantiated by the actual, albeit incomplete application of the *jus soli* in the French juridical system.

On the other hand, we ought to bear in mind that the significant *openness* in welcoming foreigners is counterbalanced by the surprisingly weak appreciation for ethnocultural differences within its own national territory. Eugene Weber has aptly shown how the French national State's various governments between the end of the revolution and World War I set up an extensive assimilationist apparatus aimed at reducing ethnocultural differences between its various regions as much as possible (yet was unable to do so completely).

As expressed in the original title of this author's work, peasants with their local characteristics would have been transformed (and to some extent they were) into more or less standard French citizens (Weber 1976). Minorities in France, i. e., groups within the country that on the strength of real or purported ethnocultural criteria demand the recognition of their diversity and may voice claims to territorial autonomy (see Corsica and Brittany for example) are ignored or kept out of sight to this day. At best, they represent an awkward, though perforce acknowledged reality.

Moreover, the law known as *Loi Pasqua*, which reformed the renowned *code de la nationalité*, one of republican France's juridical institutions, came into force on January 1, 1993. Without delving into its legal technicalities, this law makes obtaining nationality more difficult especially for immigrants. Consequently, there is a creeping ethnicization that puts present-day France increasingly in contrast with the revolutionary ideal of *patrie ouverte*, thus also with the one of *political nation*. We can rightfully wonder whether France is undergoing a Germanization.

French model vs. German model: differences and similarities

European Nation-States have far too often been regarded as sheer geographical expressions. Though not completely off the mark, this approach is exceedingly reductive since it overlooks the fact that a nation's political-institutional architecture is also and foremost a social organization. In particular, as Rogers Brubaker aptly remarked, it disregards the fact that in the first place the national State is a political association of citizens to which the latter belong owing to specific attributed or acquired shared prerequisites (mainly cultural ones) (Brubaker 1992). Accordingly, not everyone can be fully entitled to belong to a given national State. Drawing on a well-known formula by Max Weber, we could say that as a rule a nation's political organization is *an association partially open to the outside* (Weber 1956: 26). Clearly enough, this limited openness towards the outside, namely towards the *foreigner*, i. e., most often the *culturally other*, implies creating institutional mechanisms of social selection to regulate belonging and foreignness. Citizenship and/or nationality are the fundamental instruments to indisputably determine who is fully entitled to belong to a national State and who is not. Therefore, citizenship and/or nationality are closely linked to practices of inclusion and exclusion.

If we focus on the practices of inclusion and exclusion towards the culturally different, we can observe an essential analogy, despite obvious dissimilarities, between the French and the German model with reference to the recognition of ethnocultural diversity.

Through the *subjective* and *individualistic* vision of belonging buttressed by the *jus soli* principle, the French version of the national State is grounded in the principle that a person's otherness may and ultimately should be wiped out. Once assimilation has occurred and been substantiated, the former alien is granted political citizenship, thus is welcomed into the national community. The German version of the national State, with its *objective, naturalizing* and *collective* concept of difference strengthened by the *jus sanguinis* doctrine, inevitably and unchangeably determines the alien's belonging to an ethno-national group that is clearly dissimilar to the *Volk*'s one. The alien is in principle denied the chance to obtain nationality, thus to become a full-fledged member of the German political community.

Yet, these apparently very dissimilar terms of exclusion and inclusion actually pursue the same goal, i.e., establishing, maintaining or at best restoring cultural and ethnic homogeneity on the entire national territory. In fact, a national State's territory that is not mono-cultural or mono-ethnic is perceived as an *anomaly* that needs to be modified somehow, if not indeed eradicated. For this reason, ever since their advent both the French and the German model have revealed a considerable incompatibility with pluriethnicity and multiculturalism, along with serious troubles in managing either one. This emerges very clearly in the problematic stance towards minorities and immigrants to whom the national State offers the alternative between assimilation and the supposed resulting passage from one identity to another (as in the French model), and the more or less permanent marginalization from the civic and political community (as in the German model).

The propensity for territorial homogeneity common to both in their own Nation-States stems from the fact that the prime movers of both models drew on the *Staatsnation* doctrine, a term much in use in the Germanic area, which, strangely enough, is of French origin (Pierré-Caps 1995). In this context, we need to highlight that this principle is based on the incisive formula *one nation, one State, one territory* (Altermatt 1996), i.e., on the nearly untouchable and indisputable axiom by which the area occupied by a nation must coincide with the state's territory. If the two models of Nation-States just described adhere to the above-mentioned postulate, then clearly the logical corollary is the achievement of ethnocultural homogeneity in their territory.

National States and ethnic minorities in Eastern Europe

The analysis in the previous paragraphs shows how two national State models tend to wipe out ethnocultural diversity within their territories. Despite the existence of measures established by the international community after World War I to protect minorities, in practice the relentless downfall of the multicultural empires (Ottoman, Austro-Hungarian and Russian) and the rise of the new national States led to politics of limitation, negation and even physical annihilation of groups that were culturally and ethnically different within the new political entities.

A reconstruction and analysis of modern East European history shows that during this period Nation-States constantly endeavoured to make their territories and societies increasingly homogeneous both culturally and ethnically.

In fact, the past two centuries in particular were characterized by ongoing efforts to turn each national territory into a gradually more homogenous one in terms of culture and ethnicity, especially in Eastern Europe where the *Staatsnation* principle was introduced much later than in Western Europe. These processes of "ethnocultural recomposition" aimed at making the Nation-States "ethnically pure" are achieved through a dreadful, ongoing and far from over series of boundary revisions, forced assimilations, banishments, targeted and planned immigrations, deportations, ethnic wars and cleansings, genocides, reinstatements and secessions.

A periodization of the various processes of 'ethnic separation' in which more or less all European *Staatsnationen* were involved during the past two centuries will display roughly four surges whose virulence would be fraught with consequences for the entire continent's layout.

The first surge struck the Balkans in particular soon after the creation of the first Nation-States in the 19th century. Vast contingents of population of Turkish origin or simply of Muslim religion were forced to leave the region. As administrators and civil servants of the Ottoman Empire, they did indeed represent the hated occupiers, but members of social strata that had nothing or little in common with the ruling class were involved in the expulsion process as well. During the great Crisis in the Orient, which led to the bloody Russian-Turkish war, from 1875 to 1878 alone a million and a half people were repatriated. At that time and for the area involved, it was an exceptional movement of people.

The second virulent phase took place between 1913 and 1925. It was characterized by the forced transfer of entire minoritarian ethnic groups, yet it was internationally recognized and guaranteed. In the diplomatic language of those days, it was euphemistically termed 'population exchange'. Some examples illustrate the 'homogenization' strategies through 'ethnic separation'. Substantial groups of Albanians from Kosovo and western Macedonia were transferred to Turkey at the end of the Balkan Wars (10. 8. 1913) mainly because of their religion. These in turn were substituted by Serbian, Montenegrin, Croatian and Slovenian people, especially after the creation of the Kingdom of Serbs, Croats and Slovenes, with the intention of 're-Slavizing' the region. The alleged 'population exchange' between Greece and Turkey was even more dramatic. It was decreed by the Treaty of Lausanne in 1923, which ratified a series of reciprocal expulsions and hasty repatriations caused by the Greek military catastrophe during the reckless campaign in Asia Minor. After the tremendous defeat, Greece was overrun by refugees from the coasts of western Anatolia plus the Greeks (as well as the Armenians) from the Black Sea area and the Caucasus who had been fleeing the new Bolshevik regime's repressions since 1917. A country with a population of 4,5 million thus faced the arrival of 1,3 million refugees. At the same time, the 'population exchange' provided for the departure of the 'inhabitants of Muslim religion', mostly Turks but also Albanians.

The third *ethnic homogenization* surge spanned the decade between 1940 and 1950 that was prevalently marked by the Nazi policy of annihilation, transfer and expulsion of entire ethnic groups or groups regarded as such and by Stalinist deportations and purges. Along with the holocaust of the so-called *transnational minorities*, namely Jews and Roma, there were massive population movements in all of Central and Eastern Europe that would considerably alter the ethnic map of this part of the continent. Eleven and a half million Germans were expelled from the *Ostgebiete*, while three million Poles, two million of which from the regions that were assigned to the Soviet Union after World War II, would settle in Silesia and in the southern part of eastern Prussia. As a result, Poland became an almost monoethnic country, quite consistent with the *Staatsnation* ideal. The treaties between Czechoslovakia and Hungary and between the latter and Yugoslavia, which likewise provided for reciprocal 'population exchanges', date back to the same period immediately after World War II.

Finally, Stalin consolidated his conquests in the western part of the Soviet Union through a policy of 'planned' and often imposed 'mobility'. On the one hand, this involved the deportation of populations considered 'accomplices of the enemy', thus 'traitors of the great patriotic war' (Latvians, Lithuanians, Estonians, etc.), to Siberia or central Asia. On the other hand, it involved substituting them with immigrants mainly of Slavic origin such as Russians, Belorussians and Ukrainians who were considered more 'reliable' (Conte and Giordano 1993: 28 ff.).

The fourth virulent phase of *ethnic homogenization*, which may be termed *the return to the national State,* is the wave of ethnic separations that devastated Central and Eastern Europe over the past fifteen years. It can be traced back to Socialist Bulgaria with its alleged *solution of the nationality issue*, namely with the expulsion and/or forced assimilation of the 'ethnic Turks' in the second half of the 1980s. The phase continued with the disintegration of the three countries born after World War I (Yugoslavia, Soviet Union and Czechoslovakia) via a multiethnic and multinational 'logic'. All the new and old States generated by this process are based on the *Staatsnation* principle. Thus, the war in Bosnia was fully in line with this tragic but centuries-old logic of homogenization. Given the historical antecedents, it would have been rather surprising if the war had not broken out, while the Dayton Agreement, despite obvious formal differences, is but a new version of the Treaty of Lausanne (1923) dissembling a project of *ethnic recomposition*. Present-day Bosnia, in fact, is a sham multicultural State since it is divided into two different ethno-political entities. On the one side is the *Muslim-Croat Federation* in which the two communities are territorially and socially separate, and on the other side is the *Republika Srpska* with its practically autonomous political life.

The war and the independence of Kosovo have notoriously led to a double *ethnic cleansing* in Kosovo. At first, the Serbs tried to annihilate or expel the ethnic Albanian population from the region. Then, when Slobodan Milosevic lost the war declared on him by NATO, a Kosovar State with a vast Albanian majority was created. At the same time, most of the ethnic Serb population was expelled. The entire process of the double ethnic cleansing was once again in accordance with the founding principle of European Nation-States: ethnic homogeneity.

The separation between Serbia and Montenegro had a similar ethnic connotation, though for once there was no violence involved. The *long-standing conjuncture* is not over yet! In any case, thanks to these homogenization policies in the name of the ideal of a monoethnic and monocultural national State, the multiculturality of many East European States has dwindled if not disappeared over the past two centuries.

National States, ethno-cultural groups and social mistrust in this volume's articles

Most of this volume's articles show that mistrust between the national States' various ethnic or cultural components, or between the national States that emerged after the collapse of Soviet hegemony in Eastern Europe, is still rife. The article by Ingrida Gečienė shows that in Lithuania, despite a more tolerant attitude towards other ethnocultural components, also in terms of policy-making, relations between the titular nation and the various minorities are still shaky even after the country's newly reacquired independence. Therefore, the traditional relations grounded in mistrust are still in place.

The contribution by Nino Chikovani makes clear how history texts, including schoolbooks, have always negated or underplayed the reality of the country's cultural diversity, although to some extent this situation is now being addressed. The case of the new schoolbooks highlights how they are based on the old textbooks' narratives. Though looking forward to changes, the various groups' trusts remains unsteady since the monoethnic ideal persists in historical discourses.

The historical approach of the article by Nino Pirtskhalava, essentially based on the case of the Jewish community and the one of German origin, reconstructs the past and by now minimal multiculturalism of Tbilisi, the capital of Georgia. In the name of cultural purity and of a purported ideal of homogeneity, these important religious and ethnic communities were systematically discriminated against and for the most part physically eliminated.

Nebi Bardhoshi's anthropological analysis based on a detailed and complex empirical field research along the border between Greece and Albania and between Albania, Macedonia and Kosovo, illustrates how in these regions with centuries of multicultural and ethnically mixed populations the national States have endeavoured to exhibit and legitimize their authority by constructing and protecting the ethnic minorities belonging to their titular nation but located beyond their borders. These strategies have reinforced boundaries and heightened the existent, thus traditional mistrust that characterizes relations between these national States of southeast Europe.

In her contribution, Caroline Hornstein Tomić explores the topic of migration in Croatia. The author shows that immigrants build an idealized vision of their belonging to their nation of origin. Yet, when they permanently return to their country, they realize they are not regarded as true Croatians, thus are not welcome. Returning migrants also experience problems of economic integration because they lack informal political-bureaucratic networks. This generates a feeling of mistrust and disappointment.

Magdalena Slavkova analyses the case of the Rudari, an ethnic minority group, transhumant or migrant especially between Bulgaria and Greece. Though identifying itself as Bulgarian, this group is facing significant problems with its recognition by this nation. In this case, too, there is a noticeable relationship of mistrust between titular nation and minority. There is also a difficult relationship between migrant or transhumant Rudari in Greece and the citizens of this national State. Ultimately, neither of these national States seems willing to make room for this group.

In his article, Sorin Gog examines the situation of a small ethno-religious minority in Romania: the Old Believers or Lipovans. His contribution illustrates how the secularizing efforts of the socialist national State failed to achieve the desired result. Nowadays this community is divided along religious lines, since one part still adheres to the old creed whereas the other has converted to Adventism. In any case, the secularization prognosticated by several modernist authors did not occur.

Political elites, citizens and public mistrust in East European States

Much in the same way as the subjects of the countless past dominations, i. e., of the previously mentioned multinational empires, or of the authoritarian regimes between the two World Wars and of the Soviet era, the ordinary citizen in present-day Eastern Europe perceives the political and bureaucratic system and the elites' power practices as extraneous and alien, for the most part shadily intertwined and above all inherently dishonest and corrupt. Yet, we need to underscore that in Eastern Europe there is a marked identification with the nation as an *imagined community,* but not with the State that should represent it. This is certainly the most significant paradox that characterizes Eastern Europe's societies.

In this region, therefore, there is a deep fracture between State and society. The political and administrative systems as well as the succession of elites in power have a chronic lack of legitimacy. This fracture and the citizens' consequent mistrust imply the existence of two divergent and hierarchic orders of norms, roles and institutions. In accordance with Max Weber's terminology

(Weber 1956: 1, 122 ff.), in these societies one can observe a marked discrepancy between the State's legality and the citizens' belief in its legitimacy as illustrated in the following diagram:

State norms and institutions	*Socio-cultural norms and institutions*
legal	partially illegal
illegitimate	legitimate

Thanks to this Weberian, thus interpretative perspective, the motivations and legitimations that Western observers too often discount as shady, irrational, backward or even uncivilized, come to light. In fact, the above diagram, which takes into due account the negative *longue durée* experiences, highlights the rationale, thus the sociocultural logic of specific behaviours that cannot be interpreted simply as phenomena linked to the postsocialist transition or transformation or to the purported current crisis in Europe's east.

Citizens develop no feeling of allegiance to the powers of their State (Weber 1956: 1, 122). Due to their lack of legitimacy, both the empires and the modern national States of Europe's east were and still are unable to factually implement that justice they ought to guarantee in their society. Social actors systematically and wittingly bypass laws, norms and decrees for the simple reason that they have no legitimacy despite being legal. In this type of society, which may be defined as one of public mistrust, the State is perceived as an undeniable reality, but also a corrupt one. However, it would be incorrect and ethnocentric to think that the citizens of East Europe have no virtuous representations of the State and of political power in which legality and legitimacy go hand in hand. These societies, therefore, do have an ideal model of legitimacy. The interesting point, though, is that the citizens reckon that this model has not been or cannot be realized in their own State. From their point of view, a fair and properly functioning State is a utopian fantasy due to corrupt politicians and bureaucrats, though every change kindles hopes of improvements that are consistently disappointed every single time.

The abuse of power, instead, is a constant because the state's legality is permanently exploited to the advantage of a succession of various elites and individuals at the helm of the State. For the average citizen, therefore, the abuse of power is not the exception but the rule.

The corollary of this constant abuse of power is that members of public mistrust societies in Eastern Europe have never been a passive body. In the past in particular, the Ottoman Empire had to face endemic forms of rebellion in several parts of the Balkans (Landsberger 1974: 1 ff.). The spread of social and political banditry of the famed Hajduks was even more significant (Hobsbawm 1972). These brigands' feats, often idealized, accurately illustrate the thesis of the illegitimacy of the state's institutions despite their formal legality.

Mentioning only behaviours of open protest or active resistance such as rebellion and banditry would be too limiting. East Europe presents several functional equivalents that reveal the lack of legitimacy of the State, its laws and politics in general. There is a vast array of implicit strategies based on social practices of infiltration that do not include behaviours of anti-state rebellion, but rather aim to weaken the state's structures and neutralize legal norms not regarded as legitimate. Under this aspect, typical examples are the various forms of clientelism and corruption as well as Mafia-like behaviours. These action strategies are characterized by a specific ambivalence since on the one hand the actors view public institutions and laws as illegitimate and on the other hand the State's order and the common good are exploited to the advantage of one's own interest and personal needs. A Western observer would ethnocentrically speak of citizens with a *double standard.*

Over the past twenty-five years, however, East Europe's societies have undergone major processes of social and cultural change. Citizens are no longer excluded from the State's activity and are familiar with civil society institutions. Yet, there has been no substantial increase in trust towards the public sphere. To this day, personalizing social relationships within the public sphere is still indispensable; cultivating personal relationships with whoever is in a position of power in the public sphere helps to avoid the snags and hurdles inherent to public institutions and the legal apparatus. For the average citizen, clientelist relationships between governors and governed are highly useful, thus of crucial importance. Yet, the governed view these relationships as something definitely disagreeable and unfair but also indispensable. The patron, therefore, is perceived as a *necessary exploiter.* Clientelist relationships within the political system are regarded as inevitable and invaluable so that the clients will strive to put them into effect and keep them in place at all costs. Accordingly, one can speak of a generalized patronage system that infiltrates all public structures. The average citizen firmly believes, and rightly so, that having *angels in paradise,* i. e., politicians and bureaucrats in positions of power who can satisfy their client's needs, is essential. As I was able to observe during my field researches in the Bulgarian Dobrudja in particular, politicians and bureaucrats are mobilized especially to obtain state or EU subsidies. They are called *those in Sofia*, but they could easily be *those in Warsaw, Budapest, Bucharest, Tirana, Belgrade, Skopje* etc., who are considered inept, arrogant, lazy and distant but at the same time useful and inevitable (Giordano 2009: 89 ff.). Instead of dying out, clientelism in East Europe is currently updating itself since it is increasingly based on the systematic exchange of public resources for private use and on a methodical vote-grabbing, thanks also to the exploitation of civil society institutions such as associations, trade unions, personalized political parties, NGOs etc. A modern mass clientelism, therefore, is becoming a widespread feature. This implies that relations between the average citizen and the State have undergone a process of rationalization, as defined by Weber (Weber 1956: 559 ff.), but in essence have not improved. The average citizen is now aware that the State, its institutions and the legal system provide great opportunities, which, thanks to specific relationships with politicians and bureaucrats, can be turned to one's personal advantage. And though the State is regarded as necessary and important, mistrust, i. e., a *mental reservation*, is still in place.

Politics, public mistrust and informal behaviour in this volume's articles
Though not always conspicuous, the theme of public mistrust is the *leitmotiv* of this book's last two contributions. The article by Antoinette Primatarova implicitly questions how Bulgaria can develop a political culture founded on public trust and based on Western European values and strategies that would neutralize and supersede the currently widespread public mistrust. The strategies illustrated by the author are definitely significant, yet rather alien for the time being, as Sonja Schüler points up in her article. Drawing on a considerable amount of hard ethnographic data, this last author highlights the various dimensions of public mistrust, showing how differentiated and above all widespread this phenomenon is among all strata of Bulgaria's population. This aspect casts further doubts on the legitimacy of the democratically elected political class as well as on the structure and roles of the bureaucratic apparatus.

References

Altermatt, Urs 1996: Das Fanal von Sarajevo. Ethnonationalismus in Europa. Zürich: Verlag NZZ.
Böckenförde, Ernst-Wolfgang 1968: Die Teilung Deutschland und die deutsche Staatsangehörigkeit. In: Hans Barion, Ernst-Wolfgang Böckenförde, Ernst Forsthoff, Werner Weber (eds.): Epirhosis. Festgabe für Karl Schmitt. Berlin: Duncker und Humblot, 423–464.
Brubaker, Rogers 1992: Citizenship and Nationhood in France and Germany. Cambridge Mass.: Harvard University Press.
Conte, Edouard and Christian Giordano 1995: Sentiers de la ruralité perdue. In: Etudes Rurales, 138–140: 11–33.
Dumont, Louis 1991: L'idéologie allemande. France-Allemagne et retour. Paris: Gallimard.
Finkielkraut, Alain 1987: La défaite de la pensée. Paris: Gallimard.
Giordano, Christian 2009: Sozioökonomische Prosperität und privates Vertrauen. Zur verblüffenden Karriere kapitalistischer Grossunternehmer im bulgarischen Agrarsektor. Das Fallbeispiel Dobrudscha. In: Wilfried Heller and Josef Sallanz (eds.): Die Dobrudscha. Ein neuer Grenzraum der Europäischen Union: Sozioökonomische, ethnische politisch-geographische und ökologische Probleme. München, Berlin: Verlag Otto Sagner, 89–105.

Gosewinkel, Dieter 2001: Einbürgern und Ausschließen. Die Nationalisierung der Statsangehörigkeit vom Deutschen Bund bis zur Bundesrepublik Deutschland. Göttingen: Vandenhoek & Ruprecht.

Grawert, Rolf 1973: Staat und Staatsangehörigkeit. Verfassungsgeschichtliche Untersuchung zur Entstehung der Staatsangehörigkeit. Berlin: Duncker und Humblot.

Hobsbawm, Eric J. 1972: Bandits. London: Pelican.

Landsberger, Henry A. (ed.) 1974: Rural Protest: Peasant Movements and Social Change. London, Basingstoke: Macmillan.

Lochak, Danièle 1988: Etrangers et citoyens au regard du droit. In: Cathérine Withol de Wenden (ed.): La citoyenneté. Paris: Edilig-Fondation Diderot.

Montesquieu, Charles-Louis de Secondat, baron de La Brède et de (1949): Mes pensées. In: Oeuvres complètes. Paris: Bibliothèque de la Pléiade, Vol. 1, 975–1574.

Pierré-Caps, Stéphane 1995: La multination. L'avenir des minorités en Europe centrale et orientale. Paris: Odile Jacob.

Sundhaussen, Holm 1997: Nation und Nationalstaat auf dem Balkan. Konzepte, Konsequenzen im 19. und 20. Jahrhundert. In: Jürgen Elvert (ed.): Der Balkan. Eine Krisenregion in Geschichte und Gegenwart. Stuttgart: Franz Steiner Verlag, 77–90.

Talmon, Jacob Laib 1967: Destin d'Israël. Paris: Calmann-Lévi.

Weber, Eugen 1976: Peasants into Frenchmen: The Modernization of Rural France, 1870–1914. Stanford Ca.: Stanford University Press.

Weber, Max 1956: Wirtschaft und Gesellschaft. Grundriss der verstehenden Soziologie. Tübingen: J. C. B. Mohr, Paul Siebeck.

Weil, Patrick 1988: La politique française d'immigration (entre 1974 et 1986) et la citoyenneté. In: Cathérine Withol de Wenden (ed.): La citoyenneté. Paris: Eidilig-Fondation Diderot, 187–200.

Weil, Patrick 2002: Qu'est-ce qu'un français? Histoire de la nationalité française depuis la Révolution. Paris: Grasset.

Weil, Patrick and Randall Hansen (eds.) 1999: Nationalité et citoyenneté en Europe. Paris: La Découverte.

The Situation of Ethnic Minorities in Lithuania from the Perspective of Their Self-Perception

Ingrida Gečienė

Introduction

Despite the fact that Lithuania has been a multinational state for centuries and has a long-lasting tradition of peaceful cohabitation between different ethnic minorities, the events of World War II, as well as the Nazi and Soviet occupations of Lithuania, left a dramatic mark on the history of the country and on its ethnic minorities. Lithuanians, Jews, Poles and people of many other nationalities fell victim to chauvinism, xenophobia, political mistakes and crimes against humanity. The turbulent times in Lithuania before and after regaining independence in 1990 again highly affected the situation of ethnic minorities.

Researches on different ethnic groups revealed that non-titular nationalities in Lithuania and countries of similar historical context "have encountered a double adaptation stress: adaptation to market economy and adaptation to new ethno politics and minority status" (Kasatkina 2002: 22). Social adaptation in this context is understood as "a process of the combination of an individual's aspirations and expectations with his/her possibilities and expectations, and the requirements of society" (Kasatkina 2003: 68). In this aspect, social adaptation encompasses both "external" social conditions and "internal" individual skills to participate in the surrounding society. External conditions can involve various aspects from geopolitical environment, political regime, economic situation and level of social security, etc. This paper will rather focus on one aspect – ethnic politics, as all other aspects are similar for all ethnic groups in Lithuania and differences lie more in the reaction of these groups towards changes of these aspects (for example, towards economic crises, etc.). Therefore ethnic politics is one of most distinguishing external conditions, which can either be favourable for ethnic minorities or create obstacles for better adaptation.

The internal possibilities of integration in a society are related to different kinds of resources that form the social position or status of a person and the subjective perception of his/her social status as satisfactory or not. As Kasatkina revealed, "the satisfactory economic situation of individuals does not tell everything about their perception of social life", as it can be influenced by the subjective evaluation of one's own social position and the perception of its change as well as "perception may be greatly influenced by symbolic interaction and lack of recognition" (Kasatkina 2003: 16).

The aim of this paper is to reveal the contemporary situation of ethnic minorities through their own understanding and examine the main factors that influence this perception. For reaching this goal three main tasks are formulated: 1) to analyse how the ethnic politics helps or hinders the social adaptation of ethnic minorities in Lithuania; 2) to indicate what kind of problems ethnic minorities face during the process of social adaptation; 3) to examine the situation of ethnic groups from the perspective of their self-perception and the main factors that influence this perception. The main hypothesis, based on a social adaptation theoretical approach, is that the different attitudes of ethnic groups towards their social situation in Lithuania is mainly determined by ethnic identity, social status and the coherence of the social adaptation process.

The latest results from the quantitative survey of the Lithuanian population in 2012 will serve as an empirical basis for the analysis. The representative survey was conducted by the Lithuanian-British market research and public opinion company Baltic Surveys Ltd. for the scientific research project "Representations of Democratisation Process in Lithuania in Individual Consciousness", which was funded by a grant (No. SIN-12012) from the Research Council of Lithuania.

According to the 2011 Lithuanian Population Census, in 2011 people of 154 ethnicities lived in Lithuania: 84.2 % Lithuanians, 6.6 % Poles, 5.8 % Russians, 3.4 % – other (1.2 % Belarusians, 0.5 % Ukrainians), approximately 0.1 % Jews, Germans, Romany, and Latvians, significantly fewer Armenians, Azerbaijani, Moldovans, Georgians, Estonians, Karaites (Lithuanian 2011 Population Census in Brief, 2012, 20–21). The distribution of the respondents in the 2012 survey corresponds to the data from the Census. However, it must be admitted that the percentage of ethnic minority respondents in the total number of respondents (N=1008) does not constitute a sufficient number of respondents to draw conclusions about the whole population of ethnic minorities. Therefore the analysis provided in this paper is indicative for tendencies in the opinions of ethnic minorities rather than forming a strict representation of these opinions.

The biggest advantage of this research lies in the possibility to compare Lithuanians and the ethnic minorities regarding their evaluation of their previous, current and future political, economic and social situation, their opinion on ethnic tolerance and the protection of human rights, and also their perception of their social situation and quality of life. The majority of other researches in Lithuania on ethnic minorities usually includes only ethnic minorities respondents and informants into their research methodology.

In the first part of this paper, a brief overview of ethnic politics is provided for examination of the opportunities and obstacles for ethnic minorities for their better adaptation to new societal contexts. In the second part the previous results of ethnic minority studies in Lithuania are presented in order to identify the main problems that ethnic minorities face during the period after the country's regaining of independence. This part partly shows the context, which potentially can have influence on the perceptions of ethnic minorities, expressed in the newest research, and in this way complements the finding of this research. In the third part of the paper, the data from the 2012 survey are analysed in order to investigate the subjective perception of Lithuanians and ethnic minorities of their current social situation.

I Ethnic politics after regaining independence

According to analysts, ethnic policy in Lithuania is quite favourable for ethnic minorities in comparison to that of other Baltic countries (Best 2013: 49, Andrlik 2009: 11, Fearon and Laitin 2006: 16). According to the 1989 Law on Citizenship, almost all permanent residents were guaranteed the right to gain Lithuanian citizenship irrespective of their nationality, duration of residence in the country or knowledge of the state language (Kasatkina and Beresneviciute 2010: 11). The New Law on Citizenship from December 1991 made regulations for naturalization somewhat stricter, similar to the regulations of Latvia and Estonia. However, according to Lottman, in reality the law was interpreted in a much milder manner, which in fact reflected the positive experience with the integration of non-Lithuanian ethnic minorities on the basis of inclusive elements of the previous law (Lottman 2008: 510).

The 1992 Constitution of the Republic of Lithuania prohibits any discrimination or granting any privileges on the basis of ethnic background, race, sex, language, origin, social status, region, conviction or opinion (article 29). The Constitution guarantees the fundamental rights and political, economic and social freedom (among them a freedom to vote and form political parties and other organizations, articles 34–36) for all citizens independently of their nationality. Besides, there are some articles directly addressed to national minorities: "Citizens who belong to ethnic communities shall have the right to foster their language, culture, and customs" (article 37); "Ethnic communities of citizens shall independently administer the affairs of their ethnic culture, education, organisation, charity, and mutual assistance." Article 45 of the Constitution also binds the state to support ethnic communities, however, it does not indicate to what extent. Thus, this article is rather laconic and other laws elaborate the role of the state more explicitly.

The Law on Equal Treatment was adopted in 2003 in order to ensure the implementation of the provisions of Article 29 of the Constitution enshrining the antidiscrimination of persons. However, the implementation of the law still remains difficult in practice, as "the Equal Treatment Ombudsperson [...] still receives few cases alleging discrimination, as knowledge of and trust in the institution among minority communities reportedly is still limited" (Advisory Committee on the Framework Convention for the Protection of National Minorities 2014: 6).

The 1989 Lithuanian Law on Ethnic Minorities became the very first law of this type in the whole of the former Eastern Bloc. The Law did not formally define a minority and each individual's nationality was defined by their own subjective choice (Kasatkina et all 2006: 352). The Law contained provision regarding the right to equal protection, to obtain aid from the state to develop their culture and education, to establish own media, to freedom of religion, to establish ethnic cultural organisations and to contact persons with the same ethnical background abroad, to equal political representation and to hold any post in institutions, organisations and enterprises. It is important to mention, that articles 4 and 5 guaranteed the use of the language spoken by a minority in addition to the Lithuanian language in offices and organisations located in areas serving substantial numbers of a minority and the use of bilingual signs in the same areas. In these aspects the Law on Ethnic Minorities of 1989 was in conflict with the Law on the State Language, which states that "in all institutions, offices, undertakings and organisations operating on Lithuanian territory, the language used will be the State language and requires having all public signs written exclusively in Lithuanian with the exception of the use of minority languages only for the names and signs of organisations representing national minorities". As a result the Law on National Minorities was terminated in 2010 manly because of "a need to replace the outdated and inconsistent terminology and to remove the inconsistency of the legal code" (Andrlik 2009: 11).

In 2013 an attempt was made to improve the Law on Ethnic Minorities by providing the right for ethnic minorities to use their ethnic language in public space (for services in municipalities, topical information, names of streets and other public signs in territories where these minorities form more than 25 % of the concrete municipality population). However, such improvements and some other statements of the Law faced harsh criticism from Lithuanian patriotic organisations, as well as from smaller ethnic minorities as being too favourable only for the most numerous ethnic minorities, because only Polish and Russian minorities can match the proposed requirements on the concentration of ethnic minorities in some regions (Vasilevich 2013: 12). For this reason, the project of the improved Law on Ethnic Minorities is still under discussion in the Lithuanian Parliament (Seimas). The lack of a specific Law on Ethnic Minorities, according to Vasilevich, results in the situation that "in recent years the minority issues in Lithuania have become a subject of increasing politicisation" (Vasilevich 2013: 11).

Lithuania has signed and ratified various international agreements directed towards the protection of ethnic minorities, among them: The United Nations Universal Declaration of Human Rights; The United Nations International Covenant on Civil and Political Rights; The United Nations International Convention on the Elimination of All Forms of Racial Discrimination; The Council of Europe Convention for the Protection of Human Rights and Fundamental Freedoms; The Council of Europe Framework Convention for the Protection of National Minorities. However, the European Charter for Regional or Minority Languages has not been ratified yet, again mainly because of the contradiction regarding the provision of the Law on the State Language. Therefore, according to Vasilevich, the Charter provides "no protection for minority languages in Lithuania, leaving the national legislator to determine whether the country's domestic legislation should comply with the provisions of the Charter" (Vasilevich 2013: 8).

Before 2010 the Department of National Minorities and Lithuanians Living Abroad was responsible for the planning and implementation of state policy towards national minorities. However, after the reorganization of this department its functions were transferred to the Ministry of Culture, the Ministry of Education and Science and the Ministry of Foreign Affairs. The responsibility for the minority policy was transmitted towards the National Minorities Affairs Division of the Ministry of Culture. However, this change worsened the minority rights protection, as there were only 5 persons in the department now, instead of 15 persons in the previous department and as a result the scope of activities was insufficient, particularly at an international level. In 2014 the decision was made to re-establish the Department of Ethnic Minorities under the Government. This new department is expected to start its activities in mid-2015. It is expected that this department will keep efficient relations with the ethnic minority communities, cooperate with international institutions and that it will contribute to the analysis and formation of minority politics, as states government press release (delfi.lt 2014).

Another institution of ethnic minorities – The Council of Ethnic Minorities – represents 18 ethnic communities. Its members participate in the legislative process, various commissions and work groups, they act as consultants in decision making in strategic issues concerning the preservation of ethnic minority identity and the development of minority culture, monitor the implementation of international law and obligations on national minority issues, propose principles and priorities of support for ethnic minority organisations and ethnic minority target programmes.

There are no granted sets for minorities in the Parliament (Seimas), however both largest minorities – Poles and Russians – established minority parties at an early stage of the development of the party system. In 1992 the Polish minority started in the elections as Movement of Lithuania's Poles. In 1994 it was transformed to a new party, namely Electoral Action of Poles in Lithuania (EAPL). The Russians also have got a political party which has started in the elections – Lithuanian Russian Union (LRU) and later Russian Alliance (RA), a more regional party, which has its electorate in the Lithuanian port town Klaipeda. These parties use to make different coalitions in parliamentary, municipal and European Parliamentary elections, "although these parties representing major minorities in Lithuania have always had a different ideological orientation" (Frejute-Rakauskiene 2011: 21). Sometimes, as in the case of municipal elections, they participate by presenting separate lists of candidates as well as by proposing their candidates in the formed coalition. The EAPL party achieved the best results in the last parliamentary elections in 2012 when it got 8 seats and was involved in the ruling coalition.

There are about 300 NGOs founded by ethnic minorities in Lithuania. A wide spectrum of their cultural, educational and social projects receives state funding every year. Ethnic minorities can get news and information in their native languages: "more than 20 newspapers and magazines are published in Russian; and the Polish, Belorussian, German, Jewish, Tartar and Greek national minorities have their own publications" (Analytical Report PHARE RAXEN_CC Minority education 2004: 20). A number of periodical publications are printed in Russian, Polish and Yiddish. The Lithuanian National radio and television broadcast daily and weekly news and cultural programmes in Russian, Belarussian, Polish, Yiddish and Ukrainian.

It remains true, however, that the biggest problems for ethnic minorities occur in the area of education. In Lithuania, children of ethnic minorities get elementary, basic and secondary education at schools with their mother tongue as the language of instruction. Students originating from national minorities also have the possibility to learn their native language at schools where the language of instruction is Lithuanian. However, Lithuanian schools are not ready to accept pupils not knowing or only knowing poor Lithuanian, since in such cases teachers would need to provide bilingual instruction and would be forced to devote more time to linguistic difficulties during classes. There is a need "to develop and implement a more effective system of bilingual instruction that could satisfy the various needs of language learning which minority pupils have" (Analytical Report PHARE RAXEN_CC Minority education 2004: 7).

Universities and colleges in Lithuania train linguists and teachers of ethnic minority languages, however, students of ethnic minorities receive their training in other professions at tertiary level largely in the state language. Therefore, there is a need to ensure equal opportunity for all pupils to study at the Lithuanian institutions of higher education. In this regard, "it is important to develop the level of teaching of Lithuanian in the minority schools and to organise the final Lithuanian language examination for pupils leaving general education schools according to the same programme" (Analytical Report PHARE RAXEN_CC Minority education 2004: 13). Actually, for this reason, attempts were made in a new amendment of the Law of Education in 2011 to create more favourable conditions for mastering the Lithuanian language by increasing the number of subjects taught in Lithuanian in schools for ethnic minorities. Additionally, graduates from minority language schools have to take the same Lithuanian language exam as students from Lithuanian language schools. Despite the benefits these measures brought in providing better preparation for entry competitions to higher educational institutions and for participation in the public sphere, these amendments "sparked a number of protests from the Polish speaking population" (Freedom House Report 2012). Knut Vollebaek, the National Minorities High Commissioner for the Organisation for Security and Co-operation in Europe (OSCE) noted that "the requirements of the Law did not violate EU norms or standards", but, following his recommendation "the government established an eight-year transition period for the language examination, during which minority students will receive preferential grading" (Bureau of Democracy, Human Rights and Labour Report 2012: 21).

Therefore, and despite the fact that Lithuanian ethnic policy is quite favourable in comparison to that of other countries in the region, there is still a need for further improvement of the political protection of ethnic minority rights and for more attempts to develop effective educational policies for ethnic minorities to ensure equal opportunity to enter higher educational institutions.

II Main problems and aspects of discrimination faced by ethnic minorities during the last two decades

According to the findings of previous research, Lithuanian ethnic minorities have experienced difficult changes in the perception of their status in the Lithuanian society during the last two decades. First of all, according to the results of an investigation in the adaptation context and process of Lithuanian ethnic groups in the year 2000, the majority of Lithuanian nationality respondents believes that they have risen in the social hierarchy, and in the case of Russian nationality respondents, that they have descended, although a comparison of family income does not indicate that these ethnic groups are essentially different in this respect. Researchers assume, that "for this feeling, symbolic aspects of social interaction are more important than an objective material differentiation". The transition of the Russian ethnic group from a majority to a minority status had a major influence on this perception, and "the political dimension is not really important: despite the Russians 'social feeling' being worse than that of others, they do not speak about violations of rights more than others" (Kasatkina 2002: 18).

Tadas Leoncikas reveals a decline in political loyalty between some ethnic groups: while in 1990, according to the European Values Study survey, 67 % of Russian nationality respondents in time of war would go to defend their country, in 1999 this figure dropped to 38.3 %; among Lithuanians this figure also decreased from 60.8 % to 48.4 %, among Polish nationality respondents it increased slightly from 53.8 % to 60 %, and among other nationalities it decreased from 70.5 % to 50 % (Leoncikas 2000: 426). Other studies show that reluctance to fight for one's homeland is characteristic for those who are most unhappy with their life and are pessimistic about the future (Ester et al. 1997: 189).

Growing intolerance for certain ethnic minorities, especially for Jews, Chinese, Chechens and the Roma (Leoncikas 2007: 104, Vildaite and Zibas 2010: 125) can also be noticed. This circumstance is peculiar, because, due to the small number of people comprising these ethnic minorities, it is unlikely that the majority of the Lithuanian population has experienced a real relationship with them, so this intolerance is not mainly related to ethnic minority identity, but to the prevailing ethnic stereotypes (Leoncikas 2000: 422, Leoncikas 2007: 104). According to a media survey, the following stereotypes are supported in the mass media: Roma, for example, are often described as criminals, they are presented as asocial and as a marginal group (Beresneviciute and Nausediene

1999), in the same way that Chechens in 2005–2007 and Georgians in 2011–2012 were associated with criminal activity and their illegal presence in the country was emphasised (Frejute-Rakauskiene 2012: 87). Such a negative presentation of these ethnic minorities in the mass media may partially affect the perception that the Lithuanian population has towards these groups (Tereskinas 2001: 8, Frejute-Rakauskiene 2012: 90).

While the socio-economic inequalities between ethnic groups are not very large, studies reveal certain social differences between these groups: some ethnic minorities (Poles and especially Roma) have a lower level of education and thus their unemployment rate is higher (Kasatkina and Beresneviciute 2010: 12). The research study on the Lithuanian ethnic groups' adaptation context and process in the year 2000 shows a perception of ethnic discrimination characteristics in the case of job searches. Respondents from ethnic minorities stated that it is easier for Lithuanians to find a job or to get a good one. The researchers also point out that "it does not mean clear ethnic segregation in employment, it may also mean that failures of the social causes are treated as interethnic relations", but in any case, "it shows the importance of subjective ethnicity". A general social sense of security has an impact on social self-awareness and about one-fifth of Russian and Polish nationality respondents indicate that they feel a threat for their family members losing jobs, in comparison to 7 % of Lithuanian nationality respondents (Kasatkina 2002: 19). This is also related to Lithuanian origin and language knowledge. According to Kristina Sliavaite, ethnic minorities emphasise that Lithuanian roots and Lithuanian origin ensure favourable conditions for Lithuanians to find employment or to compete successfully in the labour market (Sliavaite 2013: 117). These provisions reveal a "feeling of vulnerability and insecurity, an unequal relationship with the ethnic majority (Lithuanians)" (Sliavaite 2013: 121). For this reason, mono-ethnic segments can be observed in the labour market: "nearly half of the Russian and the Polish respondents (44–45%) maintain that they work in an ethnically homogenous environment" (Kasatkina and Beresneviciute 2010: 14).

Vida Beresneviciute in her study concludes that ethnic minorities participate less in the public sector than the ethnic majority (Beresneviciute 2005: 114). Natalija Kasatkina and Vida Beresneviciute have also shown that ethnic minorities are less involved in political parties or the government than the ethnic majority. This is due to the fact that the society is heavily dominated by one ethnic group despite the preconditions created in favour of equal political participation, and the public sector is inclined to adopt and to implement a national capability offered by the advantage of the majority group (Kasatkina and Beresneviciute 2010: 25). This is primarily connected with speaking the state language, which is required in order to work in the public sector (Kasatkina 2002: 19; Kasatkina and Beresneviciute 2010: 13).

To sum it up, the situation was described by a statement from a report on human rights in Lithuania, written by the Bureau of Democracy, Human Rights and Labour (2012) stating that "the law prohibits discrimination against ethnic or national minorities, but intolerance and societal discrimination persisted" (Bureau of Democracy, Human Rights, and Labour 2012: 19). The aspects of discrimination and the subjective perception of a decreased social status which have been identified show a link between the ethnic peculiarities of the process of adaptation and the social stratification analysis. As Kasatkina and Beresneviciute argue, "a correlation between ethnicity and socio-economic outcomes can be observed" (Kasatkina and Beresneviciute 2010: 14). On the one hand, members of the same ethnic group differ in perceiving their status and its change, but on the other hand, the subjective perception of the worsening of one's own social situation correlates to marginality. Thus, even if the success of the adaptation and the marginalization of the provisions are related, it is difficult to talk about a one-way causal relationship: "those who are higher in a social hierarchy have less distrust" and have greater satisfaction with the current situation (Kasatkina 2002: 20). Accordingly, it can be assumed that the evaluation of the situation of ethnic minorities regarding their own understanding is affected not only by the change of the ethnic minority status in society, but also by the social, economic and cultural aspects of the adaptation of these minority groups during the independence period in Lithuania.

III The perception of the current situation by different ethnic groups

The latest quantitative research in 2012 opened up an investigation into the comparative evaluation made by Lithuanians and by ethnic minorities of the previous, current and future political, economic and social situations, their opinion on ethnic tolerance and the protection of human rights, as well as their perception of their social situation and life quality. The comparison aims at revealing the different attitudes of ethnic groups towards their social situation in Lithuania, which can be explained by ethnic identity, their social status and the coherence of their social adaptation process. Three main ethnic groups have been selected for the analysis: Lithuanians, Poles and Russians. Other ethnic minorities had such a small representation in the survey that they have been excluded from deeper analysis.

Demographic characteristics and the subjective evaluation of social status

The demographic characteristics of the respondents are crucial for the deeper analysis of the perception of the current situation of ethnic minorities. The following shows the profile of the three main ethnic groups in this survey:

- Lithuanians: younger (only 26 % are over 60, 23.6 % are pensioners), better educated (25 % with higher education), among them there are fewer workers (27.2 %) and more specialists (20.6 %) and accordingly more persons (49.3 %) with higher than minimal monthly income (about 200 EUR) for each family member.

- Poles: older (40 % are over 60, 36.7 % pensioners), less educated (22 % have no secondary education and the rest have only secondary or lower professional education), more workers (38.3 %) and fewer specialists (6.7 %), a smaller income for each family member (35 % have less than the minimal salary; 33.3 % have more);
- Russians: older (40 % are older than 60, 30.2 % pensioners), well educated (30 % have high professional education, 16.3 % – higher university education), more workers (37.2 %), but also a higher number of specialists (11.6 %) and even managers (heads, directors, etc.) (4.7 %); accordingly, one group (41.9 %) has less than the minimal monthly salary for each family member, and the other group (26.9 %) has more.

In order to measure the subjective perception of social status the question "To which social group (class) do you assign yourself – lower, middle, or upper?" was given (see Figure 1).

Lithuanians and Poles are quite similar in their subjective evaluations of their social status, however, no Poles declare that they belong to the upper social group. Russians evaluate their social status as significantly worse, despite the fact that their demographic characteristics are quite similar to those of the Poles; and the Russian minority even includes more educated people than the Polish minority. In addition, Russians evaluate their material situation as similar to that of the Lithuanians (see Table 1). This can be partially explained by a different social adaptation process after the regaining of independence in Lithuania in 1990. Russians drifted from being a nationality with major symbolic status during the Soviet times to becoming an ethnic minority; in addition, the Russian language was gradually disappearing from public space. Such a negative evaluation of the status brings some researchers to the conclusion, that "social status and the issue of recognition rather than formal political rights are a barrier to the successful adaptation of the Russians" (Kasatkina 2003: 20).

The subjective assessment of the level of material well-being in Figure 2 shows that differences of assessment between different ethnic groups are minimal and actually remain within the interval of statistical error. Only Poles, similarly to their subjective evaluation of social status, did not declare their material well-being as good, corresponding to the revenue declared for each family member. This can be partially explained by the persistent problem of their level of education being lower than that of other ethnic groups. The Polish minority significantly underperforms in relation to the national average in terms of educational attainment, partly because of having an insufficient knowledge of the Lithuanian language to enter higher education institutions, and also because of the fact that "a considerable proportion of the Polish population lives in rural areas where educational attainment rates, particularly at the higher education level, are significantly lower than average compared to urban areas" (Kasatkina and Beresneviciute 2010: 12).

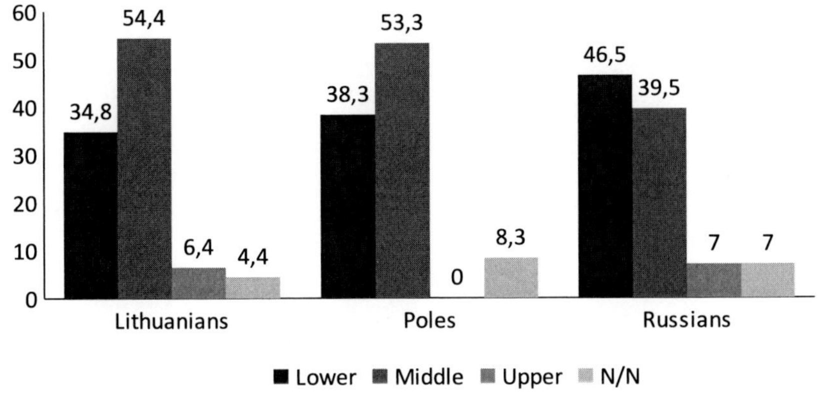

Figure 1. Subjective evaluation of social status (per cent)

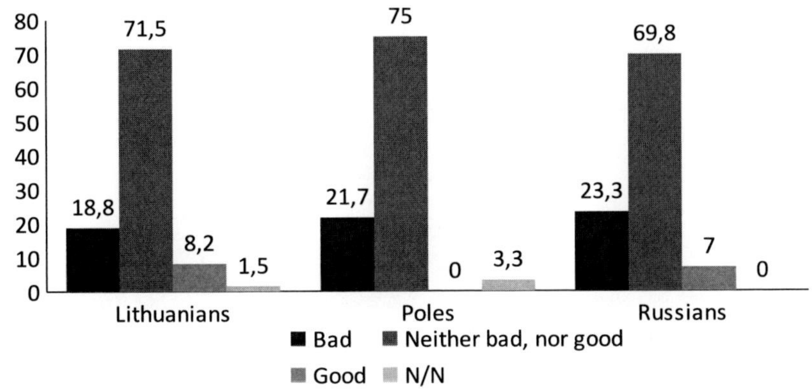

Figure 2. The subjective assessment of the level of material well-being (per cent)

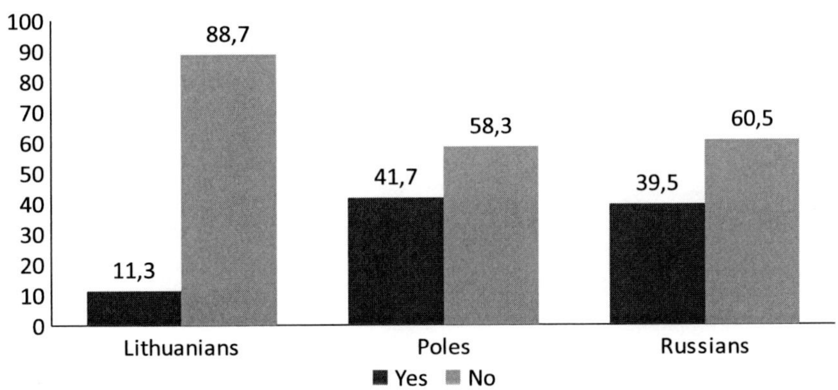

Figure 3. Perception of discrimination based on language (per cent)

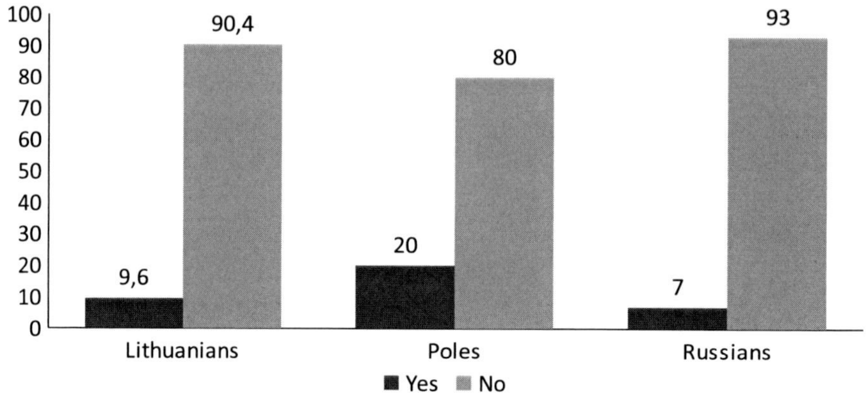

Figure 4. Perception of discrimination based on citizenship (per cent)

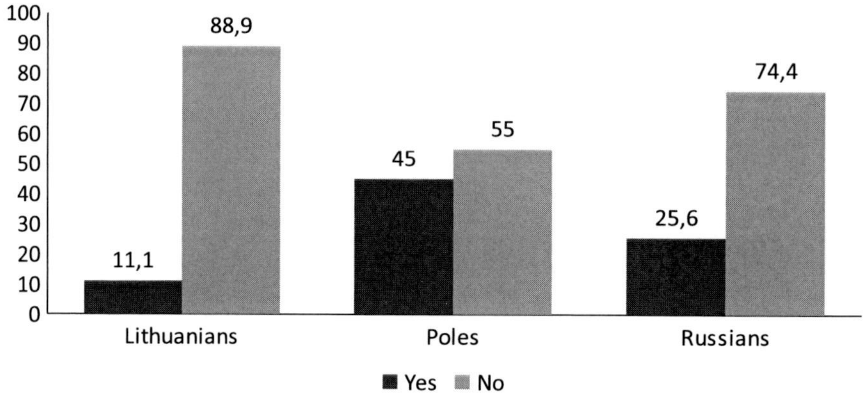

Figure 5. Perception of discrimination based on nationality (per cent)

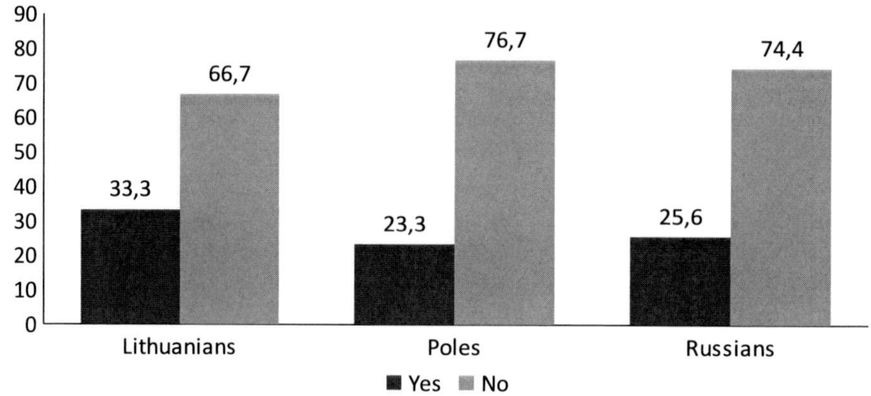

Figure 6. Perception of discrimination based on social status (per cent)

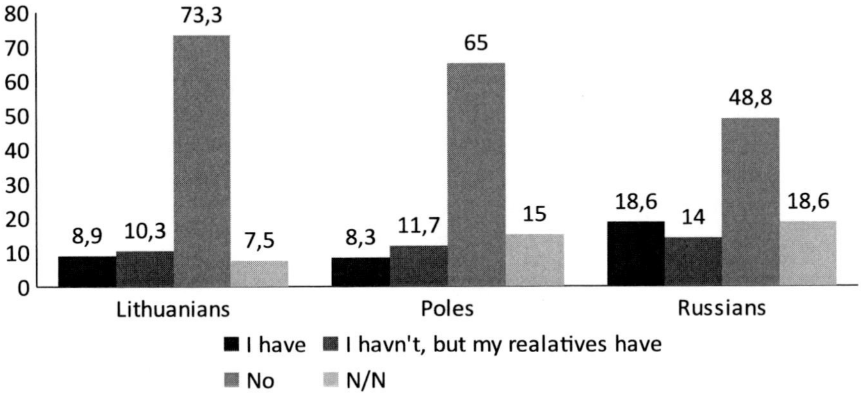

Figure 7. Experience of discrimination (per cent)

Perception of discrimination of ethnic minorities

The study also gives insights into the perception of discrimination against different ethnic groups in the following sections: language, citizenship, nationality and social status. The results of the question "In your opinion, are people in Lithuania discriminated against because of language?" are shown in Figure 3.

As predicted, Russian and Polish minorities feel greater discrimination based on the language: Poles (41.7 %) and Russians (39.5 %) state that people in Lithuania are most frequently discriminated against on the basis of language. The survey results did not reflect the increased tension in the media at that particular time connected with the use of the Polish language in public space. This can, however, be seen in the perception of discrimination based on citizenship (Figure 4) and nationality (Figure 5).

The analysis of perceptions of discrimination based on nationality (Figure 5) reveals that the Polish minority more often declares that people in Lithuania are discriminated against on grounds of nationality (45 %) than does the Russian ethnic minority (25.6 %). It can be assumed that this perception is strongly influenced by the discussions in Lithuania and Poland on the recent tense situation regarding the status of the Polish language.

Another aspect of the issue is related to the perception of different ethnic groups regarding discrimination based on social status. As shown in Figure 6, Lithuanians more than Poles and Russians claim that in Lithuania people are more often discriminated against on the grounds of social status.

It can be assumed that, compared to the ethnic majority (Lithuanians), ethnic minorities feel less discrimination based on social status because they associate discrimination more with language and nationality, but not with their social situation. This shows the sensitivity of ethnic minorities to their ethnic identity and their relationship with the ethnic majority.

In order to investigate how the perception of discrimination differs from the actual subjective experiences of discrimination, respondents were asked whether they or their relatives had experienced discrimination. Figure 7 shows that the actual experience of discrimination is less than the expressed perception of discrimination, especially the one based on language and nationality. On the other hand, Russians more often than Lithuanians and Poles claim that they or their relatives had already experienced discrimination.

Perception of tolerance/intolerance

The level of tolerance/intolerance among different ethnic groups is the other important aspect of the subjective perceptions of ethnic minority situations. The majority of all the ethnic groups studied (from 80 % of Poles to 91 % of Russians) agrees with the statement that people of all nationalities are be tolerated in Lithuania. Only the Polish ethnic minority expresses greater disagreement with this statement.

The analysis of the answers to the classical question about intolerance "which group of people would you not like to have as your neighbours?" shows that almost all ethnic groups respond similarly regarding drug users, alcoholics, criminals, homosexuals and HIV-infected persons. Large differences can be seen, however, in the answers about people of other nationalities, Muslims and immigrants (Table 1). It can be noted that Russian ethnic minority respondents are more tolerant towards these groups than Lithuanian and Polish ethnic respondents. Possibly such a more tolerant attitude reflects the migration experience of Russian ethnic groups, as 22 % of Russians immigrated to Lithuania during the last decade of Soviet regime (Taljunaite and Sviklas 2013: 101).

Nationality	Muslims	Immigrants	Jews	Roma people	Other nationalities
Lithuanians	19	4	3.3	37.9	4.1
Poles	18.4	6.7	3.4	43.6	1.7
Russians	9.4	2.4	2.3	28.4	0

Table 1. The level of intolerance for different social groups (per cent) (multiple answers)

Other studies have provided similar results. Tadas Leoncikas notes that different ethnic groups in Lithuania have the same hierarchy of undesirable groups (Leoncikas 2007: 105). Most of the ethnic groups – both the so-called majority and minorities – are united by a similar level of intolerance towards Roma, Jews and Chechens (Kasatkina and Leoncikas 2003: 259).

In order to investigate the importance of education for tolerance, the respondents were asked whether increasing the level of tolerance and trust should be the most important government priority. The findings show that, despite the relatively high level of intolerance, most of respondents from different ethnic groups do not think that increasing the level of tolerance and trust should be the most important government priority. and only a few respondents answered positively. All ethnic minority groups felt that the main priorities are: combating rising prices, creation of well-being for all people and encouraging entrepreneurial skills.

The comparison of the Soviet and the current systems

The comparison of the Soviet and the current systems reveals how different ethnic groups have different approaches to the current social situation. The comparison is presented in three sections: political, economic and social system assessments.

Ethnic group	The evaluation of the Soviet political system				The evaluation of the current political system			
	Bad	Neither good, nor bad	Good	N/N	Bad	Neither good, nor bad	Good	N/N
Lithuanians	24.8	57.2	12.5	5.5	29.2	38	12.9	19.9
Poles	23.4	68.4	0	8.2	15	36.6	30	18.4
Russians	34.9	48.8	4.6	11.7	11.7	51.3	16.3	20.7

Table 2. Evaluation of the Soviet and the current political systems

As shown in Table 2, the evaluations are rather paradoxical, because Lithuanians, more than Russians and Poles, are favourable to the former Soviet political system and dislike the current democratic political system. Furthermore, despite the Polish ethnic group having a more critical approach to discrimination than the other groups, this group favours the current political system: 30 % of Polish respondents said that the current political system is good, and only 16.3 % of Russian and 12.9 % of Lithuanian respondents answered the same. This distribution of opinions may be associated with the fact that the current political situation does not comply with the expectations of some members of these ethnic groups.

Ethnic group	The evaluation of the Soviet economic system				The evaluation of the current economic system			
	Bad	Neither good, nor bad	Good	N/N	Bad	Neither good, nor bad	Good	N/N
Lithuanians	7.6	51.7	22.8	17.9	17.6	70.2	5.2	7
Poles	6.7	36.7	40	16.6	31.6	58.3	6.7	3.4
Russians	7	28	48.9	16.1	28	58.1	11.7	2.2

Table 3. Evaluation of the Soviet and the current economic systems

These results clearly show the differences between the Lithuanian ethnic group and the Russian and Polish ethnic minorities. Russians and Poles evaluate the Soviet economic system much better than the current system. As income level differences are not statistically significant among the ethnic groups, this assessment may not be much related to income, but to other aspects of the economic system – the threat of unemployment, social security etc.

Ethnic group	The evaluation of the Soviet social system				The evaluation of the current social system			
	Bad	Neither good, nor bad	Good	N/N	Bad	Neither good, nor bad	Good	N/N
Lithuanians	32	54.9	9.8	3.3	9.1	44.9	27.5	18.5
Poles	35	53.3	6.7	5	3.3	46.7	38.3	11.7
Russians	48.8	41.8	7.1	2.3	0	48.9	34.9	16.2

Table 4. The evaluation of the Soviet and current social systems as regards social equality

The evaluations of the Soviet and current social systems regarding social equality are even more paradoxical (Table 4). All three major ethnic groups evaluate the Soviet social system equally poorly and have a good opinion of the current social system with regard to social equality. This casts doubts on whether the idea of social equality is considered an asset by all ethnic groups.

General evaluation of the current situation

In order to determine the overall evaluation of the democratisation process, the respondents were asked if they liked to return to live in the Soviet system (Figure 8).

As shown in Figure 8, 45 % of Poles and 55.8 % of Russians would like to return to live in the Soviet system, if it was possible. Only 26.4 % of Lithuanians think the same. This may be due to a better assessment of the Soviet economic system and due to the respondents' age, as both Russian and Polish respondents are older than Lithuanians and were thus more adapted to life in the Soviet system. Still, the strong egalitarian attitudes of ethnic groups can also be a partial explanation: only about one fifth of the Lithuanians and Russians (only 10 % Poles) believe that the state must ensure that everyone is provided with housing, jobs, pensions etc.

Another explanation may be related to satisfaction or dissatisfaction with life today. As shown in Figure 9, about a quarter of Lithuanians, one-fifth of Russians and only one-tenth of Poles are satisfied with their lives. On the other hand, about one-sixth of Lithuanians and Poles, and one-fourth of Russians are dissatisfied with their lives. It can be assumed that ethnic identity perception has little influence on the evaluation of the quality of life in the current situation.

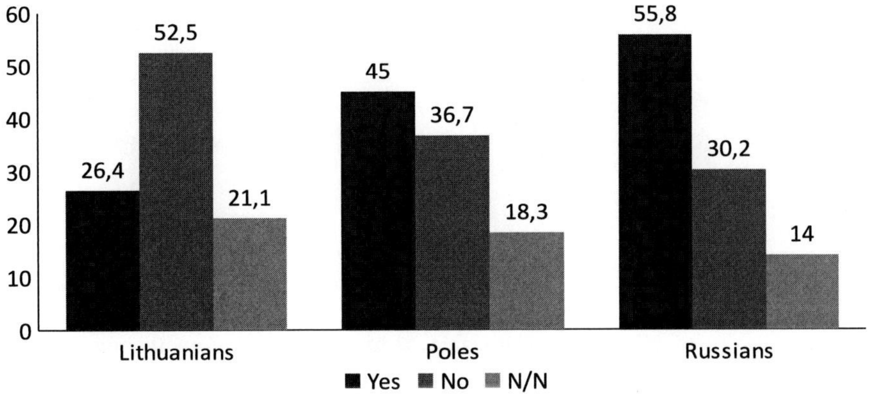

Figure 8. The desire to return to live in the Soviet system, if the choice was possible (per cent)

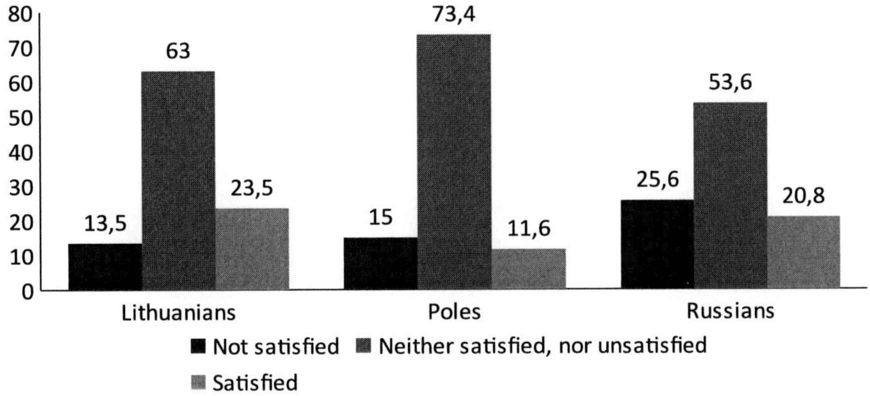

Figure 9. Life satisfaction (per cent)

Finally, the general evaluation of today's situation can be measured by the desire to emigrate from Lithuania. The answers to the question "If the situation deteriorates in Lithuania and you had a choice, what would you choose?" provided us with interesting results. 43.6 % of Lithuanians, compared to 23.3 % of Poles and 27.9 % of Russians would choose to live an easier life abroad (Figure 10).

This choice is possibly affected not only by a certain dissatisfaction with one's life, but also by the age of the respondents because in terms of age the Lithuanian ethnic group is significantly younger, and the older Russian and Poles can see fewer possibilities and are less willing to change their situation.

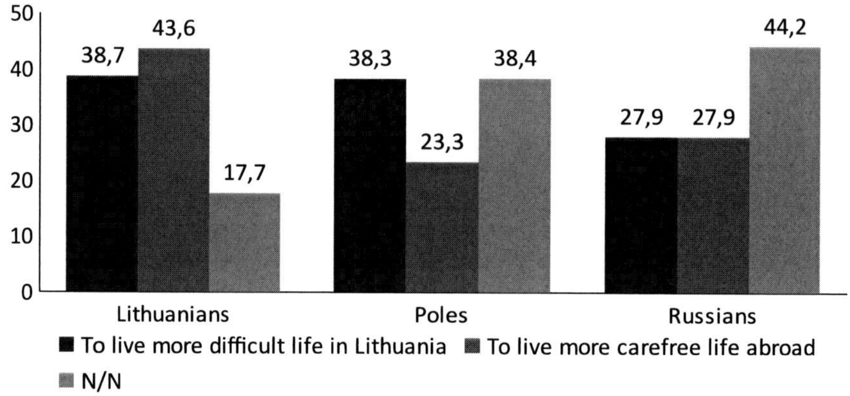

Figure 10. Choice to emigrate (per cent)

Conclusion

During the last two decades, Lithuanian ethnic minorities have experienced difficult changes in the perception of their status in the Lithuanian society. On the one hand, Lithuanian ethnic policy after the restoration of independence was, in the context of the Baltic region, uniquely liberal, inclusive and tolerant as is manifested by the issues of citizenship, culture and minority education supported by the state. However, recent ethnic politics complications with a delay of agreement on the new law on ethnic minorities and unresolved issues on the use of minority languages in public space show slightly worsened conditions for the social adaptation of ethnic minorities.

On the other hand, according to the results of previous research, Lithuanian ethnic minorities during the last two decades have experienced difficult changes in the perception of their status in the Lithuanian society: a deterioration in the assessment of their social status; the decline in political loyalty among some ethnic groups; the growing intolerance for certain ethnic minorities; an increased sense of social inequality; and weaker integration of ethnic minorities into the public sector.

The latest research results show that the self-perception of the ethnic minority social status, the evaluation of material well-being, the current economic situation, and even the wish to return to the Soviet system can be explained not so much by the level of income and the material situation, but by the social or symbolic sensitivity of ethnic minorities to their ethnic identity and their relationship with the ethnic majority.

However, it can also be assumed that the evaluation of the situation of ethnic minorities in their own understanding is affected not only by the change of the ethnic minority status in society, but also by the reflection of the external public discourse on discrimination of some ethnic minority rights and politicisation of these issues during the period of Lithuania's independence, as the situation regarding the use of the Polish language in public spaces shows.

The comparison of opinions about discrimination based on language, nationality and social status reveals differences: ethnic minorities link discrimination to language, citizenship and nationality, whereas Lithuanians link it to social status. The comparison of opinions about ethnic tolerance reveals an ambiguous picture: on the one hand, ethnic tolerance in Lithuania is important for all nationalities, but on the other hand, a large percentage of all ethnic groups (especially Poles) would not want to live in the same neighbourhood with Roma, Chechens, Muslims and immigrants. However, the reduction of discrimination or increase of tolerance and trust are not considered as one of the most important government priorities, the main priorities being: combating rising prices, the creation of well-being for all people and encouraging entrepreneurial skills.

Therefore, the analysis of ethic policy, problems of social adaptation and the analysis of research data confirm the main hypothesis that different attitudes of ethnic groups towards their social situation in Lithuania are mainly determined by ethnic identity, perceived social status and the coherence of their social adaptation. According to Leoncikas "in order for a society to be consciously tolerant and able to resist a variety of impulses promoting intolerance, discrimination, fear and violence, it has to reinforce knowledge of human rights, law enforcement expertise and social integration mechanisms" (Leoncikas 2007: 106).

Thus the current situation shows that there is still a need for further improvement in the political protection of ethnic minority rights. The main areas for improvement would be: developing effective educational policies for ethnic minorities to ensure equal opportunity for higher education, decreasing discrimination in the employment sphere and empowering their public and political participation.

References

Advisory Committee on the Framework Convention for the Protection of National Minorities 2014: Third Opinion on Lithuania Adopted on 28 November 2013. URL: https://rm.coe.int/CoERMPublicCommonSearchServices/DisplayDCTMContent?documentId=0900001680099360, accessed 12. 11. 2014.

Andrlik, Jan 2009: Ethnic and Language Policy of the Republic of Lithuania: Basis and Practice. The Annual of Language & Politics and Politics of Identity (ALPPI). Institute of Political Studies Faculty of Social Sciences Charles University, Prague. URL: http://alppi.eu/wp-content/uploads/2009/11/Andrlik_2009.pdf, accessed 24. 9. 2013.

Beresnevičiūtė, Vida 2005: Etninių grupių socialinės integracijos dimensijos šiuolaikinėje Lietuvos visuomenėje [Dimensions of Social Integration of Ethnic Groups in the Contemporary Society of Lithuania]. Etniškumo studijos [Ethnicity Studies]. Vilnius: Social Research Institute.

Beresnevičiūtė, Vida and Inga Nausėdienė 1999: Trys Lietuvos dienraščiai apie tautines mažumas Lietuvoje' [Three Lithuanian Newspapers about the Ethnic Minorities in Lithuania]. In: Sociologija. Mintis ir veiksmas [Sociology: Thought and Action], No. 1 (3): 67–78.

Best, Marina 2013: The Ethnic Russian Minority: A Problematic Issue in the Baltic States. In: Verges: Germanic & Slavic Studies in Review (GSSR), 2.1: 33–41. URL: http://journals.uvic.ca/index.php/verges/article/view/11634/3698, accessed 11. 11. 2014.

Bureau of Democracy, Human Rights and Labour 2012: Lithuania 2012 Human Rights Report. URL: http://www.state.gov/documents/organization/204518.pdf, accessed 19. 9. 2013.

Constitution of the Republic of Lithuania, Official Gazette Lithuania, No. 33–1014 (6. 11. 1992).

Ester, P., L. Halman and V. Rukavishnikov 1997: From Cold War to Cold Peace? A Comparative Empirical Study of Russian and Western Political Cultures. Tilburg University Press.

Fearon, James D. and David D. Laitin 2006: Lithuania Narrative, pp. 1–24. URL: http://www.stanford.edu/group/ethnic/Random%20Narratives/LithuaniaRN1.3.pdf, accessed 19. 9. 2013.

Freedom House Report 2012. URL: http://www.freedomhouse.org/report/freedom-world/2012/lithuania, accessed 24. 9. 2013.

Frėjutė-Rakauskienė, Monika 2011: The Impact of the EU Membership on Ethnic Minority Participation. Parties of Lithuanian Ethnic Minorities in the European Parliament Elections. Politikos mokslų almanachas [Almanac of Political Sciences], Kaunas, Vytautas Magnus University, Vol. 10: 7–30. URL: http://vddb.laba.lt/fedora/get/LT-eLABa-0001:J.04~2011~ISSN_2029-0225.V_10.PG_7-30/DS.002.1.01.ARTIC, accessed 4. 12. 2014.

Frėjutė-Rakauskienė, Monika 2012: Lietuvos spauda ir visuomenės nuostatos apie rusų, ukrainiečių bei baltarusių etnines grupes ir naujuosius imigrantus [Lithuanian Press and Public Opinion about the Russian, Ukrainian and Belarusian Ethnic Groups and New Immigrants]. In: Etniškumo studijos [Ethnicity Studies], No. 1–2: 71–102.

Kasatkina, Natalija 2002: Lietuvos etninių grupių adaptacijos ypatumai [Adaptation Peculiarities of Ethnic Groups in Lithuania]. In: Filosofija, sociologija [Philosophy, Sociology], No. 4: 15–21.

Kasatkina, Natalija 2003: The Adaptation of Ethnic Minority Groups: Defining the Problem (Case of Lithuania). In: Etniškumo studijos [Ethnicity Studies]: 8–29.

Kasatkina, Natalija and Vida Beresnevičiūtė 2006 [reprinted 2010]: Ethnic Structure, Inequality and Governance of the Public Sector in Lithuania. In: Etniškumo studijos [Ethnicity Studies], No. 1–2: 7–25.

Kasatkina, Natalija, Giedrius Kadziauskas and Kristina Sliavaite 2006: Ethnic Minorities and Public Policy: The Case of Lithuania. In: S. S. Akermak (ed.): International Obligations and National Debates: Minorities around the Baltic Sea. Mariehamn: The Aland Peace Institute, 347–396.

Kasatkina, Natalija and Tadas Leončikas 2003: Lietuvos etninių grupių adaptacija: kontekstas ir eiga [The Adaptation of Lithuanian Ethnic Groups: Context and Process]. Vilnius: Socialinių tyrimų institutas, Eugrimas.

Law on Equal Treatment of the Republic of Lithuania, Official Gazette, Lithuania, No. 114–5115 [5. 12. 2003].

Leončikas, Tadas 2000: Vertybės ir visuomenės mažumos [Values and Societal Minorities]. In: Kultūrologija, vol. 6: 413–431.

Leončikas, Tadas 2007: Nepakantamo hierarchija ir socialinė distancija visuomenės mažumų atžvilgiu' [Hierarchy of Intolerance and Social Distance Social Minorities]. In: R. Žiliukaitė (sudarytoja): Dabartinės Lietuvos kultūros raidos tendencijos: vertybiniai virsmai [The Current Lithuanian Cultural Trends: Values Transitions]. Vilnius: Kultūros, filosofijos ir meno institutas, 89–107.

Lithuanian 2011 Population Census in Brief (2011). URL: http://www.stat.gov.lt/uploads/Lietuvos_gyventojai_2011.pdf, accessed 5. 11. 2012.

Lithuanian Human Rights Association 2004: Analytical Report PHARE RAXEN _CC Minority Education. URL: http://fra.europa.eu/sites/default/files/fra_uploads/276-EDU-Lithuania-final.pdf, accessed 19. 9. 2013.

Lottman, Annelies 2008: No Direction Home: Nationalism and Statelessness in the Baltics. In: Texas International Law Journal, Vol. 43, No. 3: 503–519.

Okunevičiūtė, Neverauskienė L. 2010: Tautinių mažumų integracijos į darbo rinką aspektai [The Ethnic Minorities' Integration into Labour Market Aspects]. In: Filosofija, sociologija [Philosophy, Sociology], Vol. 21, No. 4: 245–256.

Resler, Tamara J. 1992: Going It Alone: Post-Soviet Lithuania. In: Swords and Ploughshares, Vol. VII, No. 1, Fall 1992: Stories from Russia and the Post-Soviet States: 14–16. URL: http://acdis.illinois.edu/assets/docs/367/articles/GoingitAlonePostSovietLithuania.pdf, accessed 24. 9. 2013.

Šliavaitė, Kristina 2012: Etninės mažumos darbo rinkoje:kalbos, pilietybės ir socialinių tinklų reikšmė (Visagino atvejis) [Ethnic Minorities on the Labour Market: the Importance of Language, Citizenship and Social Networks (the Case of Visaginas)]. In: Etniškumo studijos [Ethnicity Studies], No. 1–2: 103–125.

Special Department Will be Restored for Ethnic Minorities (2014). Lithuanian government press release published in online news portal delfi.lt. URL: http://www.delfi.lt/news/daily/lithuania/tautinems-mazumoms-grazinamas-specialus-departamentas.d?id=66356062#ixzz3NKnB7HRk, accessed 12. 11. 2014.

Taljunaitė Meilutė and Eduardas K. Sviklas 2013: Lietuvos rusai Lietuvos nepriklausomybes išvakarėse: santykis su Lietuva [Russians in Lithuania at the Dawn of the Restoration of the Lithuanian Independence]. In: Meilutė Taljūnaitė, Andrius Marcinkevičius (sudarytojai): Lietuvos socialinė raida:

migracija ir etniškumas nuo totalitarinės iki demokratinės visuomenės [Social Development of Lithuania: Migration and Ethnicity; From Totalitarity to Democracy]. Vilnius: Lithuanian Social Research Centre, No. 2, 101–112.

Terskinas, Arturas 2001: Ethnic and Sexual Minorities in the Lithuanian Mass Media: Images and Issues. URL: http://www.policy.hu/tereskinas/policypaper.html, accessed 19. 9. 2013.

Vasilevich, Hanna 2013: Lithuania's Minority-Related Legislation: Is there a Legal Vacuum? The European Centre for Minority Issues (ECMI) Working Paper #70. URL: http://www.ecmi.de/uploads/tx_lfpubdb/WP_70_Final.pdf, accessed 19. 11. 2014.

Vildaitė, Dovilė and Karolis Žibas 2010: Etninių tyrimų instituto visuomenės nuomonės tyrimų apžvalga (2005–2010 m.) [Overview of Public Opinion Polls Carried out by the Institute for Ethnic Studies (2005–2010)]. In: Etniškumo studijos [Ethnicity Studies], No. 1–2: 121–137.

Ethnic Minorities in the History of Georgia: the Post-Soviet History Textbooks

Nino Chikovani

Introduction

This article deals with the problem of perception of the role of ethnic minorities in the Georgia's history. The main research questions are: how did the importance of forming the feeling of national belonging regardless of ethnic, cultural or religious identity come to the forefront? How was this complex and contradictory process reflected in the post-Soviet history textbooks? The study is based on the method of content analysis. In particular, the transformation of the Georgian master narrative and school history textbooks is explored. Several projects aiming at overcoming the ethnocentric vision of history are analysed as well. The study demonstrates that the process of overcoming the ethnocentric vision of history started on the level of the secondary educational institutions; positive dynamics could be observed in the representation of ethnic and religious minorities in the history textbooks of the post-Soviet period.

Georgia is a country with a multi-ethnic, multicultural and multi-religious population. According to the census of 2002, non-Georgian ethnic groups form 16 % of the population of the country. The Azerbaijani minority is the largest one – 6,5 %, followed by Armenians – 5,7 %, Russians – 1,5 %, Kurds – 0,5 %, Greeks – 0,3 % and other ethnic groups. As for the religions, Orthodox Christians represent 65 % of the whole population, Muslims – 11 %, Russian Orthodox Christians – 10 %, Monophyzit Armenians – 8 %, others – 6 %.

Why history textbooks?

It is a generally accepted idea that our perception of *self* and of *others* is mainly formed during childhood and is highly determined by the mode and style of how history is taught. Conceptions of history teaching and textbooks created on this basis are one of the most important tools for shaping national identity and collective historical consciousness. As Hanna Schlissler puts it, there is an inevitable political dimension to what knowledge is being imparted in school books. It can be extracted from textbooks what a society believes should be handed on to the young as a part of their historical consciousness (Schlissler 1987: 26). "History textbooks communicate a contemporary past, one which matches the prevailing social and political needs. ... Textbooks manifest the mass historical transmission of a historical knowledge from one generation to another ... They represent a point of social negotiation between different groups whose prime concern is passing down to students a common past for a mutual future" (Porat 2001: 51); perception of one's own nation, as well as its place in history and those of "others" are formed on their basis.

The goals and standards of history teaching, as well as the main principles of representation of national and World History are defined by the state. They reflect the image that a society holds on its past and, indirectly, the way of how it imagines its future.

History textbooks are produced within the historiography tradition, which is reflected in the master narrative – the "dominant narrative as expressed in the key texts, which were widely received as being particularly subtle, masterful and authoritative. ... National historical master narratives thus provide a narrative framework" for perception and interpretation of the past, demonstrate who are actors of national history, who are perceived as enemies. "It is through such historical master narratives that people make sense of the past and identity with particular versions of the past" (Berger 2009: 33–34).

The Georgian historical master narrative

The Georgian historical master narrative was formed in the last decades of the 19th century, being termed as an era of "inventing traditions" by Eric Hobsbawm. It was shaped in confrontation with the Russian imperial policy which was aimed at the re-construction of the historical memory of Georgians according to imperial goals. Similar to other cases where the professional historiography was formed as a response to the imperial challenge, the Georgian master narrative tried to strengthen the Georgian's ethnic identity; therefore, history should fix their difference from "others" – inside the country and outside as well. As Stephen Jones argues, Georgians referred to their distant past history to support claims of priority over Russian colonizers (Jones 1994: 158). As in other similar cases, a nation was perceived vis-a-vis *others*, who were often constructed as "national enemies". Themes of suffering and repression enabled the Georgians to mark out a national history in opposition to an oppressive "other" (Berger 2009: 30–32).

Imposition of the Soviet rule brought significant changes in the study and teaching of history. The nationality policy of the Soviet Union was aimed at the formation of the common Soviet identity. As A. Miller notes, the Soviet nationality policy was based on two deeply contradictory principles: the imposition of the Russian language and the Soviet culture combined with the system of fixed national belonging of individuals that blocked the possibility of full assimilation (Miller 2008: 61). On the one hand, the ethnic belonging of the Soviet citizens was determined by their birth; on the other hand, ethnic belonging was declared a temporary category that should wither away over time. The state took care of the development of local cultures and identities of nations, nationalities and peoples who should mingle in the "Soviet family". The Marxist framework of history writing was combined with the propagation of national characteristics (Berger 2009: 32).

The Georgian master narrative formed in the beginning of the 20th century was mainly maintained, although rearranged according to the new methodological requirements. As in other authoritarian societies, the emotive potential of national history remained strong in Georgia (Velychenko 1994: 17). It can be said that the national history successfully confronted the official Soviet narrative in Soviet Georgia. On the other hand, ethno-territorial institutionalization and cultivation of national, political, economic and cultural elites appeared as a foundation for inter-ethnic tensions in the second half of the 1980s.

In the period of "Perestroika", the general process of the revival of national identity was accompanied by the growing interest towards the national history. Already from the mid-1980s on the history of Georgia became a compulsory course for secondary as well as higher educational institutions. Filling in the "white spots" of history and the re-creation of the "true history" became the main task for historiography. A great deal of factual material, covering themes that had been forbidden in the Soviet time, now appeared in the narrative. These were mainly issues of the modern history: political movements of the beginning of the 20th century, political parties formed in Georgia, their programs and leaders; developments from February 1917 to May 1918; detailed history of the Georgian Democratic Republic; struggle against the Soviet regime in the 1920–1930s; Soviet political repressions, etc. The names of the political and public figures of the period of the Georgian Democratic Republic, as well as those of Soviet political leaders and intellectuals, who became victims of the Soviet repressions, leaders of anti-Soviet uprisings and the rebellion of 1924 in particular, appeared in the narrative for the first time.

Since the end of 1980s, with the easing of constraints, the master-narrative has become more ethnocentric. In this period, the struggle for national rights took a political overtone. This was followed by the sharpening of the "Combat for History", which had started at the beginning of the 20th century and later on was stamped with the legacy of the Soviet nationality policy. The Georgian master-narrative was confronted by Abkhazian and South-Ossetian counter-narratives. The themes of national guilt, victimization by "other", historical justice and historical truth became central aspects for the nationalist rhetoric and national narratives in Georgia at the end of the 1980s.

After the dissolution of the Soviet Union, the process of re-consideration of national history emerged as an integral part of the state-building process in Georgia. Setting the role and place of different ethnic groups in the past as well as in the present life of the country was one of the most important tasks for the multi-ethnic, multi-religious and multicultural state. History has come under the scope of the titular nation and the ethnic minorities as well. The debates on the new narrative – different from the Soviet one – and the methodology of history teaching have been sharpened by the ethnic conflicts and complicated by the formation of the post-conflict traumatic memory.

Though the methodological constrains disappeared, the inertia of the past had quite a strong influence on future developments. The traditional mono-methodological Marxist approach made the task of the historians easier as it equipped them with the sole possible discourse of interpretation; that is why it was not abandoned enthusiastically. Difficulties and sometimes even the lack of will to comprehend new theoretical approaches may have been observed during this period. Emancipation from the Marxist ideological discourse was an important goal for the post-Soviet historiography, but this was not an easy task. Instead of the deideologisation, the communist ideology was replaced by the unqualified or para-patriotic narrative (Reisner 1998: 414). A sudden shift took place, from one "correct" history (where everything was evaluated from the aspect of the class struggle) to another "correct" one (where everything was interpreted from the perspective of the Georgian people) (Gundare 2007).

As expected, in terms of the re-consideration of history, the public discourse was much more active than the professional historians. Ultra-patriotic sentiments appeared in the public speeches of the political leaders, printed media, TV. The paradigm of victimhood re-emerged and was strengthened by stressing the facts of constant attacks and threats of aggression from neighbours. The principle of "autochthonous population" became the subject of manipulation. Portions of political parties started to talk about the "guests"; residence of different ethnic groups on the territory of Georgia was declared as a result of tolerance of the titular nation, in the meantime the notion of "ungratefulness" was set. Some of the activists of ethnic minorities were no less radical in their political rhetoric, using the concept of "historical lands". A tendency similar to that of the Georgian nationalist discourse was revealed in the narratives of ethnic minorities. Mutual blaming for falsification of the "historical truth" appeared. Consequently, difference was constructed negatively as an exclusion and marginalization of those who were defined as "others" or "outsiders" (Woodward 1997: 35).

As for the professional historical narrative, it reflected the above mentioned tendency rather moderately. The traditional conservativeness of the academy played a positive role in this case: academic historians had difficulty in giving up not only the old methodological framework, but the traditional narrative of the Soviet period as well.

The situation was aggravated by the conflicts of the early 1990s in Abkhazia and South Ossetia. They were preceded and accompanied by the contested memories/history wars; motives, aspirations and actions of the confronted sides were differently narrated by the conflicting parties, based on myths, stereotypes, preconceptions and prejudices formed within a long period of time. The experience of coexistence and shared history was suppressed, as the conflicts were followed by the rule of the post-conflict traumatic memory.

It took some time to realize the importance of overcoming the conflicting memory and forming the feeling of national belonging regardless of ethnic, cultural or religious identity. At the end of the 1990s, reconfiguration of historical narratives and collective memories found their way into the history textbooks for secondary educational institutions. It should be stressed that by this time there had been no remarkable changes in the master narrative; hence, the history textbooks could not be built on the novelties offered by the academia.

Post-Soviet history textbooks: Introducing new methodological approaches

In the last quarter of the twentieth century a different rationale for school history emerged on the international level, which reflected a change of thinking about what qualities "good citizens" need to have and the ways in which history might contribute to these. A kind of move towards more critical and detached approaches to the national past could be observed at that time (Haydn 2004: 89–90). The transmission of a comprehensive historical "canon" was seen as less important than the ability to learn new skills and understandings in the context of the perceived need for flexible, adaptable learners living in a modern information society.

After attaining independence, Georgia came to face the need of compiling new textbooks of national as well as world history. The principles of history education were not re-defined, thus the changes were not based on a more or less clearly structured system. The first post-Soviet textbooks were in conformity with the master narrative. They were full of facts and still compiled in the Soviet style. Marxist methodology was denied, but attaining methodological pluralism and establishing multi-perspectivity turned out to be a hard task. There was nothing new in terms of integrating ethnic minorities in the general narrative; like in the Soviet times, they were mentioned randomly in the lessons on the topics of cultural history. "History of Georgia" and "World History" were strictly separated.

It took some time to realize the importance of overcoming conflicting memory and forming the feeling of national belonging regardless of ethnic, cultural or religious identity. At the end of the 1990s, the process of overcoming ethnocentric history was started through the secondary school textbooks. Elaboration of the new curriculum and of new textbooks on national and world history became the major task.

The first step was made in 1997 when the Low on Education and the National Educational Standard in Georgia's History were adopted (Lomashvili and Vardosanidze 1997: 5) and the new curriculum for the school subject "History of Georgia" was elaborated on their basis. They established main principles of history teaching. The new textbooks were introduced.

In the introduction of the Standard, the authors pointed out the influence that state ideologies have on history teaching conceptions. In this case, the example of the Soviet period was brought up when history teaching was used as a tool for justification of the Soviet regime. The new Standard, as opposed to the Soviet one, tried to elaborate a conception of history teaching which would correspond to the political orientation of post-Soviet Georgia. According to the Standard, it was particularly important to have a "model of historical education which corresponds to the perspectives of complete democratization of the country and contributes to the raise of ... political, cultural, religious ... tolerance in pupils" (Lomashvili and Vardosanidze 1997: 5). The Standard put the emphasis on "pluralistic-alternative teaching of history" which was rejected in the ideologized Soviet programs. The authors of the Standard tried to elaborate a conception of history teaching which would correspond "to the perspectives of complete democratization of the country and contribute to the raise of ... political, cultural, religious tolerance in pupils" (Lomashvili and Vardosanidze 1997: 5). The importance of "pluralistic-alternative teaching of history" was accentuated. However, the content of the Standard did not fully correspond to the declared principles. According to the Standard, the only aim of the presentation of alternative perspectives was to achieve historical truth: "There might be different perspectives on the same historical fact but only one of them is true" (Lomashvili and Vardosanidze 1997: 31). It was not quite clear how to handle the ethnic, cultural and religious diversity of the country and how the role of ethnic minorities in Georgia's history should be presented.

The second post-Soviet generation of the national history textbooks, created on the basis of the Standard of 1997, represented history as a collective memory aiming at strengthening national, or – to be more precise – ethnic identity rather than a form of knowledge, with the particular disciplinary procedures and methods. The way of presenting historical events and facts did not allow pupils to keep distance from them. It led to the creation of an impression of history as a destiny, a legendary story about the past. Enormous factual material given in a positivist tradition did not contribute to the development of critical and independent thinking. Textbooks were based on the single narrative. No alternative vision and possibility of different interpretations were given. The emphasis was put on learning as many facts, events, dates and names as possible. Besides, the context in which national history was presented was narrowed almost to the national borders. The glorious times of the Georgian history were presented as a consequence of the efforts of ethnic Georgians while hard periods were mentioned as a result of unfair destiny. The ethnic minorities were not adequately addressed and they were referred to as foreigners or newcomers, if mentioned at all. The problem of the representation of Georgia's history as being created not by the "hosts" and "guests" but rather by the citizens, united by a common past, shared values and a common future, remained unresolved.

Together with the Georgian officials, international actors were involved in the process of reformation of history education; they became more active from the second half of the 1990s on. On 25–27 September 1997, under the initiative of the Council of Europe, the Regional Seminar on "The reform of history teaching in secondary schools" was held in Tbilisi and Tabakhmela, Georgia. It brought together specialists from Georgia, Armenia, Azerbaijan, Moldova, the

Russian Federation and Turkey, as well as experts invited by the Council of Europe. The problems of preparation of the new history curricula and textbooks, issues regarding the standards and their implementation were discussed at the seminar.

Some other international initiatives were aimed at overcoming conflicting narratives and creating common history textbooks for the South Caucasus. The "Tbilisi Initiative" is the best-known among them. The idea was proposed by Georgia's Ministry of Education at the above-mentioned seminar in 1997 and was further supported and financed by the Council of Europe. Although the main goal of the project was not fulfilled, the participants gained substantial experience of collaboration. Apart from this, the working process revealed problems, which had to be carefully comprehended.

Changes in the perception of "other"

From 2003 on, a radical shift from ethnic to civic nationalism could be observed in the Georgian political discourse. The political elite started to stress ethnic and cultural diversity of Georgia as the source of its might; "Diversity is our strength" became the main message. In general, setting the principles of education (history education in our case) is the prerogative of a state; consequently, realization of the statement set by the political discourse was started through secondary school textbooks.

The new Law of Education (2005) more thoroughly addressed a challenge of civic integration. Legitimization of the multi-ethnic but integrated Georgian state has become the main concern of history teaching. The reform in the teaching of history involved the following goals: establishing a multi-perspective approach; presenting history as an interpretation; overcoming traditional national/ethnic discourse; shaping civic consciousness (inclusion of ethnic minorities in the history of Georgia). It was particularly underlined that "the material should be presented from different points of view. This contributes to the formation of the critical thinking and adds to overcoming the stereotypes. School should support diversity through raising respect towards religious, linguistic and ethnic differences" (Lomashvili and Vardosanidze 1997: 35). Beginning from 2005, textbooks created in accordance with the national Standard are to be submitted to the Centre for National Curricula for approval. Several textbooks may be approved for one and the same grade. One of the approved textbooks is translated into the other languages of instruction (defined by the Law): Azeri, Armenian and Russian. Schools are entitled to select a textbook from the list of those approved by the Centre. Until that time, in the regions with compact ethnic minorities, teaching history had been based on the textbooks supplied from ethnic homelands. They were studying both the history of their ethnic homeland as well as Georgia's history through the Armenian and Azerbaijani reflection. Unification of teaching history as well as other social sciences throughout the country was declared as one of the main goals. According to the National Curriculum, the pupils should get information on political, social, cultural, religious, and ethnic diversity both in Georgia and worldwide. Different perspectives on historical events should be introduced for making pupils understand different interpretations of and reasons for their existence.

The third generation of post-Soviet Georgian history textbooks represents the first attempt on the way to overcoming an ethnocentric vision of history. Georgia is portrayed as a multi-ethnic and multi-religious country which has been shaped throughout centuries. The ethnic minorities have appeared in the textbooks in order to show their participation in Georgia's history and their role in the building of the Georgian state. The tone of the textbooks has become more neutral and Georgians are no longer represented as victims of external forces. The textbooks are mostly cleared up from the ethnic and religious stereotypes. Another important innovation is that there have been attempts of keeping distance with the historical events, including those of the 1990s. Responsibility of the Georgian side is raised even concerning a sensitive and painful issue of the Abkhazian conflict. The attempt of planting the multi-perspective approach appears to be having some success. History is shown as a science based on interpretation. Nevertheless, the problem of inclusion of ethnic minorities in the history of Georgia still remains a significant issue. The impression is that these groups reside separately, not interacting with each other. Their participation in the common past is mentioned, but statements are not supported by facts.

The form of provision of material appeared to be one of the most contentious issues: the authors' narrative practically disappeared, being substituted by fragments from sources with brief comments. The authors of the textbooks considered that it was the most appropriate way for the representation of different perspectives, contributing to the formation of critical thinking and perception of history as an interpretation of the past. Exactly this approach is hotly debated by Georgian historians. The new type of textbooks requires high professionalism of teachers: this is not a traditional textbook with the narrative to be learned by a student; a teacher should check to what extent the material was memorized.

In 2006, the research project was implemented by the CIMERA, which was finalized in a publication under the title "History Teaching in Georgia: Representation of Minorities in Georgian History Textbooks" (2007). Another attempt of summarising the results of the first stage of changes in the sphere of history education at the secondary school level was initiated by the Association for Internal Affairs, Czech Republic in 2008. The project "Contemporary History Textbooks in the South Caucasus" was realized and a collection of the articles was published under the same title. The above-mentioned studies revealed achievements and problems on the way to the implementation of the new approach to history teaching; the most important issue was that history as interpretation was hardly perceived and accepted, not only by the school teachers but by the academicians as well. "History is history! We have to write the real history [as it was], and nothing else!" (Gundare 2007: 34). Most of the history teachers strongly believed in the sole real history: "History is comprised of facts. How could we say that something did not happen? There could not be an alternative opinion" (Gundare 2007: 34). The phrase fully reflects an attitude of most of the teachers towards the "right way" of history teaching. This attitude even exists today.

In 2010, the three-year project "How We Lived Together in Georgia in the 20th Century" was accomplished. The project had been initiated by EuroClio and the Georgian Association of History Educators in June 2008, under the wider name "Tolerance Building through History Education in Georgia". Historians and history educators from different regions of Georgia, ministry officials, as well as international observers, trainers and lecturers were involved in the working process at different stages. The project was aimed at representing the role of different ethnic and religious groups in Georgia's history in the 20th century. Understanding tolerance represented one of the most important issues for the project participants. The working process revealed the fact that in spite of the belief and proud of our traditional tolerance, the concept of tolerance was not always addressed adequately and often came as "the genetic characteristic" of the concrete ethnic group *(We are tolerant, and thanks to it different ethnic and religious groups found a shelter here)*. As a result of the project, the teaching tool "How We Lived Together in Georgia in the 20th Century" was published (2011). The book comes along with a 150-page teachers' guide indicating the compliance of each module with the national curriculum. As mentioned in the introduction of the book, "These are the topics which make your neighbour more aware of different ethnic and religious identity. They make sure that ethnic and religious diversity is the main heritage of our country, and only peaceful coexistence, mutual understanding and respect, knowledge of culture, traditions and values of each other pave the way for its future success." Materials presented in the book demonstrate "why people with different ethnic and religious identities considered themselves as a part of the society, and what made them feel marginalized" (How We Lived Together ...: 2). More time will be needed to evaluate the long-term impact of the project on various levels, to observe to what extent the project is noticed and referred to among the teachers, stakeholders, policy makers and the wider audience.

In 2010, the Ministry of Education and Science of Georgia initiated a new subject for the 10th–12th grades of secondary educational institutions, named "World Culture". Teaching standard and syllabus were elaborated and the piloting materials were prepared for the 2010–2011 academic year. Trainings for teachers were conducted. After the successful piloting in the secondary schools of all regions of Georgia, the subject was included in the list of elective courses and introduced from 2012–2013 when it was elected by more than 860 schools (of about 2000 ones existing in the country). The subject is aimed at the formation of the new knowledge regarding the phenomenon of culture and its related issues. Pupils should comprehend culture as a basis of the similarities and differences between societies; positive attitude towards the cultural diversity should be raised; students should be equipped with the skills of orientation in diverse cultural environments, successful communication and tolerance.

An ongoing 3-years project under TEMPUS "Development of International Model for Curricular Reform in Multicultural Education and Cultural Diversity Training" (started in 2012) has aimed at the promotion of multicultural education. Cultural diversity training will add much to the preparation of the teachers who will ensure the implementation of the new approaches to history teaching and adequate representation of the role of ethnic minorities in Georgia's history.

In the 2012–2013 academic year, the new history textbooks approved by the National Centre for the Development of the Quality of Education were introduced in the 7th–12th grades of the secondary schools. They have not thoroughly been analysed yet, however, at a glance, it is visible that the authors have returned back to the old style of presenting materials. Currently, some new changes are expected in the educational sphere, including the system of preparation, evaluation and publication of the textbooks. Hopefully, the experience gained during the past years will contribute to the comprehension of existing problems and serve as a basis for further advancement of history teaching in Georgia.

Conclusion

Representation of ethnic minorities in Georgia's history turned out to be the problem which became the subject of special interest in the last two decades of the 20th century. Setting the role and place of different ethnic groups in the past as well as in the present life of the multi-ethnic, multi-religious and multicultural country turned out to be one of the most important tasks. Hard experience of the bloody conflicts of the 1990s and hardships of the transitional period and state-building process led to understanding the importance of overcoming conflicting memory and forming the feeling of national belonging regardless of ethnic, cultural or religious identity of all citizens of Georgia. Academia appeared to be more conservative in changing the tradition of ethnocentric narrative of the positivist historiography. The process started on the level of the secondary educational institutions. Positive dynamics could be observed in the representation of ethnic and religious minorities in the history textbooks of the post-Soviet period. However, the trajectory of transformation of the historical narrative is not easy and continues to be affected by the contradictory political developments in Georgia.

References

Berger, Stefan 2009: The Comparative History of National Historiographies in Europe: Some Methodological Reflections and Preliminary Results. In: Susana Carvalho and Francois Gemenne (eds.): Nations and Their Histories. Constructions and Representations. Basingstoke: Palgrave Macmillan, 29–45.

Gundare, Ieva 2007: The Teaching of History in Georgia. With Special Focus on the Armenian and Azeri Minorities and Their Representation in Georgian History Textbooks. In: Levan Gigineishvili and Ieva Gundare: History Teaching in Georgia: Representation of Minorities in Georgian History Textbooks. Geneva: CIMERA. URL: http://www.cimera.org, accessed 21.3.2008.

Haydn, Terry 2004: History. In: John White (ed.): Rethinking the School Curriculum. Values, Aims and Purposes. London: RoutledgeFalmer, 87–103.

How We Lived Together in Georgia in the 20th Century. 2011. Tbilisi.

Jones, Stephen 1994: Old Ghosts and New Chains. Ethnicity and Memory in the Georgian Republic. In: Rubie S. Watson (ed.): Memory, History and Opposition under State Socialism. Santa Fe: University of Washington Press, 149–165.

Lomashvili, Pharnaoz and Sergo Vardosanidze 1997: National Educational Standard in History of Georgia. Tbilisi.

Miller, Aleksei 2008: The Romanov Empire and Nationalism. Essays in the Methodology of Historical Research. Budapest, New York: CEU Press.

Porat, Dan 2001: A Contemporary Past: History Textbooks as Sites of National Memory. In: Alaric Dickinson, Peter Gordon and Peter Lee (eds.): International Review of History Teaching, Vol. 3. Raising Standards in History Education. London: Woburn Press, 36–45.

Reisner, Oliver 1998: What Can and Should We Learn from Georgian History? Observations of Someone Who Was Trained in the Western Tradition of Science. In: Internationale Schulbuchforschung, No. 20: 409–424.

Schissler, Hanna 1987: Perceptions of the Other and Discovery of the Self. What Pupils Are Supposed to Learn about Each Other's Past. Perceptions of History. In: Volker Rolf Berghahn and Hanna Schissler (eds.): International Textbook Research on Britain, Germany and the United States. Oxford: Berg Publishers Limited, 26–37.

Velychenko, Stephen 1994: National History and the "History of the USSR": the Persistence and Impact of Categories. In: Donald Victor Schwartz and Razmik Panossian (eds.): Nationalism and History. The Politics of Nation Building in Post-Soviet Armenia, Azerbaijan and Georgia. University of Toronto: Center for Russian and East European Studies, 13–39.

Vesely, Lubos (ed.) 2008: Contemporary History Textbooks in the South Caucasus. Prague: Association for International Affairs.

Woodward, Kathryn 1997: Concepts of Identity and Difference. In: Kathryn Woodward (ed.): Identity and Difference. London: Sage Publications, 7–62.

The Model of the Multi-Ethnic City and the Question of a Linguistic-Cultural Identity of the Minorities in Georgia

Nino Pirtskhalava

Introduction

Effectively, within the Caucasian region Georgia is a multilingual and multi-religious country even today, with particularly strong inclinations towards the West and Europe. Speaking of a multidimensional diagnosis of the situation of the national, confessional, ethnic and language minorities in European states, means to take note of various aspects of life of the different communities in the cultural and historic context of these states. Correspondingly, for Georgia as a typical multi-ethnic state between Europe and Asia, it is of extreme importance to take into consideration the particular role of the different ethnic communities especially during the last two centuries (19th and 20th century). Emphasising the importance of this period should enable a more systematic approach and affords to focus on the essential issues of the study of the identity of national and cultural minorities in Georgia in the space of the Tsarist Empire and later in the modernised Tsarist Empire as Soviet Empire. The research will concentrate on finding out the forming of the identity narrative,[1] for example of the Georgian-speaking Jews, known as the "Georgian Jews", on the one hand, and the forming of the identity of the so called Russian-speaking population (Russians, Germans, Poles, most of Armenians, Greeks), on the other hand.

The concentration on the above named epoch helps to express the inimitably cosmopolitan atmosphere typical of fin-de-siècle Tbilisi. In this context one should note the fact that for several years, thanks to the development of a unique

[1] The forming of the identity narrative means the analysis of the correlation of the power to narrate and the power to block other narratives, which is crucial to culture and history. Narrative or story is the main rhetorical device used in historiography or in literary theory. In terms of Edward Said the "narrative is crucial" and his basic point is "that stories are at the heart of what explorers and novelists say about strange regions of the world; they also become the method colonised people use to assert their own identity and the existence of their own history". All the issues – who owned the land, who kept it going, who won it back or who plans its future – "were reflected, contested, and even for a time decided in narrative". And as Said agreed to the suggestion of one critic "nations themselves *are* narrations". Cf. Said, Edward 2007: Culture and Imperialism. London: Vintage Books, XIII.

spiritual ambiance – strong international colouring of the population (Jews, Armenians, Azeris, Russians, Germans, Poles etc.) – Tbilisi was crucially important within the Caucasus as the model of a multi-ethnic, multiconfessional and multicultural city, characterised by an active exchange between the nationalities. Around the turn of the century it became the meeting place of different oriental and occidental phenomena.

Considering the above-mentioned circumstances, during the analysis of the cultural, historical or literary processes particular attention should be devoted to the study of the interference and interrelations of all these fields. The research dedicated to the processes taking place in the multicultural society of Georgia is aimed at the comprehension of the processes taking place in Georgia in the 19th and 20th century on the basis of the comparative analysis of the historical and literary texts. It also points to the sharply set interdisciplinary nature of the designated research.

Considering the general context of the interconnection between literary criticism, history, philosophy, sociology, cultural studies, psychology and art history, the research pays special attention to the crucial aspect of the comparative study – the issue of the interference of literature and history.

The above mentioned method of comparative study, which denies the narrow disciplinary framework and strives for overcoming the boundaries separating them, will eventually contribute to a better understanding of the historical reality of Georgia in the past two centuries. This kind of interdisciplinary study will entail some positive results for the analysis of the range of unusual changes and the genesis of the fatal transformations. It will also highlight some of the problems, still keeping their importance for Georgia.

For further discussion of this problem, beside the abstract theoretical consideration of this thesis, the topic will be analysed on an artistic level, too. Furthermore, we can affirm that it was Alexandre Dumas who started an absolutely unique tradition of the perception of Georgia ("la Grèce, c'est Galathée encore marbre, la Géorgie, c'est Galathée animée et devenue femme") and especially of Tbilisi (Dumas 1990: 378). During the 19th and 20th century this perception became determinative not only for all Europeans, but also for the Georgians' auto-identification of their own existence as a culture situated at the hinge of Occident and Orient. Dumas' perception of the Tbilisian boundaries between Occident and Orient is explicitly musical. The polyphonic palette of its tonal colours becomes even more patent against the background of the Persian poems of Saadi sung in the district of the sulfur baths as well as of the execution of Verdi's "Lombards" by a remarkable company at the magnificent opera house, all the more embellished through the presence of beautiful Georgian women "embellie encore plus par la présence de très belles femmes". Thus, it was between the Belcanto of the Italian opera and the sung Persian poetry that the 19th century French writer perceived the multinational Tbilisi resounding in the context of the Tsarist multinational Empire (Russie qui est un "sombre souverain" dont la splendeur foudroyante lui fait perdre la faculté de se réjouir et elle se tient ainsi morose devant la Géorgie, cette "joyeuse esclave", "que sa servitude ne peut assombrir") (Dumas 1990: 347). Precisely this is what gave birth to the European tradition of the perception of Tbilisi.

National minorities in Georgia between state and homeland during the 19th and 20th centuries

Concerning the investigation of the historical experience and the question of a linguistic-cultural search for identity of the different ethnic communities in Georgia of the mentioned epoch we can discern three general periods:
1. from the end of the 19th century to 1917 (Tsarist Empire),
2. from 1917 to 1921 (Independent Republic of Georgia),
3. from 1921 to the end of the 1920–1930s (Soviet Empire).

As already mentioned, emphasising the importance of this period should create a more systematic approach and affords focussing on the essential issues of the study of the identity of national and cultural minorities in Georgia in the space of the Tsarist Empire and later in the modernised Tsarist Empire as Soviet Empire. At the same time the research will concentrate on finding out the forming of the identity narrative not only of the Jews in Georgia as "Georgian Jews" but also of the identity of other national and cultural minorities in Georgia; especially of the Germans from Swabia. To concentrate on the above named epoch helps to express the inimitably cosmopolitan atmosphere typical of fin-de-siècle Tbilisi and emphasising the importance of the last two centuries (19th and 20th century) should enable a more systematic approach on the essential issues of Jewish identity in Georgia as a *country* that lost its independence twice, once after the Georgian annexation by the Russian Empire in 1801 and later by the modernised Soviet Empire. For example the 1920s are the crucial period in the historical and cultural development of Georgia. The sovietisation in 1921 and, later on, the transformation into being part of the Soviet Union brought serious changes to the country. One of the main aims of the new state was the upbringing of the new human being - with new ideals and a new Soviet identity. History and literature - the two powerful tools of the formation of the collective memory - were ascribed the crucial role in this respect. Both became strongly ideologised, although the processes took different shapes in these two spheres.

The research will concentrate on finding out the formation of the identity narrative of the Jews in Georgia as "Georgian Jews" within the Russian Empire as the *state* including its whole oppressive system on the one hand and within Georgia as the *homeland* or *fatherland* on the other hand, where despite their attempts, the authorities could not completely annihilate the practice of Judaism. Even in the late 1960s and 1970s, most Georgian Jews managed to observe their traditions.

At the same time emphasising the importance of this historical period of the last two centuries is decisive for demonstrating that anti-Semitism as a secular nineteen-century ideology in Central and Western Europe was unknown in the Georgian culture. The fact is that modern anti-Semitism grew in proportion as traditional nationalism declined, and reached its climax at the exact moment when the European system of nation-states and its precarious balance of power crashed. In this historical epoch we cannot speak about Georgia as an independent nation-state, where, like in most European countries, the outburst of violent popular hatred against Jews and an anti-Jewish feeling, nourished by an economic conflict was an important factor in politics. As an annexed part of the Russian Empire, Georgia could not be a typical nation-state in which the "eternal anti-Semitism" or Jew-hatred was a normal and natural reaction of the society.

Thanks to this tragic political situation, the lack of statehood allowed Georgia to escape responsibility for one of the most chauvinistic and aggressive anti-Semitism of the Russian Empire with all its well-known pogroms. In Georgia there has never been a political movement against the Jews, neither special discrimination nor special favour determined to form of a Jewish type and to establish them as a special clique like in Europe. Since the 19th century the "Georgian Jews" as well the Georgians received their citizenship from the Russian government. Hence being citizens not of Georgia but of the Russian Empire they did not have to be tolerated as a "nation within the nation", in contrast to the European or Russian Jews.

In this period the Georgian Jews like the Jews from different Central and Western European countries obviously fulfilled some of the functions of the middle class, because they were mostly shopkeepers and traders. As a group they stood between the landowners and propertyless classes and were thus middlemen between the nobility and peasantry. Small property holders, however, can exist in a feudal as well as in a capitalist economy. In this context the social situation of the "Georgian Jews" is more or less comparable to the situation of most Central and Western European countries. It should also be mentioned that the historical and cultural reality of South-Eastern Europe and the Caucasus are comparable from several points of view particularly interesting for us (e.g. existence in the framework of the multinational empires, problems of identity in multi-ethnic and multi-cultural societies, etc.).

But there are some differences: The Jews very clearly were the most important inter-European element within a nationalised Europe, but the situation was different in Georgia, where the Jews were quite isolated from the international Jewish framework.

Tbilisi as the model of the multi-ethnic city

In this context one should note the fact that since several years in Tbilisi there is a sumptuous, self-confidently central synagogue which is filled with festively dressed families on Saturdays, a mosque praises God with the verses from the Qur'an or the Khutbah, while on the other side of the city in the Evangelic

Church the Biblical Word is preached in Luther's translation. This enables not only to find particular approaches to a Euro-Asiatic coalescence, but also to experience differently the word of one's own culture. Or in terms of Goethe: *Gottes ist der Orient! Gottes ist der Okzident! Nord- und südliches Gelände / Ruht im Frieden seiner Hände.*[2] Thanks to a unique spiritual ambiance Tbilisi has gained crucial importance within the Caucasus as the model of a multi-ethnic, multiconfessional and multicultural city.

In this context the function and semiotics of Tbilisi as a multi-ethnic city during the fin de siècle within the Caucasus is comparable to important cultural centres in Europe. When we speak of the European-Jewish tradition, of a critical utopia of Jewish intellectuals, it is of extreme importance to take into consideration the particular role and function of cities like Prague („Dreivölkerstadt", where *Hussitentum, Deutschtum* and *Judentum* shaped the city's unique history) and Vienna. For these represented, around the turn of the century – alongside to the rest of German cultural centres like Berlin, Leipzig, Munich and Dresden – the spiritual centres. By using the example of these cities we can show the cooperation of the literary-cultural and urban semiotics with particular clarity.

When we speak of germanophone literature or philosophy (cf. „Der deutsche Idealismus der jüdischen Philosophen" – Habermas) of this epoch in the cultural context of the Danube monarchy or Germany, the account of the prominent role of the Jewish intellectuals with a German tongue is indispensable. Using the example of the spiritual life within the cultural centres of the Danube monarchy – (Prague and Vienna) or Germany, one should note the fact that these cities became decisive centres for the liberal tradition of Jewish intellectuals and the Jewish educated middle-class within the German-speaking intellectual space. On the one hand, the physiognomy of Jewish thinkers of the past century was shaped by the cult of Kant, Goethe or Nietzsche. On the other hand, Jewish intellectuals were again those who remained fascinated, be it by the Marxian doctrine or by the ideas of Martin Buber.

At the same time, it was because of the tragic constraint of a historical irony of role play that in a Marxian context an intimate animosity on the part of the *Bildungsjuden* emerged against the *Geldjuden* – a sublime inner-Jewish anti-Semitism against a class whose imago had been strongly shaped by, for instance, the Rothshilds.

Though, in Europe at that time there were places like Vienna and Prague where thanks to a unique spiritual ambiance – strong international colouring of the population development, Bohemian traditions, the insular position of the language and the fibrous Jewish self-understanding – germanophone Jewish intellectuals were confronted with a choice between extreme assimilation and militant Zionism. This brought up, as a necessary consequence, the search for

---

2 Goethe, Johann Wolfgang 1977: West-östlicher Divan. Werke in 6 Bänden. Frankfurt am Main, 1977, S. 344.

identity on their own ground and meant an intense debate around the problematic concept of fatherland-haunting Austria for decades for the original citizens of the Danube monarchy.

In Europe at the same time there was a place like Paris where the quarrel and conflict between the anti-Semitic catholic "true" patriots or "les antidreyfusards" and the pro-Semitic minded cosmopolitans or "les dreyfusards" gave rise to the fad of the highly questionable philosemitism of certain glamorous saloons in Paris. In addition, typical for the mental atmosphere of these sophisticated circles in Europe are accentuation and emphasis on the affinity of German and Jewish phenomena. For further discussion about this problem, besides the abstract theoretical consideration of this thesis, the topic will be analysed on an artistic level, too. Therefore a qualitative content analysis of the literary works by Marcel Proust who speaks not only about "dialecte mi-allemand, mi-juif" (Proust 1954: 773) but also about "l'internationalisme juif" of the Parisian Jewish intellectuals similarly to Thomas Mann ("Wir sind international - aber wir sind pro-deutsch, sind es wie niemand sonst in der Welt, schon weil wir gar nicht umhinkönnen, die Verwandtschaft der Rolle von Deutschtum und Judentum auf Erden wahrzunehmen") (Mann 1975: 553) is undoubtedly very useful. But we have to bear in mind that the roots of the theoretical background for the interpretation of Judaism as an intermediate-international-pro-German phenomenon reach back to Nietzsche's doctrine and his dream of producing a crossbreed of Europeans as a consequence of continuous intersections that implied the annihilation of national animosities and of an "artificial nationalism", which is as dangerous as the "artificial Catholicism". This was the fundamental precondition for the attainment of his aim of life – the education of a "good European" (Nietzsche 1980: 309). In this process of a mingling of nations the Germans were assigned the role of "the nations' interpreter and mediator". The Jews were considered to be an indispensable "ingredient" for the education of a strong European crossbreed, because thanks to their activism, high intelligence and the accumulated historical experience they are to be seen as the "purest race at present living in Europe" (Nietzsche 1968: 201).

This intermediate-international-pro-German pathos gives distinction to the liberal tradition of Jewish intellectuals to which the middle of the 20th century in Europe, also because of the catastrophic history, has put an end. It can be considered paradigmatic for the common destiny of a Jewish-European intellectual of this epoch. It was in general more or less a typical characteristic feature of the assimilated well-educated representative of the Jewish community in Europe between two World Wars that reacted with an irritably nervous dynamic to the dissolute aggressive anti-Semitism as well as to the Parisian temporary fashion of philo-Semit (so called "cheap philosemitism") (Arendt 1976: 23) craze.

This nervousness, this ambiguous tremulous seesaw and "ulterior demonical possession of the switching of masks" = Maskenwechsel (G. Simmel) or "das von Proust so ausführlich besprochene Augurenlächeln der Clique" (Hannah Arendt) that signify the Jewish-European intellectuals "to be Jews, but not like Jews" (Habermas 1981: 56) is totally alien, different in nature and foreign to the Jewish nature of the "Georgian Jews". This Jewish nature has created and still occupies a unique niche of "Georgian Jews", which defines the cultural dimension of their Judaism and Jewish Existence. This precise concrete term that has been the commonly used term since the 19th century describes the essence of the idea of the particular case of the age-long unique relationship between Georgians and not simply general and abstract Jews but exactly the "Georgian Jews".

The most crucial difference to the European Jews was the absence of the "exception Jews" (Ausnahmejuden) among the Georgian Jewry, that was synonym to the assimilation that formed two types of Jews in Europe, what Hannah Arendt calls "Pariah and Parvenue". They were not excepted to become exceptional specimens of humanity without any ambiguity "to be and yet not to be Jews" (Arendt 1976: 56). According to Hannah Arendt "for the formation of a social history of the Jews within the nineteenth century, it was, however, decisive that to a certain extent every Jew in every generation had somehow at some time to decide whether he would remain a pariah and stay out of society altogether, or become a parvenue". And the result of the ambiguity of this situation was that "Jews felt simultaneously the pariah's regret at not having become a parvenue and the parvenue's bad conscience at having betrayed his people" (Arendt 1976: 66). For Georgian Jewry this "complex psychology of the average Jew" from Europe was totally alien.

At the same time it is important to bear in mind that assimilation as a group phenomenon really existed only among Jewish intellectuals and is not typical for Georgian Jewry of the 18th and 19th centuries. The ambiguity of this alternative social situation to that above-named period was untypical for the life style of Georgian Jewry and became familiar only after the emigration of the Ashkenazy Jews from Russia who, at the beginning of the 19th century, were forced by the Russian government to move to Georgia. The Ashkenazi Jews and the Georgian Jews began establishing contact with each other, but relations were strained. Georgian Jews considered the assimilated Ashkenazim to be godless and secular, while the Ashkenazim looked down to the "non-emancipated" Georgian Jews.

In the 19th century a differentiation between native Jews and those who "invaded" the country from the East was made in all Western and Central European countries. In this context the "Georgian Jews" were considered as native Jews and the Russian-speaking Ashkenazim from Russia as foreigners. The restricting differentiations between native and foreign Jews could not be avoided. At the same time this differentiation was the line of demarcation between conservative (native or Georgian Jews) and assimilated (Russian-speaking Ashkenazim) Jews.

An excellent formula, which may serve as a motto for Western European assimilation and which was propounded by the Russian Jew Judah Leib Gordon in Hebrew (be a man in the street and a Jew at home) "Ein Mensch auf der Straße und ein Jude zu Hause" (Arendt 2003: 142) or as Herder characterised the pathos of the new humanism of the eighteenth century which expressly wanted "new specimen of humanity" (neue Exemplare der Menschheit) (Arendt 1976: 57) is irrelevant for Georgian Jews of the two past centuries.

The birth and growth of modern anti-Semitism has been accompanied by the Jewish assimilation, the secularisation and withering away of the old religious and spiritual values of Judaism. Therefore, emancipation of the Jews as granted by the national state system in Europe during the nineteenth century had a double origin and an ever-present equivocal meaning.

Concept of the "Georgian Jews"

The detailed definition of the concept of the "Georgian Jews" should enable a better specification of the domain of definition. For that matter, it will be necessary to analyse two different, but complementary aspects of the relation between Georgians and Georgian Jews. On the one hand, this concerns the historical, cultural and religious aspects of the Jewish community in Georgia; on the other hand, we need to analyse the image of the "Georgian Jews" in the context of the Aliyah and its coherency to the history and culture of Jewish Diasporas or world Jewish community.

Specific characteristics of this binary-coded singular term of the "Georgian Jews" face a challenge which is at least two-fold. The twofold nature of the concept of the "Georgian Jews" with a specific bonding capacity means cohesive energy for two phenomena – the Georgian one and the Jewish one. Apparently the effects became doubly because this idea is part of the identity for both of them. According to this the separation of the "Georgian Jews" from their Jewishness as well as from their existential orientation towards the Georgian language and culture is not really possible.

To speak of a dual and multiple meaning of this inseparably connected elements of the above-named term of "Georgian Jews" at least two aspects should be considered. First of all, as a typical near-Eastern country, Georgia has always been looking towards Europe and apprehended its own mediatorial function between Orient and Occident. Since the 19th century self-consciousness of the mission of being the intermediate-interpretational culture mediator of this country situated between Europe and Asia could be one of the basic principles for the narrative, not of the ordinary "Georgian-Jewish commensal symbiosis" but rather of the Georgian-Jewish Mutualism. This is because of the particular character of the class of relationship between these two organisms where one element benefits but the other is neutral (there is no harm or benefit). In this case there is rather another type of association: mutualism, where both organisms benefit.

Furthermore, with this unique term of "Georgian Jews" the fibrous Jewish self-understanding has increased twofold and means for the members of the Georgian speaking Jewish community to be not common Jewish but something particular, namely "Georgian Jew". This extraordinary linguistic-ethnic-cultural construction is not simply a geo-ethnological term denoting the Jewish populations living in Georgia. It can also explain certain social hostility and the sense of superiority of "Georgian Jews" towards the Russian-speaking Ashkenazi Jews who later in the 19th century migrated, mostly eastwards from Russia, forming communities in Georgia after Georgia's annexation by the Tsarist Empire.

The eye-catching difference between the "Georgian Jews" and the Ashkenazi Jews attracted the attention of the famous German-speaking Jewish writer and journalist, also well-known as *the Raging Reporter,* Egon Erwin Kisch, born in Prague, who visited Georgia in the nineteen-twenties. Around the turn of the century he experienced in real life a masked ball of Tbilisi titled "An der Grenze Asiens und Europas". Kisch speaks about "absolute unikale Besonderheit der kaukasischen Juden, die besonders der 'Bergjuden'", who migrated from Kutaisi to the capital and who according to Kisch are unsimilar to their compatriots, even visually: "Hochgewachsen, mit breiten, eher auf- als abwärts gekrümmten Nasen". In this context Kisch's expression "wer weiß, sie können die einzigen Arier dieser europäisch-asiatischen Bezirke sein!" (Kisch 1993: 201) is a symbolic one. It is underlined that these Jews are very different from the Ashkenazi and that in contrast to the Russian Jews they speak neither Yiddish nor Russian. This is how Kisch perceives the Jewish Russian-speaking population of Georgia.

The use of the name "Georgian Jews" in a Georgian-speaking area mirrors the century-old sense of togetherness and with this beloved saga also accents two aspects:

1. For Georgian-speaking Jews it means enhancement of the unique position as "Georgian Jews", at the same time it means to excel and to be distinguishable by superiority within the world's Jewish population and the international Jewish community.
2. For Georgians, thanks to an insular isolated position of their language and confession in the region and thanks to the lack of diaspora, who consider themselves as "orphan-nation" and are suffering from this mental trauma, the self-declaration of the Georgian-speaking Jews as "Georgian Jews" means to find relatives connected with them by language and affinity, which become something like a connecting bridge that channels the way of Georgia to the world political-cultural space.

Today a specific bonding capacity of this age-long tradition of an intercultural Jewish-Georgian dialogue acquires particular importance. This dialogue has lost none of its relevance today. By the observation of this tradition not only the Jewish life in history and present age in Georgia has been shown but also the importance of the reception of the ideas of the European and Jewish Enlightenment as precondition for the political and cultural emancipation. In this context the accentuation of the importance of the last two centuries (19th and 20th century) should enable not only a more systematic approach and the focus on the essential issues of the Jewish identity in Georgia as a *country* that lost its independence twice, but also provides an insight into the precedent 18th century. This is correlated with *Haskalah*, the *Jewish Enlightenment*, a movement among European

Jews and the Jewish emancipation in Europe, as precondition for the integration into the European society.

As Jürgen Habermas said, there was no "jüdisches Abendland" (Jewish Occident) before the 18th century (Habermas 1981: 54). And in this context one should note that for the history of Georgian Jewry the version of the Occidental Enlightenment with its origins in Berlin, the capital city of Germany, is largely unknown. Instead of Haskalah, this essential and indispensable phase of the Jewish culture, an endless string of wars and invasions characterised the 18th century in Georgia.

According to Habermas before the 18th century "liegt vielmehr das Mittelalter des Gettos" (Habermas 1981: 54) and to that effect if *Haskalah* followers advocated the "coming out of ghetto" in order to assimilate among gentile nations, which implied both the struggle for Jewish emancipation and the integration in the wider European society, this resulted in the Jewish political movements and Jewish Nationalism.

The situation in Georgia is totally different in nature. The engagement of Jews in a variety of competing ways within the country where they lived is alien to the nature of the Jewishness of the "Georgian Jews". Possibly because of the lack of challenge, the Haskalah movement with all the positive and disputable consequences was non-existing in Georgia in this concrete historical period. Also, there is nothing like the crowding of the cultural sphere by Jews which was especially marked in Germany and Austria and later even in Russia, where a great proportion of cultural institutions, like newspapers, publishing, music and theatre, became Jewish enterprises.

Thanks to this contradictory matter of fact, in contrast to the German-speaking Jewish intellectuals who were confronted with a choice between extreme assimilation and militant Zionism, the "Georgian Jews" were distant from the acute conflict between the enlightened and the orthodox Jews on the one hand and the conflict between the Jews and the Georgian society on the other hand.

A necessary consequence in this context was that the function and semiotics of Tbilisi as a multi-ethnic city during the fin de siècle within the Caucasus is comparable to the most important cultural centres in Europe like Berlin. At the same time, like Berlin, Tbilisi is a city that witnessed a rising middle class and intellectual elite of Jews. But this process of rising has extremely decelerated and is erratic.

This fact shows the contradiction of a lack of challenge. The lack of aggressiveness and of religious persecution on the part of the native society as a potential advantage provoked a certain inactivity. This excluded the struggle for Jewish emancipation characteristic for the European life of the late 18th and early 19th centuries and caused what the nation-state had once feared so much, namely the birth of a Jewish intelligentsia.

It is regrettable that cultural, political and metaphorical functions of the Georgian-Jewish mutualism forming narrative have not been sufficiently been thematised, even if the newest German literature about Georgia argues that "Georgien ist vielleicht das einzige Land der Welt, in dem es nie einen organisierten Antisemitismus gab".[3]

Concerning the investigation of the historical experience and the question of a linguistic-cultural search of identity of the Jews in Georgia it is of extreme importance to take into consideration the issue of the political status of Georgia, where Georgian-speaking Jewry is one of the oldest communities (with an approximately 2,600-year history in the region), tracing back their migration into the country during the Babylonian captivity.

Due to Aliyah[4] Georgia's Jewish population has steadily decreased over the years during the last two centuries. In the second half of the 19th century (1863) groups of Jews began to return to the Holy Land, mostly for religious reasons. Later, after the Russian Revolution, the Red Army invaded Georgia in February 1921, prompting a mass exodus from the region. Approximately 1,500–2,000 Jews left Georgia. In the middle of 20th century huge numbers of Georgian Jews applied for exit visas to immigrate to Israel. In 1969 several families addressed the Human Rights Commission of the United Nations, demanding permission to make Aliyah. This was the first public insistence by Soviet Jews for immigration to Israel. In July 1971 a group of Georgian Jews went on a hunger strike outside a Moscow post office. As a result, the determination of the Georgian Jews led the Soviets to lessen their harsh anti-Jewish policies. During the 1970s about 30,000 Georgian Jews moved to Israel and thousands of others left for other countries. Approximately 17 percent of the Soviet Jewish population emigrated at that time.[5]

In this context one could argue that Georgian Jews did not leave their fatherland, but the state, a Soviet Empire modernised version of the Russian Tsarist Empire or so-called "jail of the nations" (de Custine). The Georgian Jews perceived this state from the perspective of a double or even triple detachment. It is precisely this detachment, obtained by the triple alienating experience, through which an acuity was gained, making the lack of intimacy with the state bearable. Because unlike Georgia as a *fatherland*, the Russian Empire could only be a *state* thanks to the chimeric functioning of the state machinery, but would never become a *homeland*.

---

[3] Wackwitz, Stephan: 8½ Spaziergänge in Tbilissi. URL: http://www.eurozine.com/articles/2012-03-07-wackwitz-de.html, accessed 8. 7. 2015.

[4] (Hebrew: עֲלִיָּה *aliyah*, "ascent") is the immigration of Jews from the diaspora to the land of Israel *(Eretz Yisrael)*.

[5] Cf. *грузинские евреи*. Электронная еврейская энциклопедия. The Jewish Encyclopedia in Russian on the Web. Электронная еврейская энциклопедия ... URL: http://www.eleven.co.il/article/11322, accessed 8. 7. 2015; ჭიჭინაძე ზ., «ქართველი ებრაელები საქართველოში», თბ., 1990; მეტრეველი რ., «ებრაელები საქართველოში», თბ., 2002; მამისთვალიშვილი ე., «ქართველ ებრაელთა ისტორია», თბ., 1995; ციციაშვილი ა., «ებრაელები და საქართველო», თბ., 2003.

In conclusion it should be made clear that be it because of geographical, linguistic, political or even cultural reasons, the Jewish Identity Narratives in Georgia still waits for a sufficiently profound study as well as for a study and analysis of the tracks of the Germans or other Europeans in the culture and history of Georgia.

The tracks of the Germans from Swabia in the culture and history of Georgia

In the course of the ever-expanding investigations on the transnational and transcultural phenomena of the history of literature and culture the boundaries of what may be called the history of "German" literature and culture have greatly changed. Besides the phenomena of migration noticeable within Germany and by now marked with the controversial concept of "migration literature", especially the historical and actual migration of Germans to foreign countries has become a major and much-researched topic. The emigration and re-emigration of Germans to the East, i. e. to Romania, the modern Czech Republic, Hungary, Serbia etc., has been studied not only within the framework of particular projects, but has also gained a major place in the current debates of culture theory by means of institutionalisation. The research results are important not only for historical and literary studies, but also have a political relevance.

As mentioned above, there still needs to be a sufficiently profound study on German migration to Georgia. This deficit could be rectified through the intensification of the cooperation and exchange between German and Georgian scholars from the fields of literary, linguistic and cultural studies.

For that matter it will be necessary to analyse two different, but complementary aspects of the relation between Georgia and Germany. On the one hand, this affects the historical, cultural and religious aspects of the emigration of Germans, especially of Swabians, to Georgia; on the other hand, we need to analyse the image of Georgia in the German-speaking literature and culture. To be more precise, this concerns the mythical image of the Caucasus, which is identified with Georgia as the complement of what is considered as the "Orient". Since the studies of Edward Said concerning the Western "Orientalism" we know how world regions become areas for the projection of cultural fantasies of origins. However, Orient has always meant India or the Arabic world. The imaginations of the Caucasus and the mythical and metaphorical functions of this mountain situated between Europe and Asia has not been sufficiently been addressed. The Caucasus functions as an intersection between East and West and at the same time represents something like a "pure" no man's land. It is both a borderline and a passage – a liminal region that instead of separating has rather the function of mediating.

Effectively, within the Caucasian region Georgia is a multilingual and multireligious country even today, with particularly strong inclinations towards the West and Europe. In the context of various movements of migration or colonization the German migration plays a particularly important role. Hölderin's hymn "Die Wanderung" is a pertinent example for the connection of historical events with metaphorical interpretation.

This hymn, published in 1802 and rightly considered as enigmatic, names the homeland right from the beginning: "Glückselig Suevien, meine Mutter." In the description of the journey of the "lieben Verwandten" from the Alps, from the central-European Suevia to the Caucasus, we should not only see a metaphysical search for a new transcendent centre. It also alludes to the historical facts that Hölderlin learned at school – "Auch hat mir ohnedies / In jüngeren Tagen Eines vertraut" (Hölderlin 1969: 145 f.). The Hölderlinian description of the migration of his fellow countrymen "deutschen Geschlechts" to the Caucasus certainly contains a historical core. In fact, some of the Hölderlin researchers (Friedrich Beißner and Jochen Schmidt, cf. Hölderlin 1969: 145 f.) suppose that the poet thought of this migration along the lines of the emigration of the Swabian settlers to the Black Sea prompted by Catherine II the Great in 1770, and which still belonged to the poet's near past.

Not all historical facts are correctly reproduced in Hölderlin's hymn: The Germans came from their Swabian homeland in two waves. The first one arrived in 1817, the second in the 20s of the 19th century. On 21st of September 1917 the first 31 families arrived in Tbilisi and settled down in Sartichala near Tbilisi. The first colony was named Marienfeld. Until the end of 1819 six colonies were founded in the Caucasus: Mariendorf and Petersdorf in Sartichala, the Tbilisi colony on the territory of the Aghmashenebeli-avenue, Alexanderdorf in the area of the Samtrediastreet in Tbilisi, Elisabethtal (today Assureti), Ekaterinenfeld (today Bolnisi). In 1842, close to Zalka, the new colony Alexandershilf was founded, which was then re-named to Rosenberg. In 1884 Neudorf and Gnadenberg were founded – two colonies near Sokhumi. In general, throughout the 19th century the migration from Germany to Russia and to South Caucasus had a permanent character. The newcomers settled down in big cities or joined the already existing colonies. "Colonists" was the official designation of the German immigrants. Until 1884 these villages were named "German colonies in Georgia", then "German colonies in the South Caucasus".

At the beginning of the Second World War nearly all Germans were subjected to forced resettlement. After Stalin's death a small number came back. Some of the Germans who had formerly lived in Azerbaijan came to Georgia and founded two new villages in the region of Gardabani: Botanika and Rosa (Luxemburg). However, in the period of "Perestroika" many of the native Germans returned to Germany for social reasons.

Along with the immigrants not only the German language, but also some other culturally and ideologically interesting phenomena came to Georgia. Since the 19th century Georgian and foreign scientists have done research regarding the history, religion, economy, morals and customs of the German colonists in Georgia. Unfortunately, the architectonic heritage of the settlers has only rarely been taken into consideration. The importance and the artistic value of these buildings are mostly unknown to both Georgians and Germans. The result is that these houses, which are already derelict and officially unpreserved, slowly lose their face or disappear.

Besides the material tracks there are also tracks related to the history of mentality: this was first of all the proverbial Swabian assiduity, the "inner-worldly asceticism" which inspired Max Weber for his thesis of the connection between Protestantism and capitalism. This assiduity manifested itself particularly in the history of the agriculture and handicraft enterprises of the colonies. It is noteworthy that the German colonies owe their advancement and wealth to the viniculture; in the homeland of grape-vine in the South Caucasus they founded their own winegrowing schools that became exemplar places of German trade diligence. The prosperity and success in viniculture was rather due to the particular working morale in the sense of a consequent rationalisation and to the harmonic unification of the innate and the learned than due to permanent and hard physical work, which the country's excellent terrain and favourable climate did not even need. During several decades many other crafts were exclusively in the hands of the Germans. After the mass deportations in the 1930s and 1940s only few successors of these precision engineers, opticians, clockmakers and gunsmiths remained in the country, predominantly by means of marriages into Georgian or Russian families.

Conclusion

As a typically near-Eastern country, Georgia had always been looking towards Europe and according to Hegel, "was darin hervorragend ist, hat dieses Land nicht bei sich behalten, sondern nach Europa entsendet. Den Anfang aller religiösen und aller staatlichen Prinzipien stellt es dar, aber in Europa ist erst die Entwicklung derselben geschehen" (Hegel 1995: 132). For decades German had been the language which channelled the way of Georgians to the European cultural space. Today this long lasting tradition of intercultural Germano-Georgian dialogue could gain particular importance, as well as the century-long Jewish-Georgian dialogue.

The analysis of Jewish-Georgian, German-Georgian or Polish-Georgian etc. cultural contacts would comprise not only the opening and reworking of unknown sources and data of the literary tracks in the culture and arts of Georgia, but also makes the investigation of the substance of the strong international colouring of the multi-ethnic population between *state* (Tsarist or Soviet Empire) and *homeland* (Georgia) during the last two centuries (19th and 20th century) possible. Besides, in this context a platform should be created for the consideration of the history of Georgian culture in the context of European and World developments. With regard to the investigation of the historical experience and the question of, for example, a linguistic-cultural search for identity of the Jews in Georgia it is of extreme importance to consider the issue of the political status of

Georgia, where Georgian-speaking Jewry is one of the oldest communities in the world (with an approximately 2,600-years of history in the region). Jewish history, whose central concern since the Babylonian exile has always been survival, received a peculiar room for development in Georgia, where the aggressive anti-Semitism as well as the "cheap philosemitism" as the European fashion of philo-Semitic craze is totally alien, different in nature and foreign to the nature of the interpretation of the Jewishness of the "Georgian Jews", which defines the cultural dimension of their Judaism and Jewish Existence.

Decisive in our context is that the well-organised anti-Semitism as an ideological force is different from primitive, banal anti-Jewish feelings or attitudes of everyday life without any political relevance. And the ability to distinguish between them is crucial not only for the investigation of the history of Jewry in Georgia but first of all for the systematic study of the historical essence of Georgian culture. At the same time it is of extreme importance to take into consideration how so-called "nationalistic anti-Semitism" is harmless when compared with modern movements and well-organised anti-Semitism as ideology.

As mentioned above, the history of German migration to Georgia and the forming of their identity still waits for a sufficiently profound study. This also applies to the study of migration history of the other minorities, the so called Russian-speaking population (Russians, Poles, most of Armenians, Greeks) in Georgia. This deficit could be rectified through the intensification of the cooperation and exchange between scholars from the fields of literary, linguistic and cultural studies.

In the course of the ever increasing researches concerning transnational and transcultural phenomena of the history of culture the borders of what one may call "Georgian" cultural history have changed considerably. This context makes the problem of a Georgian-Jewish or Georgian-German dialogue as well as of the historical and contemporary migration of Jews and Germans an important subject. A multilateral and exhaustive exploration of these intercultural and interconfessional questions, which yet have to become prominent subjects in contemporary debates in cultural theory, requires an integrative and interdisciplinary analysis of historical, linguistic and cultural relations. Hence, the future results of this research will be important not only for historical, cultural and literary studies, but will also have political relevance.

Therefore, it will be necessary to address two different, but at the same time complementary aspects of the communication between Georgia and the Jewish or German culture. On the one hand, we will have to examine the historical, linguistic and religious aspects of the Jewish or German phenomenon in Georgia, which still is a metalinguistic and multiconfessional country and shows particular interest in increasing its bonds with the West. On the other hand, we will have to deal with comprehensive cultural-historical and socio-cultural aspects, which will be analysed through detailed and reciprocally complementing studies in the history of languages, culture, literature and religion. Only by means of an interdisciplinary perspective is it possible to thoroughly analyse the question of the linguistic-cultural quest for identity among national, confessional, ethnic and language minorities in Georgia in the socio-cultural context of European developments.

It is in this context that the exploration of the semiotics of Tbilisi as a model for a multi-ethnic, multiconfessional and multicultural city as well as for a liminal experience between Orient and Occident gains decisive importance.

References

Arendt, Hanna 1976: The Origins of Totalitarianism. San Diego, New York, London: Harcourt Inc.

Arendt, Hanna 2003: Elemente und Ursprünge totaler Herrschaft. 9th Edition. München, Zürich: Piper.

Dumas, Alexandre 1990: Impressions de voyage. III, Le Caucase. Paris: Editions François Bourin. URL: http://gallica.bnf.fr/ark:/12148/bpt6k9935c/f1.image, accessed 7. 7. 2015.

Goethe, Johann Wolfgang 1977: West-östlicher Divan. Werke in 6 Bänden. Frankfurt am Main: Insel Verlag.

Habermas, Jürgen 1981: Der deutsche Idealismus der jüdischen Philosophen. In: Jürgen Habermas: Philosophisch-politische Profile, extended edition. Frankfurt am Main: Suhrkamp.

Hegel, Georg Wilhelm Friedrich 1995: Vorlesungen über die Philosophie der Weltgeschichte. Werke, Vol. 12. Frankfurt am Main: Suhrkamp Verlag.

Hölderlin, Friedrich 1969: Hölderlin Werke und Briefe. Vol. I. Eds.: Friedrich Beißner and Jochen Schmidt. Frankfurt am Main: Insel Verlag.

Kisch, Egon Erwin 1993: Gesammelte Werke in Einzelausgaben, Vol. 4: Zaren, Popen, Bolschewiken; Asien gründlich verändert; China geheim. Berlin: Aufbau Verlag.

Mann Thomas 1975: Doktor Faustus. Berlin, Weimar: Aufbau-Verlag.

Nietzsche, Friedrich 1968: Zur Genealogie der Moral. Eine Streitschrift. In: Friedrich Nietzsche: Werke. Kritische Gesamtausgabe, Bd. VI, 2: Jenseits von Gut und Böse. Berlin: Walter de Gruyter.

Nietzsche, Friedrich 1980: Menschliches, allzu Menschliches. In: Giorgio Collo and Mazzino Montinari (eds): Friedrich Nietzsche: Sämtliche Werke. Kritische Studienausgabe in 15 Bänden, Vol. 2. München, Berlin, New York: Deutscher Taschenbuch Verlag.

Proust, Marcel 1954: À la recherche du temps perdu: A l'ombre des jeunes filles en fleurs. Paris: Gallimard.

Said, Edward 2007: Culture and Imperialism. London: Vintage Books.

Wackwitz, Stephan: 8½ Spaziergänge in Tbilissi. URL: http://www.eurozine.com/articles/2012-03-07-wackwitz-de.html, accessed 8. 7. 2015.

грузинские евреи. Электронная еврейская энциклопедия. The Jewish Encyclopedia in Russian on the Web. Электронная еврейская энциклопедия … URL: http://www.eleven.co.il/article/11322, accessed 8. 7. 2015.
მამისთვალიშვილი ე., «ქართველ ებრაელთა ისტორია», თბ., 1995.
მეტრეველი რ., «ებრაელები საქართველოში», თბ., 2002.
ციციაშვილი ა., «ებრაელები და საქართველო», თბ., 2003.
ჭიჭინაძე ზ., «ქართველი ებრაელები საქართველოში», თბ., 1990.

Small Numbers, Big Issues: the Border Areas as Social Arena of Legal Systems

Nebi Bardhoshi

Introduction

It has been argued that the function of the legal system is not only keeping the social order intact through justice projections and dispute settlements but it has, also, the capacity of representing and creating a classificatory scheme of people, of things and human activities. In addition, the law creates a social field in which people participate, interact and negotiate their social status and identities. The laws on citizenship, the legal status of any minority, and the national discourse of the nation state are closely related and depended on each other. On the one hand the law on citizenship needs the national discourse to get its legitimacy as national discourse and ideology needs the law as an instrument of governmentally through classification and categorization of peoples' lives and activities within the borders of the state. The legal status of any minority, on the other hand, as the notion of minority itself becomes a product of the above interrelations and interdependencies between the national discourse and the law on citizenship. Therefore, the national discourses on citizenship should be seen as a classificatory structure rather than a representative of any kind of collective consciousness (Hart 1999: 198) with the function to legitimize the laws and state's politics on minorities.

The legal system on minorities and citizenship, for many post-socialist societies, has rapidly and drastically changed as a result of the politics of state to meet the standards of a Western type of market oriented democracy. The process of democratization itself, in post-socialist nation-state societies, seems to be a result of both national and transnational processes and forces. The question of minority rights and citizenship is rearticulated and redefined in order to meet the standard of the new economic, political, legal, social and cultural contexts represented by the market oriented democracy which is part and parcel, as the case of Balkan societies represents, of the process of Europeanization and European Union integration.

The anthropological works on Eastern Europe have shown us how nation-states have behaved in this new geopolitical context (Hayden 1992, Verdery 1996, Herzfeld 2005, Cohen and Dragovic-Soso 2007). Regardless of the new geopolitical and ideological milieu, the nation-states once again domesticate and shape the whole language of human rights, democracy and Europeanization to fit in the scheme of national discourse. In fact, the nation state acts as one of the many agents with the capacity to tailor the cloth of ideology to fit the body of their societies (see Hutchinson 2005, Creed 1998, 2013). Ethnographic data show that the states have not given up their classical position in proving to the nation where its borders are. By drawing light on how members of two different ethnic minorities living in two different border areas articulate their identity within the legal systems of different nation states, I will argue in this article that the law does not only create a social field but also an economic sphere of prestige where the material world finds its meaning. The case studies used in this article will show how the rhetoric of human rights, rule of law and Europeanization is used by the state as an instrument, on the one hand, to prove and to create, on the other hand, new socio-cultural realities for the nation. In turn, the law on minorities and citizenship under this context, embedded as a suitable economical offer, becomes an instrument in the hand of the nation-state through which the national identity is extracted from many people and communities, especially inhabiting the border areas. We need, thus, to expand the idea that the nation-state does not only make everything possible to prove the cultural homogeneity of the nation within its borders (Brubaker 1994: 59). But it also stretches to the other side or far beyond the actual border area by proving to all interested parties the actual historical borders of the nation (de Rapper 2007: 569).

Notes on fieldwork and minorities

The ethnographic data used for this work derive from two different ethnic minorities that live in border areas. The first set of data originates from the Aromanian/Vllachs community of Albania living in the areas near the Albanian and Greek border. The second set of data comes from the Slavic Muslims community living in Gora and Zhupa villages located in the border area between Kosovo, Albania and Macedonia (FYROM). These case studies are not chosen for comparison purpose, but they should be seen as instructive cases for future studies and further inquiries within a wider research project. In this paper the Aromanian/Vllach people, besides the data collected from fieldwork, are analysed also from the legal perspective set by the state law on minority and citizenship of Albania, Greece and Romania. The same logic is applied also in the second case of the Slavic Muslim community where the ethnographic data are combined to foster our arguments about the law on minorities and citizenship of the states of Kosovo, Serbia, Macedonia, and Bulgaria.

To analyse our ethnographic data I made use of the theoretical lenses deriving from a legal pluralism approach in understanding the life of law, the local meaning attributed to it, and above all the daily life of people (Griffiths 1986, Merry 1988, Rouland 1994, Benda-Beckmann 2002, Vanderlinden 1971, 1989). In terms of methodology, in order to comprehend how the states produce their laws on citizenship and minority right, I combined the polymorphous engagement of studying up strategy (Nader 1972: 285–311, Gustterson 1997: 114–119) with the long term ethnographic exploration of the everyday life of people and communities living in the border areas. Nations states and their politics have been observed and analysed by keeping in mind two relevant issues. Firstly, the state law is a social fact (Nader 2002). Secondly, the law is a product of power relations within a society. Consequently, the study of law cannot and should not be separated from the concrete geographies of power, power relations, and social contexts from where it originates (McGrew 1998: 337–338).

In a broader view these border areas represent a social arena where different nation states try to show their authority aiming toward the protection and/or creation of ethnic minorities. By defining the border areas as the locus of ethnographic exploration, such perspective gives us the possibility to see how the legal categories of different nation-states operate and take form in the daily life of people who are subject to such categories. At the same time the border areas become the arena of continuous formations and exchanges of national identities by the people who inhabit them. Moreover, the issue of minority numbers inhabiting these areas has, for some time now, has become an important public issue. Referring to Appardurai's work "small numbers" of ethnic minorities are considered as sources and as key element of geography of anger (Appardurai 2006). Once again the law is called by the nation-states to play its role in categorizing and classifying the people of the border area as minority or national majority. The logic, rhetoric and ideology of the numbers and the specific importance attributed to them by the nation-states in relation to the border communities will also be regarded throughout the analysis of this work.

The Aromanian community and the border area: between Greeks and Albanians

The border area between Greece and Albania has become an anthropological *locus* as well as an anthropological *topos* during the last two decades. Some of the issues explored by scholars were related to the border impact in the life of people, collective identity and migration (i.e., de Rapper 2006, 2007, 2009, Green 2005, 2007, Lelaj and Bardhoshi 2008, Schwandner-Sievers 1999). The national origin has once again become a topic in the daily life of people. The reasons are partly related to the post-socialist or post-dictatorial conditions of people and communities living in the border area especially in Albania, as well as to the border itself which embeds the life of the people inhabiting it with a sense of "ambiguity" (de Rapper 2007, 2009). We can add that post-dictatorial Albania, partly because of a negative social memory on the nation-state in general, partly because of dictatorship and also because of state failure after the dictatorship, was a fertile social environment for the social production of mistrust towards state institutions (Giordano and Kostova 2002).

The state discourse upon which, on the one hand, the national identity was forged, created and enforced was strongly challenged as the post-dictatorial state weakened and continuously delegitimized. On the other hand, the pluralisation of truths about the national or ethnic identity, once a state domain, are rearticulated on different levels through the same conceptual categories and social memory created by the state from self-proclaimed, regional and local intellectuals, nationalist historians and other groups. The post-dictatorial Albanian public opinion has been shaped the subject by a flux of information that derives not only from state institutions such as formal education but also from the neo-liberal market and social media where *national language, the cult of ancestors, the belief on common blood origin* are presented. Parts of this symbolic market of the nationhood – *folklore and traditions* – are presented by different state and non-state agencies as products to be sold and consumed in the form of books, songs and cultural artifacts. In a broader view, the articulation and dialectics between state and non-state agents, when it comes to the issue of national identity and the mechanisms used for its creation and eventually its legitimization are unthinkable without strategies of collective memory production for the sake of the present (Halbwachs 1992: 119, see also Connerton 1989). It also cannot be understood without taking in consideration the legal system of citizenship and minorities at which such social memory aims to communicate as well to be politically and morally legitimized.

The members of the Aromanian community in Albania who live in or originate from the border areas near Greece make use of state criteria to classify themselves. On the one hand, the members of this community who want to promote their affiliation to Greece emphasize their common religious background, territory and ancestors. Their discourse does not neglect to underline the contribution of Aromanian personalities throughout the history of the Greek nation-state. Other members of the same community, on the other hand, who want to promote the community's affiliation to Rumania, emphasize issues related to language, race and history to prove their Romanian ethnic origin (Dino and Puriqi 2003). In both written publications and daily life conversations members of the Aromanian community make use of either *ius soli* and/or *ius sanguinis* criteria in order to legitimize their belongingness to the legal categories created by the law on citizenship and minorities in the countries to which they claim affinity as well as in the country where they live, which – in this case – is Albania.

What is the number of Aromanians in Albania? Different agencies have raised different numbers as an answer to this question. Since the creation of nation-states in the Balkans, the uncertainty about the numbers of a given minority has always been present. Regardless of the data we have at hand, it can be said that throughout the history of the censuses, it is observable with naked eye that nation states have made titanic efforts to decrease, on the one hand, the number of minorities inside the state territory and, on the other hand, to increase the number of their minorities outside the state border. The number of the Aromanian community in Albania is very debatable. A governmental document on minorities reports that in 1955 approximately 4249 people lived in Albania[1]. On the other hand, a prominent figure and researcher on the Aromanian community in the Balkans, John Winnifrith, evaluated that in Albania there live approximately 200000 Aromuni (Winnifrith 1995: 68). Leaders of the Aromanian community support the idea that this number is for sure more than 200000 Aromanian in Albania (Dino and Puriqi 2003).

The Aromanian community in Albania, after the fall of communism, was organized politically into an association aiming at the protection and promotion of the community's collective identity (Schwandner-Sievers 1999: 7). Besides the protection of the language and cultural heritage, part of the agenda was also the political lobbying and pressuring the Albanian government in order to gain the status of ethnic minority for the community. Attaining the status of ethnic minority would make the protection of language and cultural heritage for this community much easier because both language and cultural heritage would have been supported at least by Albanian governmental funds. In a conversation I had with the General Secretary of this Association in Tirana, I was told that, besides being a historical momentum for the community, this meeting was accompanied by a severe clash between the Pro Hellenic and Pro Rumania grouping. Other researchers have also referred to this clash during the meeting (Schwandner-Sievers 1999: 3, Nitsiakos 2010). In between the clash of the two groupings within the Aromanian community, a third party emerged, a Pro-Albanian one, fostering the idea that the community should simply be considered as Vllachs Albanian Citizens. Such a grouping promotes the idea of a long harmonious historical relation between Albanians and Aromanians. Through various sources it has emphasized and promoted the contribution made by Aromanians throughout Albanian history.

Progress considering the legal status of this community was made in 1997, when the Union for Aromanian Language and Culture, based in Freiburg/Germany and led by the well-known Diaspora Aromanian activist Vasile Barba, succeeded in leading the Parliamentary Assembly of the Council of Europe to formulate a recommendation for the protection of the Aromanian culture and language in the host countries.[2] This decision was made without the participation of Greece (Schwandner-Sievers 1999: 3). But the fact that Romania has not recognized Kosovo as an independent state is used as an informal argument for why the Albanian government has not recognized the Aromanian community as an ethnic minority so far. Until now, besides the work done by the Association, the Aromanian community in Albania is legally recognized as a *linguistic minority* only. To attain the status of ethnic minority, the criteria used in the Albanian law on minorities, are those following the notion of *territorial continuity*. The case of the modern Romanian and Aromanian community living in Albania

[1] Raport mbi Pakicat Kombëtare në Shqipëri, 2001: 112.

[2] Council of Europe Parliamentary Assembly AACR 18.7.

reflects a *territorial discontinuity* and therefore the community is categorized as a *linguistic minority* only.

In 2012 the community was organized into a political party called *The Alliance for Equality and European Justice Party (ABDEP)* and it took part in the national election held in the same year. The organization of minorities into political parties is not something new for Albania. Since the first post-communist elections, the Greek minority living in Albania was organized and has often more than one seat in parliament with the Human Rights Party (PBDNJ). The Macedonian minority is also organized into a political party called The Macedonian Alliance for European Integration Party (AMIEP). Despite the fact that the Aromanians were organized into a political party has not eased the frictions between the Pro-Hellenic and Pro-Romanian groupings in the community the opposite is true.

Moreover, the issue of minority numbers in Albania became a hot issue in 2011. In this year the Albanian Government started the registration of population based on the principle of *self-declaration*. The issue was then presented by the government as a condition imposed by the European Union in the light of standard fulfilment. For the first time after WW II, the Albanian state recognized people's right to freely express their ethnic identity. The vice chairman of Albania Council of Justice started a national tour accusing the Albanian Government for undertaking this process. The accusations were articulated in terms of protecting 'national interest', and it was said that the government was sold out to the Greeks. The way of how the census was structured, so further interpretation, would artificially increase the number of the Greek minority in Albania and bring water to the Greek nationalistic claims for south Albania. The anti-census movement initiated by the resigned vice chairman of the Albanian Council of Justice, first turned into an NGO, and after few months, it was organized into a nationalistic party called Aleanca Kuq e Zi (Red and Black Alliance Party or RBA) (Bardhoshi and Lelaj 2012). The party representing the interest of the Greek minority in Albania strongly reacted against the declarations made by the RBA Party. In the declarations of the representatives of the Greek minority party, the RBA was considered to be a nationalistic and xenophobic political movement that went against European Union values. In turn, the RBA Party insisted on accusing the Albanian government for participating in this big conspiracy against the Albanian nation, together with the Greek minority party, the head of the Albanian Orthodox Church, Greek diplomats and ordinary people who, by selling out their national identity, were in fact selling out a part of the territory of Albania. One of the slogans of the RBA Party used against the principle of self-declaration in the census was "KOMBËSIA NUK SHITET" (THE NATIONALITY IS NOT FOR SALE!). In one of its official declarations the RBA party stated that according to information on their disposal a whole Muslim village in the Korça district (a district near the Albanian-Greek boarder), was declared Greek. From the RBA's perspective the inhabitants did so because the Greek consul in Korça had offered money to them. Moreover, the leader of the Macedonian minority party in Albania urged the people of Golloborda to declare themselves neither Bulgarian nor Albanian but Macedonian.[3]

The Aromanian Association in Albania was part of the debate, too. According to some representatives of the association the number of the Greek minority living in Albania would be close to the numbers that the Greek state projects, if only the members of the Aromanian community were about to declare themselves as Greeks. The Association of Aromanian in Albania claims that the real number of Aromanians in Albania is between 200000 to 300000 people. Moreover, in an editorial in the bilingual newspaper named Frația published by the association, under the title "Jo Rregjsitrimit të Aromunëve Grekë" (No to the Registration of Aromanians as Greek), the chairman of the organization publicly reacted to the declaration of the Greek Consul in Korça who had stated that Aromanians living Albania are and should declare themselves as Greek. The argument in this editorial once again shows how history is used to legitimate the present. According to a story published alongside the public reaction in 1914 an Aromanian priest and leader of this community in the area was killed in Korça by a Greek military group because he wanted to protect the ethnic identity of the Aromanians. Beside the story, in the first page of Frația[4], the whole declaration was published and said:

> "The declaration of the Greek Consul that says that Aromanians/Vllachs are Greek is considered by us as a grave provocation for our ethnicity. The purpose of the declarations of the Greek Consul in Korça is to alienate the Aromanians of Albania into Greeks. The Association 'Aromanians of Albania' with centre in Tirana has 16 branches all over Albania, and works more intensively in those areas that the Greek Consul calls Vorio Epir, it makes a sharp distance from such a declaration and considers it a very dangerous diversion for Albania and for our ethnicity. Our ethnicity is unique in the Balkans and cannot be Greek in any way. Our ethnicity is Aromune/Vllachs and it carries out all cultural traits of one population, which are language, customs, folklore and religious particularities within the orthodox religion. The registration of the population (census), also based on ethnic belonging, has been very much welcomed by all of us and we have considered it a positive step from the Albanian State towards the protection of Human Rights and Minorities. It is unacceptable for us that this process continues. Equally unacceptable is also that this process is being used by members of our community to declare themselves as 'Greeks'. Instead we should declare ourselves as we are internationally known: Aromanians. [...]" (Head of Association "Vangjel Shundi", Tiranë, 7. 2. 2011).

---

[3] Gazeta Panorama, Në Korçë një fshat musliman deklarohet grek, 4 October 2011.

[4] Frația, Journal of Aromanian Community in Albania (Tiranë) No 2, February 2011.

Due to their cultural, linguistic and religious background and also favoured by the way of how state law categorizes collective identities within and outside the state borders, the Aromanian community in Albania is a *sujet de droit* not only of the state law of Albania but also of the state law on citizenship and minorities of Greece and Romania. In 2007 Greece made some changes in the law on Citizenship. Through the application of the legal category called "homogenis" a person who lives in another country and is member of the Greek Orthodox Church or of Greek orthodox background is eligible to apply for citizenship. The procedure is as follows: beside the religious ties the individual should make a naturalization statement in the country of residence and should be acting as a witness before the Greek Consul, in the presence of Greek citizens acting as witness. Such statement should be accompanied with a photocopy of the passport or any other travel document, together with the birth certificate, or in case such a certificate cannot be provided, a baptismal certificate, along with a criminal record issued by the foreign authorities (Greek Citizenship Code, Art.10/1). In practice we do not have satisfactory data to speak of how many people have used this law to get a Greek passport.

Through these seductive policies from Greece according to members of the Association of Aromanians in Tirana, more than 70 % of Aromanians living in Albania declared themselves as Greeks after the fall of communism. Moreover, being a member of the Greek Minority in Albania was economically profitable at least on two counts. First, until the visa regime between Albania and EU was lifted, by declaring him/herself Greek or of Greek origin the individual could easily access Greece and eventually all other EU countries through legally attaining permission to reside and work in Greece. Second, family members that did not migrate and proved to be members of the Greek minority in Albania were eligible to the so-called agricultural pensions. This pension was around 218 Euros. The Greek government paid an agricultural pension to the members of the Greek minority in order to retain their ties with the homeland. Based on a Ministerial Decision the members of the Greek minority living in Albania, Egypt and Turkey, following the logic that those people for a while had worked in agriculture and as long as they are part of the Greek minority were/are entitled to the agricultural pension. In Albania this pension scheme is simply known as *pensionet e grekut* (Greek pensions). It is widely seen as an instrument of the Greek state to assimilate the Albanian people into Greece. After the financial crises in Greece the "agricultural pension" became an issue. After the Samaras Government had stopped funding this pension (in 2013) the new government in Greece led by Alexis Tsipras declared that it will refund these pensions scheme again (February 2015).

The representatives of the Aromanian community have more than once reacted against such policies used by the Greek State. The General Secretary of the Association of Aromanian of Albania, in a personal conversation, considered these politics as soft assimilation of the Aromanian community into a Greek minority. In an interview with the priest of Orthodox Church in Përmet I was told that even Muslim people come and get baptized in the Church. Many Albanian emigrants in Greece have told me their stories of how they were using photos and papers from the ceremony of baptizing as evidence to prove they share a common religious background with the Greeks in order to get *letrat* (the papers).

The Aromanian minority in Albania is also subject to the Romanian law on naturalization. Based on the Romanian legislation on Citizenship (1991, 2009), the Aromanians of Albania, as everywhere in the Balkans, are legally considered a Romanian minority. Due to the protective policies of the Aromanian identity in this area, the Romanian Government applies the legal category of "positive discrimination" toward the members of the minority. Following this principle the Romanian state is legally obliged to give concrete support for the continuity and development of the people to carry on their identity.

The crucial legal concepts here are the preservation and strengthening of national identity, mother tongue, positive discrimination, wherever Romanians live. Based on the testimony of a local community Aromanian leader in the South of Albania, the Romanian government has given more than 3000 scholarships to students who came from Albania and who had legally proven their Aromanian descend to the government. The Association of Aromanians of Albania has the authority to prove community membership. Most of these scholarships have been given in fields such as law, medicine, economics, and arts. After one year of Romanian language studies in Cluj, students are allowed to spread all over Romania to study at state universities.

Gora and Zhupa people in Kosovo

The people of Gora and Zhupa are part of a Muslim Slavic speaking community in Kosovo. Many members of both communities also speak Albanian. Zhupa and Gora communities are, geographically, located in the border area between Kosovo, Albania and Macedonia. The term *Gorani* as collective identity originally derives from a small district called Gora. In the Slavic language Gora means Mountain or Alpine Area. Gora is composed by 27 villages, of which 18 villages are in Kosovo whereas the remaining 9 villages are in Albania. The administrative centre of Gora villages is the Dragash municipality in Kosovo. The municipality of Kukës is the administrative centre for the rest of the 9 Gora villages in Albania. The Gora and Zhupa people are identified sometimes by Albanians in Kosovo and Albania, as *torbesh*. This term is used also to identify members of the Zhupa community. The debate about the collective identity and more specifically about the ethnic origin of the Gorani communities is very vividly debated especially between local intellectuals in Kosovo and Albania. The arguments that local historians have presented are structured to fit both Albania and Kosovo national histories. Basically, the community's origin is traced and constructed from ancient times until today, reflecting the relations and changes that the identity of the community had in time (Hoxha 2007, Dokle 2009).

The identity of the Zhupa people is similarly debated by local, national and international historians. The Zhupa region is more heterogonous in comparison to the Gora area. According to Malcolm (1998: 23) the origin of Zhupa derives from the word *zupa* that identified a small tribal territory ruled by a tribal chief known as Zhupan. In time, the valley and the villages composing the Zhupa region, was subject to many national ideologies. Consequently the landscape is wrapped and tramped by an overlapping of old and new symbols that reflect the ideological battle to give an identity to the area. We should not neglect the very fact that the origin of the people cannot be understood outside the historical process of the politics of space and cultural colonialization the area went through in time. For example, both the Zhupa and the Gora area, including the Sharr Mountains, were specifically designated as areas to be colonised in *The Expulsion of the Albanians – Memorandum*. The *Memorandum* was coincided by a prominent figure in academic circles and supporter of the colonialist ideology in Serbia, Vaso Čubrilović (cf. Čubrilović 1937).

The real effects of the politics of colonization on the Kosovo peoples' collective identities have been discussed by historians and it still remains an issue in academic circuits (see Malcolm 1998, Dragović-Soso 2008). Beyond the politics of direct colonization, the tectonics of identity base has been very fragile because of political changes during the 20th centuries in Gora and Zhupa. These changes of identity have arisen partly due to "ambiguous identity" (Duijzings 2000: 26) and partly because this ambiguity of identity is the production of state politics regarding peoples' identity in border areas, which has changed time after time (Roux 1992, Duijzings 2000). In a census made in Yugoslavia in 1971, 80 percent of the population of the nine villages declared themselves as Albanian. In 1981 in a census in the same villages 92 percent declared themselves as Muslim Slav (see Roux 1992: 420–421). But as we referred to earlier we will look at these two communities within the reality of contemporary Kosovo.

The quest of minority numbers and their legal definition in Kosovo is different compared to many other nation-states in Europe. In legal and international discourse Kosovo is defined as a *multi-ethnic state*. The constitution of Kosovo is an expression of power games between international and local actors. The meaning of ethnic minority as a legal category within the contexts of Kosovo's constitution is very fluid as long as the legal concept of national majority is virtually none-existent because the state of Kosovo was not founded on the principal of a *nation-state*. Through the interpretation of the Constitution of Kosovo (2009) we might conclude that Albanians in Kosovo seem to be accepted as the major community but yet they are not legally considered as a national majority. One of the many problems that the state of Kosovo faces with the state of Serbia is the legal status that Kosovo has in the Serbian Constitution. In the preamble of Serbia's Constitution of 2006, it is stated that "[...] the Province of Kosovo and Metohija is an integral part of the territory of Serbia" (Constitution of Republic of Serbia 2006: 2).

In daily life conversations, especially when you speak to Kosovo Albanians and ask them about the members of the Gora and Zhupa communities they tell you that practically many people in Gora and Zhupa "have declared themselves as Serbians and to do so they went as far as Belgrade, but they do refuse to declare themselves as Serbian when Pristina demands, but they are declared as Gorani". From a legal perspective individuals who declare themselves as Serbian in Kosovo are no longer entitled to use the status of ethnic minority but they are considered as citizens of Serbia in Kosovo especially when they have also attained a passport. People tell you that most members of the Zhupa and Gora communities, as well as Kosovo Albanians or others, have attained Serbian citizenship because of the facilities that the passport gives them especially in moving and travelling around Europe. But this does not mean that they have rejected the Kosovo citizenship, many hold two passports, that of the Republic of Kosovo and that of the Republic of Serbia. When it comes to Gorani and Zhupa communities, from a legal point of view, some are classified in the Serbian legal system as Serbian citizens in Kosovo, and in Kosovo's legal system they are classified as part of the Serbian community in multi-ethnic Kosovo. During my field work in Gora people told me about the Serbian parallel institution. Some of them said that "they exist only because some people in Gora want to benefit from the money given by Serbia but nothing more behind it". Some others said that "is a very dangerous situation because it is a game between Slavs and we are caught in between because Serbia, Macedonia and on the other side of the border, Bosnia and Bulgaria are all taking efforts to assimilate us".

Reality, as fieldwork experience has shown, is far more complex. Within these two small regions people have declared themselves as Albanians, Bosnians, Bulgarian Muhamedan (Muslim), Macedonians, Serbs, Muslims, Gorani etc. For instance in the Dragashi Commune of which the Gora villages are part, out of a population of 33 997 people, according to a source, 20 287 are Albanians, 7 Serbs, 202 Turks, 4 100 Bosnians, 3 Roma, 4 Ashkali, 3 Egyptians, 8 957 Goranians, 283 other ethnicities, and 129 people did not like to declare their ethnicity (RPEFB 2011: 142). The reasons for such a plural ethnic composition are three-folded. Firstly, they are related to the context created by the legal plurality of this area. Secondly, the state of Kosovo produces as many minorities as it can through legal categories. Thirdly, the historical context of the whole region and its factual social pluralism can be seen as a product of the politics of the modern states surrounding the area. This last subject will not be discussed in this work because we need more data for our argument. For the moment we will explore the first two reasons in the following.

According to the Constitution and laws in Kosovo, a minority that gets 10 % of votes in local elections has the right to appoint the Vice President in the Municipality's Assembly, together with a certain number of representatives and positions in local administration. (Constitution of Kosovo, Art. 62/1.) The fight to be employed in the local administration, to get a chair in the local assembly or to influence matters through the power that the chair of vice-president offers in the local assembly was and still is particularly ferocious in the multi-ethnic regions of Kosovo. One day I was talking to the receptionist of the hostel where I stayed for a few nights during my fieldwork. She asked me what I was doing and I told her about my research project. She immediately replied to me "why should you do such research on Gorani or Bosnians, Albanians are now the minority in Prizren, not them (referring to Yugoslav period) ... today the best way to get a job in Prizren is to choose to be part of one of these minorities, otherwise you will be jobless. What was the point to build the state in Kosovo? Nothing, just nothing, just words ...!"

Regardless of the fact that the Albanians are legally acknowledged as the major community in Kosovo, the legal category "other communities" recognizes the following groups as communities in Kosovo: Serbians, Bosnians, Roma, Ashkali, Egyptians, Turks, Gorani. (Constitution of Kosovo, Art. 64/2). These communities have their own NGOs and they are also organized in political parties. From 112 parties in Kosovo more than 60 parties belong to these communities. Some of them are very active in representing the rights of their communities. In the region of Gora and Zhupa, among others, there are three parties representing the rights of the minorities: the Macedonian Democratic Party, SDA-Stranka demokratske akcije (Party of Democratic Action) and DIG (Draganska Incijativa Gora).

Particularly, the DIG party has been active in promoting not only the Gorani identity but, as people tell you, it has also encouraged the members of the community and pressured the local and central government to introduce the learning of the Bosnian language in the region's schools. Due to internal conflicts, some members separated from the DIG party and created a new party called Democratic Party of Vatan (origjinali). Unlike the DIG, the new political party promotes the introduction of the Serbian language in the elementary schools of the area. For instance in some elementary schools, such as in the case of the Rastelica, the biggest village of Gora, lessons are delivered using three different study programs and languages. The main programs are delivered in the Bosnian language, using textbooks published in Bosnia but approved by Kosovo's Ministry of Education. The learning of the Albanian language is compulsory and the teaching of it starts from second grade elementary school. Moreover, besides lessons in Bosnian and Albanian for some other programs pupils use text-books that are issued by the Serbian Ministry of Education but which are not recognized by Kosovo Ministry of Education. Even though these textbooks are, from a legal point of view, illegal, yet the Kosovo institutions do not stop people using them.

As mentioned before, according to the legal system in Kosovo Gorani are legally accepted as a "community" and there are 8970 people who have declared themselves as Gorani. The rest of the Muslim Slavic speaking people of this area have preferred to declare themselves as Bosnians. There seems to be the same situation also in the Zhupa villages. Being part of the Prizren districted, a multi-ethnic city, for the Zhupa villages the situation is a bit more complex. When I asked different members of these communities, they gave me different perspectives on their family or clan origin. For example, in the Mushnikova village where a Muslim Slavic community lives, whose members identify themselves as Bosnians, I was told by some members of the community that their clan ancestors came from Gabrica, a village in the Luma region, in Albania. Others who identified themselves as Bosnians when asked about their origins did not try to make any kind of genealogy to prove their origin from Bosnia but simply said that "Which nation in the Balkans is Muslim but speaks a language like ours? It is Bosnia and we are from there".

As already is mentioned during the last population registration in former Yugoslavia many people had declared themselves belonging to the category Muslim with no specific indication to a nation. In today's Kosovo reality such category does not seem to be much represented. Thus, Muslim Slavic speaking communities, as the case of Kosovo indicates, are being declared as Bosnians. Nevertheless, in Macedonia an NGO called the Association of Macedonian Muslim was created to promote the existence of a Slavic Muslim community inside and outside the Macedonian state, especially in the border areas. In 2004, in Ljubina, a village in the Zhupa area, the UNMIK forces registered an NGO called "The Bulgarian Mohammedans". According to the Bulgarian historian Kanchov Ivanov the people of Zhupa are Muslims of Bulgarian descent (Mangalakova 2004). It seems that both Macedonia and Bulgaria are competing to include both Gora and Zhupa people as their own ethnic minority, based on linguistic affiliations. The Bulgarian state has gone a step further in this process because it has granted to members of both communities the possibility to attain the Bulgarian citizenship (World Bulgaria 2000). But the Macedonian state is not behind in this process either. I was told by a representative of the Gora Association in Kosovo that more than 15 000 people from Gora and Zhupa have already taken the Macedonian citizenship. Another source declared to me that nearly 1500 Goranians have taken the Bulgarian citizenship. The number of people from Gora and Zhupa who applied for the Bulgarian citizenship has increased after Bulgaria joined EU in 2007.

In the Gora and Zhupa villages I met many people telling me how many passports they have. In Gora, once, I heard the story of two brothers who had chosen to have different nationalities – one was declared as Bosnian and the other as Serbian. They did it publically and their children had chosen to go to the same school. The Bosnian brother enrolled his children in the Bosnian classroom that uses the Bosnian language and books, while the other enrolled his children in the Serbian classroom that uses the illegal education system. When I asked one of the teachers of this school how this it possible and what he thinks about it I was interrupted by an old man – "Hey young man! Listen to me. If you want to know the truth, it is so easy to understand why ... We have always been slaves of the states and forever it will be so. Then tell me, what is the point of being faithful to the state if you starve!? What really matters is to have food to feed your children ... that is our story ...".

Conclusion

"Naming and shaming for human rights abuses now have real consequences" Ignatieff once said (2000: 293). Many elaborated and elegant contributions in political anthropology have supported the idea that the time of nation states is over. They are being replaced by non-state agencies that are playing a major role to rule the world and societies through market mechanism or non-state agencies (Sassen 2001). Maybe a fundamental question should be posed before putting the nation-state in one of *Madam Tussauds* display rooms, namely how the nation-states are interpreting or, to put it more bluntly, how the nation-states in time of globalization or Europeanization are domesticating and manipulating the international standards, including the Human Rights for their own sake? How do nation states use Human Rights to expand or to protect their regional influence? That is an issue very much related to the question of nation-state politics and border areas. What we have learned from history is that in modern times nation-states have been very elastic and resistant to any universal or non-universal ideology.

The two ethnographic case studies above show us how the legal systems of different nation-states did shape the daily life of people in boarder areas by transforming these border areas into the social arena of legal plural identities. Michael Barkun's expression that "The law is a system of manipulable symbols that functions as representations, as model of social structure" (Barkun 1968) has opened many debates in the anthropology of law. His view might look pessimistic to many, but in our case we have observed the manipulation of the law on different levels by the state and the everyday life of people. The first level of manipulation was reflected in the way of how nation-states in the name of Human Rights and Rights of Minorities shape their national law on citizenship and minorities in order to expand or retain their influences on some border area regions. In this perspective, the national-states do not leave the place to any kind of post-national state, but they simply domesticate and shape the international standards and the human rights ideology as spears to foster their agendas.

The second level of manipulation is how nation-state institutions and other non-state agencies such as NGOs or political parties, created in compliance with states law, interpret the law in everyday life. We saw how people leading political parties or NGOs play both idealist and pragmatist roles to fulfil state, community and personal agendas. There are no doubts that there are individuals who do believe in the ideals of Human Rights or national values, but in daily life very few people believe that there are people out there who still do things because they believe in some ideals. The kingdom of mistrust is not only for sceptics but as the people that live in the border area tell us it belongs to all, at least in this part of Europe.

Thirdly and probably the most important level is the grassroot manipulation of the law, which becomes the locus of legal plurality, created by the existence of many legal systems in the same society. Every day people, in a wide spread condition of mistrust toward state institutions, politics and civil society, do make practical choices to manage everyday life matters. Changing one's citizenship does not mean changing nationality, religion or personal name for real. It is a stage in terms of Goffman (Goffman 1956, Lelaj and Bardhoshi 2008). The power to manipulate the law is not only placed in the hands of people who have the power to create or to implement it. Such power is also in the hands of people subject to it. If their life is articulated within a context of legal plurality, as the case of the communities in the border area shows, then the individual can choose to declare accordingly to what is more profitable to him/her. Thus, if the main concern of modern nation-states is to use the law on citizenship to create, to protect or transform the structure of a given ethnic minority in a border area, this is, on the other hand, not a problem for the everyday life persona because his/her problems are totally different ones.

References

Appardurai, Arjun 2006: Fear of Small Numbers: An Essay of the Geography of Anger. Durhan, London: Duke University Press.

Bardhoshi, Nebi 2013: Legal Dynamics in Border Area: Between Customary Law and State Law. In: Journal of Legal Anthropology, Vol. 1, No. 3 (2013): 314–332.

Bardhoshi, Nebi and Olsi Lelaj 2012: "Hard Times for All: Economic Crisis and Millennial Nationalism in Contemporary Kosovo and Albania." International Interdisciplinary Conference, Naples.

Barkun, Michael 1968: Law without Sanctions: Order in Primitive Societies and the World Community. New Haven: Yale University Press.

Benda-Beckmann, Franz von 2002: Who's Afraid of Legal Pluralism? In: Journal of Legal Pluralism, No. 47: 37–83.

Brubaker, Rogers 1994: Nationhood and National Question in the Soviet Union and Post-Soviet Eurasia: An Institutionalist Account. In: Theory and Society, 23, 1: 47–78.

Bulgarian Citizenship on the Basis of Origin 2007 (3 pages). URL: http://www.newbalkanslawoffice.com, accessed 27. 6. 2015.

Cohen, Lenard J. and Jasna Dragovic-Soso 2007: State Collapse in South-Eastern Europe: New Perspectives on Yugoslavia's Disintegration (Central European Studies). Purdue University Press.

Connerton, Paul 1989: How Societies Remember. Cambridge University Press.

Constitution of Republic of Kosovo, 2009.

Constitution of Republic of Serbia, 2007.

Čubrilović, Vaso 1937: The Expulsion of the Albanians – Memorandum. In: Robert Elsie: Texts and Documents of Albanian History (17 pages). URL: http://www.albanianhistory.net/texts20_2/AH1937_1.html, accessed 27. 6. 2015.

Creed, Gerald W. 1998: Domesticating Revolution: From Socialist Reform to Ambivalent Transition in a Bulgarian Village. University Part: Pennsylvania State University Press.

Creed, Gerald W. 2013: Every Village, a Different Story. In: Ger Duijzings (ed.): Global Villages: Rural and Urban Transformations in Contemporary Bulgaria. London, New York, New Delhi: Anthem Press, 53–66.

de Rapper, Gilles 2006: La "Biographie": Parenté incontrôlable et souillure politique dans L'Albanie communiste et post-communiste. In: European Journal of Turkish Studies, 4 (22 pages). URL: http://www.ejts.org/, accessed 27. 6. 2015.

de Rapper, Gilles 2007: The Greek-Albanian Border and Its Impact on Local Populations. Cahiers Parisiens/Parisien Notebooks 3: 566–575. URL: https://halshs.archives-ouvertes.fr/halshs-00293784/document, accessed 27. 6. 2015.

de Rapper, Gilles 2009: Pelasgic Encounters in Greek-Albanian Borderland: Border Dynamics and Reversion to Ancient Past in Southern Albania. In: Anthropological Journal of European Culture, 18, 1: 50–68.

Dino, Thanas and Thoma Puriqi 2003: Historia vllahe në tregime njerëzore: biseda dhe intervista. Gjirokastër: Qyteti i Jugut.

Dokle, Nazif 2009: Bogomilizmi dhe etnogjeneza e torbeshëve të Gorës së Kukësi. Tiranë: Geer.

Duijzings, Ger 2000: Religion and Politics of Identity in Kosovo. London: Hurst & Co.

Giordano, Christian and Dobrinka Kostova 2002: The Social Production of Mistrust. In: Chris Hann (ed).: Post-Socialism: Ideals, Ideologies, and Practices in Eurasia. London, New York: Routledge, 74–91.

Goffman, Erving 1956: The Presentation of Self in Everyday Life. University of Edinburgh: Anchor Books.

Greek Citizenship Code (without year of publ.). EUDO-Citizenship Observatory. URL: http://eudo-citizenship.eu/NationalDB/docs/GRE%20Citizenship%20Code%20(as%20of%202010,%20English).pdf, accessed 27. 6. 2015.

Green, Sarah 2005: Notes from the Balkans: Locating Marginality and Ambiguity on the Greek-Albanian Border. Princeton, Oxford: Princeton University Press.

Griffiths, John 1986: What Is Legal Pluralism? In: Journal of Legal Pluralism, 24: 1–55.

Gusterson, Hugh 1997: Studying up Revisited. In: PoLAR, Political and Legal Anthropology Review, 20: 114–119.

Halbwachs, Maurice 1992: On Collective Memory. Edited, Translated, and with an Introduction by Lewis A. Coser. Chicago, London: The University of Chicago Press.

Hart, L. Kain 1999: Culture, Civilization, and Demarcation at the Northwest Borders of Greece. In: American Ethnologist, 26, 1 (Feb. 1999): 196–220.

Hayden, Robert 1992: Constitutional Nationalism in the Formerly Yugoslav Republics. In: Slavic Review, 51, 4 (Winter 1992): 654–673.

Herzfeld, Michael 2005: Cultural Intimacy: Social Poetics in the Nation-State. Second edition. New York, London: Routledge.
Hoxha, Shefqet 2007: Shqiptari Sinan Pashë Topojani: Qëmtime historiko-etnologjike për Lumën dhe Gorën. Tiranë.
Hutchinson, John 2005: Nations as Zones of Conflict. London, Thousand Oaks, New Delhi: Sage Publications.
Ignatieff, Michael 2000: I. Human Rights as Politics. II. Human Rights as Idolatry. Princeton: The Tanner Lectures on Human Values. 65 pages.
Law on Romanian Citizenship, No. 21, 1st of March 1991 (updated version and text in force since 17. 5. 2009) (12 pages). URL: http://www.coe.int/t/dghl/standardsetting/nationality/National%20legislation/romanian%20law%20on%20citizenship%202009.pdf, accessed 27. 6. 2015.
Lelaj, Olsi and Nebi Bardhoshi 2008: Negotiating Existence in Emigration: An Outline of Albanian Emigrants in Greece. In: Elena Marushiakova (ed.): Dynamics of National Identity and Transnational Identities in the Process of European Integration. Cambridge: Cambridge Scholars Publishing, 294–406.
Malcolm, Noel 1998: Kosovo: A Short History. London: Macmillan.
Mangalakova, Tanya 2004: Kossovo: viaggio tra i Gorani, Osservatorio Balcani e Caucaso, 2 agosto. URL: http://www.balcanicaucaso.org/aree/Bulgaria/Kossovo-viaggio-tra-i-Gorani-26420, accessed 27. 6. 2015.
McGrew, G. Anthony 1998: Global Legal Interaction and Present-Day Patterns of Globalization. In: V. Gessner and A. Cem Budak (eds.): Emerging Legal Certainty: Empirical Studies on the Globalisation of Law. Aldershot, Brookfield: Ashgate and Dartmouth, 325–345.
Merry, E. Sally 1988: Legal Pluralism. In: Law & Society Review, 22, 5: 869–896.
Nader, Laura 1972: Up the Anthropologist: Perspectives Gained from Studying up. In: Dell H. Hymes (ed.): Reinventing Anthropology. New York: Pantheon Books, 284–311.
Nader, Laura 2002: The Life of the Law: Anthropological Projects. Berkeley, Los Angeles, London: University of California Press.
Nitsiakos, Vassilis 2010: On the Border: Transborder Mobility, Ethnic Groups and Boundaries on the Albanian-Greek Frontier. Berlin: LIT Verlag.
Raport mbi Pakicat Kombëtare në Shqipëri, 2001 (123 pages).
Rouland, Norbert 1994: Legal Anthropology. Stanford: Stanford University Press.
Roux, Michel 1992: Les Albanais en Yougoslavie. Minorité nationale, territoire et développement. Paris: Éditions de la Maison des Sciences de l'Homme.
Sassen, Saskia. 2001: The Global City. Second edition. Princeton, New York: Princeton University Press.
Schwandner-Sievers, Stephanie 1999: The Albanian Aromanians' Awakening: Identity Politics and Conflicts in Post-Communist Albania. ECMI Working Paper, No. 3. Flensburg: European Centre for Minority Issues.

Stahl, Johannes and Thomas Sikor 2009: Rural Property in an Age of Transnational Migration: Ethnic Divisions in Southeastern Albania. In: Anthropologica, 51, 1: 95–105.

Vanderlinden, Jacques 1971: Le Pluralisme juridique: essai de synthèse'. In: John Gillisen (ed.): Le pluralisme juridique. Brussels: Université Libre de Bruxelles, 19–56.

Vanderlinden, Jacques 1989: Return to Legal Pluralism: Twenty Years Later. In: Journal of Legal Pluralism Issue, 28: 149–157.

Verdery, Katherine 1996: Transnationalism, Nationalism, Citizenship, and Property: Eastern Europe Since 1989. In: American Ethnologist, 25, 2: 291–306.

Winnifrith, J. Tom 1995: Shattered Eagles. Balkan Fragments. London: Gerald Duckworth & Co.

Diaspora Politics and Re-Migrant Perspectives on Identity and Belonging in Croatia Today

Caroline Hornstein Tomić

Introduction[1]

Like many other countries in Southeastern Europe also Croatia is a classic emigration country and has traditionally been less a destination for migrants, apart from seasonal labour migration and the return of labour migrants from abroad. The beginning of the process of emigration from Croatia dates back to the fifteenth century. The state agency which deals with the Croatian diaspora distinguishes four historical phases of Croatian emigration until Croatia left the Yugoslav Federation and eventually declared independence in 1991.[2] Disregarding pre-19th century emigration, the 1st phase lasted from the second half of the 19th century until World War I; destinations back then were mainly overseas (USA, Latin America, Australia, New Zealand, South Africa; less in Europe). The 2nd phase reached from 1918 until World War II, with destinations increasingly also in Western Europe, mainly Germany, France and Belgium, but also Luxembourg and the Netherlands. The beginning of the 3rd phase set off at the end of World War II and continued into the early 1960s, with destinations mainly in Latin America, (less) USA, Canada and Europe. The 4th phase began with Yugoslavia starting to tolerate and eventually to support labour migration from the mid-1960s onwards to release pressure from the domestic labour market and it continued until the end of the dissolution of the Yugoslav Federation. Migrations during that phase were mostly planned for limited periods of time, but eventually prolonged due to family reunions, chain migrations etc. Remittances were invested back home, preparing the eventual return; destinations were mainly in Western Europe. A fifth phase of emigration thus began after 1990 – war-related in the early 1990s, then mostly due to economic and professional reasons – and it still continues. Croatian scientists like Čizmić and Živić equally speak of four

---

[1] This text was completed in December 2013; besides proofreading adaptations and references to articles by the author that have meanwhile been published and to some very recent trends in skilled migration and its media coverage no changes have been made to the content, and no more recent data (including statistical) has been added.

[2] See Country Presentation Croatia by Petar Barišić, (former) Head of Independent Service for Croats abroad, Ministry of Foreign Affairs and European Integration, Republic of Croatia, at the "Workshop on Emigration Issues in the Western Balkans – joint approach to linking migration and development of the countries of origin" organised by TAIEX, Sarajevo, October 13, 2011.

emigration waves from Croatia until today, however, the dates are set somewhat differently: 1. late 19th century until World War I (mainly overseas); 2. until the end of World War II (overseas and Western Europe); 3. since the 1960s (mainly labour migration to Western European countries); 4. escape from war and emigration of the 1990s (Western European and overseas destinations) (Čizmić and Živić 2005: 8). However, during the past two decades of state-building and post-socialist transformation since Croatia left the Yugoslav Federation it also slowly turned into a country which is not only left, but to a certain extent has actually become a destination for migrants.

In the light of continuing population-shrinking processes immigration is good news as a counterbalance, however, net negative migration has consistently been the prevalent feature. The last census in 2011 for example showed a population decrease of more than 150,000 people (3.43 per cent of the total population) over one decade. The year 2011 alone showed the most pronounced migration dynamics during the past decade, with 12,699 registered departures and 8,534 arrivals. Intensive flows (both in and out) were registered between Croatia and some of its neighbouring countries, especially Bosnia-Hercegovina and Serbia. Still, more than 2,500 people left Croatia for European Union countries. With Croatia's accession to the European Union in 2014 this trend was expected to increase as was the case in other Central and Southeast European Union member states. Also, the brain drain, especially of the young tertiary educated population the country has suffered from since the early days of transition, is likely to keep accelerating. This expectation is supported by the fact that the largest age cohorts of registered emigrants are between 20 and 44 years of age. Nevertheless, according to forecasts migration flows will continue to be most intense within the immediate region.[3]

As the Croatian Bureau of Statistics points out immigration was and still is to more than 50 % mainly co-ethnic, homeland and return migration,[4] besides temporary labour migration mainly from neighbouring countries. To a certain extent also war-related migratory movements can be registered until today, with refugees from neighbouring countries permanently settling in Croatia (and vice versa), as well as domestic refugee/IDP movements (Mesić and Bagić 2011). As such (internal and regional) war-related migration, also international co-ethnic (re-)migration dynamics have on the one hand contributed to further ethnic homogenisation – and thus may be considered part of the ethno-national state building process in Croatia. On the other hand, they most likely also contribute to increasing diversification of the sociocultural fabric and of daily life in the Croatian society. Whether co-ethnic or not, any incoming migrant brings along difference: different views, values, habits, behavioural routines, languages and

3 Croatian Bureau of Statistics 2012a, 2012b. URL: http://www.dzs.hr/Hrv_Eng/publication/2011/07-01-02_01_2011.htm, accessed 14. 4. 2013.

4 For the discussion of terminology and typologies see Čapo Žmegač 2005, 2010a, 2010b.

preferences acquired elsewhere. In order to grasp how – also in the context of co-ethnic (re-)migration – such differences come afore, play out and leave traces in social life and daily interactions in the Croatian host society/„homeland", a closer look shall be taken into narratives of co-ethnic (re-)migrants who have come to Croatia since the transition.

The empirical part of this article is based on interviews which I conducted between 2010 and 2013 with Croatian re-migrants from Germany and overseas (Canada and the United States of America). Based on stories about local encounters, identifications/identity negotiations and integration experiences I am going to reflect on meanings of „home/homeland", „homeland return" and „re-migration". Marita Krauss, in her study of emigrants who returned to Germany after 1945 (Krauss 2001), proposed to study return and re-migration as de-facto migration. For return/homeland migration and the Croatian context respectively Čapo Žmegač follows the same line of arguments (2010: 227).[5] However, family ties, regular homeland visits, language skills and cultural knowledge are likely to put co-ethnic migration (and one should add: co-national migration, considering Croatian emigrant nationals of other ethnicity) in a position different to any other immigrant. Without spinning this further, one in fact may assume that like any other kind of immigration, co-ethnic (re-)migration equally contributes to the cultural diversification of the receiving (host) society.[6] Homeland return from diaspora is in Croatian domestic politics and in public discourse primarily argued for as contributing to the development of an ethno-national community and its livelihood (or on the contrary denounced as ethno-nationalistic programme). Co-ethnic migrants might unexpectedly be vanguards of a diversification process, which goes along with an accelerating mobility and an international integration process the Croatian society already is and increasingly will be exposed to in the foreseeable future.

Diaspora politics since early transition

Croatia belongs to a group of countries with a large diaspora. The last census accounted for a home population of approximately 4,290,612; compared to that roughly 3 million Croats are officially estimated to live in the diaspora – not including Croats in Bosnia and Herzegovina (today approx. 400,000, 1991:

---

5 Čapo Žmegač (2010: 227) follows the same line of argument.

6 I have meanwhile further explored this train of thought together with Sarah Scholl-Schneider in an article which compares re-migration experiences in Croatia and the Czech Republic. A sketch of the Croatian context as presented here has been taken over in the article, which was written in German (Hornstein Tomić and Scholl-Schneider 2015). An English translation of the article is in preparation for re-publication.

760,852) and Croatian minorities in 12 European countries (approx. 350,000).[7] This would mean some 50 % of all Croats live outside Croatia. International sources such as the World Bank Migration Fact-book 2011 extremely differ from these numbers. According to the Fact-book there are around 753,900 Croats abroad, slightly above 17 % of the total Croatian population (Ratha, Mohapatra and Siwal 2011).

Whatever perspective is taken, considering its significant diaspora, Croatia like most other states in post-socialist Eastern Europe has been engaging in diaspora outreach since the early transition period. Also in the Croatian case the traditional "homeland orientation" of diasporas (Brubaker 2005) is evident.[8] That the dissolution process of Yugoslavia stirred up the Croatian diaspora all over the world is well documented in personal and scholarly accounts (Sopta 2003: 27–28; see also Božić 2005, Ragazzi 2009, Winland 2005), as well as in accounts of political analysts (Hockenos 2003). Diaspora representatives and organisations were heavily involved in political lobbying in the late 1980s for international recognition of Croatia's quest for independence, and eventually became crucial for collecting humanitarian aid and financial means to purchase weapons for the "Homeland War". International recognition in January 1992 and the prospect of a UN peacekeeping mission to intervene in the armed conflict was - according to some observers - an additional encouragement for members of the diaspora to further contribute to stabilising statehood and independence, and even to return (Vidak 1998: 67). The first President of the Republic of Croatia, Franjo Tuđman, had well understood the Croatian diaspora as a capital to foster homeland developments (Winland 2005: 59–60). He had repeatedly visited diaspora organisations and representatives in Europe and overseas to win support for his ideas about Croatia's future and the mission of his party, the Croatian Democratic Union/Hrvatska Demokratska Zajednica (HDZ). He was determined to reconcile the political opponents, former partisans and nationalists, representatives of the communist nomenclature and political émigrées. He also opened up perspectives regarding their possible involvement in building the Croatian state. Indeed, members of the Croatian diaspora became key figures in his first government; 20 % of the employees in the newly established Ministry of Foreign Affairs, in embassies and consulates abroad were originally members of the diaspora. Diaspora Croats filled leadership positions in public administration and enterprises as well as in national institutions like the Croatian Heritage Foundation/Matica Hrvatska (Sopta 2003: 28).[9] It might be the case that returning political *emigrées,*

---

[7] URL: http://www.dzs.hr/Hrv_Eng/publication/2011/SI-1441.pdf, accessed 27. 12. 2013; http://www.mvep.hr/hr/hmiu/iseljenistvo/stanje-hrvatskih-iseljenika-i-njihovih-potomaka-u-inozemstvu/, accessed 27. 12. 2013.

[8] Earlier versions of the following two paragraphs have been published in Hornstein Tomić and Pleše 2013.

[9] Gojko Šušak (Canada), first Minister for Return and Immigration, then Minister of Defense; Ivan Milas (Austria) Minister of Interior/Vice Prime Minister; Ivica Mudrinić,

as well as other members of the Croatian diaspora who had cultivated a primordial understanding of belonging and of ethno-cultural identity abroad, were substantially contributing to changes in public discourse, to "the way in which Croatians see themselves" (Winland 2005: 63) and also to the de-tabooing of a new political agenda in the early transition period. Whether the concept "Croatia in Exile"/"Iseljena Hrvatska", which called on Croats abroad to return and repatriate, was meant to strengthen the Croatian ethnic nation also demographically and thus contained the logics of ethnic homogenisation, as Hockenos has argued, is, however, disputable (Hockenos 2003: 11).

In any case, until today the Croatian public perception of the diaspora is polarised. While some seem to idealise it as a prosperous expatriate community with strong homeland ties and patriotic commitment others rather demonise it as a politically reactionary community which primarily fuelled nationalism and the violent breakup of Yugoslavia. Both are influential positions in public discourse, particularly with respect to diaspora involvement in domestic politics and have been criticised as equally distorting (Perica 2011, Skoko 2013). When the Ministry of Return and Immigration was established during the first Tuđman Government it drew on Israel's "Law of Return" as original document for comprehensive legislative steps to facilitate repatriation (Barbić 2008: 7). In 1996 the Ministry was renamed into Ministry of Immigration. Also, a new law on citizenship was introduced, a step described as "one of the most striking examples of a radical shift toward post-territorial citizenship" (Balalovska and Ragazzi 2011: 7), as it granted citizenship and voting rights to ethnic Croats beyond state borders. Whether, as Balalovska and Ragazzi have argued, it also contributed to marginalising ethnic minorities (respectively Serbs as "new" minority) within the country has been disputed as well. It has been questioned that ethnic discrimination was ever officially legitimised by any law or state document. According to Koska the Croatian state de jure was consistently inclusive towards minorities (Koska 2011). Laws, responsibilities and legal bodies have meanwhile repeatedly changed; however, the emphasis on co-ethnics is still an integral part of any activity in official politics also relating to immigration in general.[10] The most recent *Law on the Relations of the Republic of Croatia with Croats outside the Republic of Croatia* more specifically than any of its precursors tries to regulate the relationship between the Croatian state and its diaspora in more detail.[11] It continues to focus on and to distinguish the following three groups: Croats in Bosnia-Herzegovina, Croatian minorities in 12 European (not specified whether EU) countries, and the Croatian diaspora in Europe and overseas. A "Welcome Office" within a recently formed governmental office dealing with

---

Minister of Maritime Affairs and Communications, later Director of the Croatian TV, then CEO of the Croatian Telekom for many years, and others.

[10] See Branko Barbić 2008, and URL: http://www.osce.org/eea/40846, accessed 27. 12. 2013.

[11] URL: http://www.hrvatiizvanrh.hr/pdf/hmiu38363467.pdf, accessed 17. 10. 2013.

Croats abroad has the task to facilitate return by providing information about legal rights and obligations. Advisors for Croatian returnees furthermore shall inform about customs regulations, special tax benefits, social services, employment or business opportunities, and about "integration into the Croatian society" in general. The legal act also specifically focuses on the offspring of former emigrants, i. e. incoming students (mentioning scholarships etc.; Article 60–62). As it intends facilitating integration and access to Croatian citizenship also for non-Croats (i. e. partners/spouses of Croatian citizens and family members), and by introducing the new category of "Croat without Croatian citizenship" it might be considered supportive of general, ethnically un-biased immigration policies. But it is mostly the *Migration Policy Framework 2013–2015*[12] which for the first time suggests a comprehensive approach by connecting immigration to economic development and restructuring and by explicitly noting a vital interest in immigration.[13] It also foresees the introduction of a population register (and other measures) to keep track of actual migration dynamics; it clearly recognises the relevance of immigration also with respect to population dynamics and ageing processes; and it finally also links immigration with labour market requirements and the sustainability of social welfare systems, which has repeatedly been urged for by experts (Barbić 2008: 10–12, Crnković-Pozaić 2008: 21–28).

It also includes incentives for supporting patterns of circular migration following dynamics of supply and demand. Both the law and the framework have to be seen as corresponding with the prognosis of a steadily shrinking labour pool in Croatia. While in the past most significant numbers of immigrants and labour migrants originated from neighbouring countries in the region it has repeatedly been suggested to orientate immigration policies towards the regional neighbourhood (Horvat 2008: 29–34). However, already some years ago scientists and highly qualified personnel were identified as the primary deficit on the labour market for supporting development and innovation in the foreseeable future (IOM Migration Profile Croatia 2007: 31–32);[14] and they have to be recruited globally. Taking into account a youth unemployment rate (age 15–24) of 51.8 % (general unemployment rate in December 2013: 17.6 %)[15] and continuing brain drain dynamics, which both point to an apparent mismatch between demands by local industry and offers of knowledge and skills produced by the domestic educational and scientific sector, a refocusing of migration policies might be timely (let alone educational reforms).

---

[12] URL: http://www.vlada.hr/hr/content/download/242728/3559216/file/74.%20-%2010.pdf, accessed 26. 2. 2013.

[13] URL: http://www.mup.hr/UserDocsImages/minstarstvo/2013/Migration%20policy%20RoC_en_2013%2002%2005.pdf, accessed 19. 10. 2013.

[14] URL: http://iom.hu/PDF/migration_profiles2007/Croatia_2007.pdf, accessed 19. 10. 2013.

[15] URL: http://europa.eu/rapid/press-release_MEMO-13-968_en.htm, http://ycharts.com/indicators/croatia_unemployment_rate, both accessed 27. 12. 2013.

As in most post-socialist Eastern European countries incentives to gain brain also in Croatia still and again mostly target diaspora instead of being linked with ethnically indifferent immigration policies. At least, fellowship schemes like the "Unity through Knowledge Fund" and "NEWFELPRO" to enhance mobility of Croatian researchers and scientists and further cooperation with international partners and institutions have learned from numbers and debates and have meanwhile pointed into the direction of overcoming the ethnic bias.[16] Concentrating recruitment efforts on the diaspora might indeed hardly suffice. A shift towards facilitating access and mobility disregarding ethnicity is a key governance but also a diversity challenge for the Croatian society in general.

Who has actually come since the transition?

In order to get a better understanding of the heterogeneity of the co-ethnic (re-) migrant community in Croatia one first of all needs to take into account the heterogeneity of the Croatian diaspora, and also the different types of return/homeland and re-migrants who have come to Croatia during the past two decades since the early 1990s – as there are also different migrant types and their initial reasons of emigration. The most basic typological distinction is usually made between political/forced and economic migration, though both may overlap, as do temporal categories such as seasonal migration, migration with the intention to return and permanent emigration. In a recently published article Ulf Brunnbauer has proposed and discussed this basic typology also as applicable to the whole region of Southeastern Europe (2013: 1–8).

For Croatia respectively Rogić and Čizmić present a further differentiated emigration typology for the period between 1945 and 1991, during the second Croatian modernisation, and hence distinguish three types of emigrants: (1) the *political* type, representing individuals who left under pressure due opposing the political regime. According to Rogić and Čizmić this type first included mostly foreign residents immediately after World War II, but soon also ideological opponents, dissidents and regime critics; political emigration culminated after the Croatian Spring when expressions of Croatian national identity and national emancipation were met with fierce state repression; (2) the *socio-cultural* type representing those who chose to depart due to socio-cultural rather than political pressures and who wished to live in a different society.

The authors distinguish this type from the previous one primarily because it refers to individuals who left without being under existential threat; it also refers to those who continued a "tradition" of emigration (in their family or wider local community); following the footsteps of family members, ancestors, friends

---

[16] URL: http://www.ukf.hr/, http://www.newfelpro.hr/default.aspx?id=63, both accessed 27. 12. 2013.

or neighbours can be observed also in the Croatian case as a widespread mobility pattern crucial for the emergence of diaspora communities, transnational social spaces and ways of life. It usually comes along with practices and attitudes inspired by different cultures that function as frames of references for individuals, families and communities both in the homeland as well as abroad; (3) the *economic* type representing all those who leave to secure or improve the personal or the family's livelihood, or to advance professional careers. As in other contexts many of Croatian migrants are likely to fit into more than one of those categories.

Furthermore, variations within the categories are equally found. Amongst political emigrants for example one could find supporters of the World War II Ustasha regime, and at the same time dissidents and opponents of the Socialist Regime and of Serb domination within Yugoslavia – as holds true for many activists of the Croatian Spring – with rather little or no affinity at all to right-wing extremist ideologies. Likewise, economic migrants could vary fundamentally in their attitudes towards the Yugoslav regime, often in coincidence with religious identification, cultural practices and attitudes (Hornstein Tomić and Ivanda Jurčević 2012: 185–192). While most Croatian families abroad would speak the Croatian language at home, not all were socialising also or primarily in diaspora networks: only some searched contacts mainly in the Croatian community and found a home in the Croatian Catholic Mission; others deliberately chose to connect as well to migrants from former Yugoslavia with whom they shared a common understanding via language, habits, tastes and customs; relations were developed with migrants from other countries or with German neighbours; children were frequently visiting schools with few or no Croatian migrants and this not only in places with little diaspora presence or community cohesion; last but not least, the emphasis on integrating into the mainstream society through language learning, sports and other leisure time activities is a pattern which runs through the Croatian communities in many countries of the world. But also other, exclusionary modes of living within diaspora communities can be found, which cannot be further discussed here.

As mentioned earlier immigration to Croatia since the political transition from Socialism has – besides seasonal labour migration – been in fact mostly co-ethnic (re-)migration. Migrants arrived in the first part of the 1990s alongside war refugees and displaced persons. Many of them came from neighbouring Bosnia and Hercegovina and other parts of former Yugoslavia, and often also via third states in Western Europe. Amongst the re-migrants were former guest workers returning after retirement, but also former political *emigrées* who returned to take part in the political transition and democratisation process. And there was – and still is – a certain influx of not only first but also second and even later generations, descendants of former Croatian emigrants, foreign citizens with Croatian ancestry who equally took the transition and eventual EU integration process as an incentive for homeland or „ancestral" return (King 2000: 10). Many of those re-migrants with often tertiary education and professional skills share the common denominator of having taken chances, the motivation of contributing to and/or profiting from political and economic transformation. As potential or actual change agents they have been part of the post-socialist transition process in countries such as Croatia (Hornstein Tomić 2011: 13–15).

Although official statistics throughout the 1990s tried to take records of migration, no clear distinction was made between return migration, immigration and war-related international migratory movements or between various migrant types (Lajić 2004). Besides census data statistical records were at the time and still are today primarily based on residency cards kept by the Ministry of Interior, which have to be filled out when residence is being taken in Croatia. Registered immigration between 1990 and 1998, for example, was differentiated only by the original country of residence. Not included in these data were refugees from countries of former Yugoslavia. What it showed, for example, was an immigration peak in 1992; about 50 % of those immigrants actually came from Germany. It has been suggested that the high numbers of arrivals in 1992 existed due to the fact that re-migration in average needed two years of preparation, especially for "... those from overseas countries such as Canada and Australia; work obligations with associated pension plans were a key factor in delays of implementation of an overseas move to Croatia" (Vidak 1998: 67). Leaving homes, moving children from school, establishing residency etc. requires if anything than time, the least.

For the first half of the 1990s, during which the majority of re-migrants came into the country, estimates range between 5,000 until up to 55,000.[17] But also a precise number of 45,967 has been circulating (Vidak 1998: 58). Since there are no accounts of how many migrants actually stayed – also due to loose registration practices – or have gone back to their original countries of residence or hold double residencies and commute or only come to Croatia for extended visits, such range does not come as a surprise. Thus, the Croatian example confirms the experience of return migration researchers that such "('new') types of migration escape the attention of statisticians and demographers (...) and are rather 'known' through anecdotal evidence, qualitative research (or) even newspaper reports" (King and Christou 2010: 167).

All in all, re-migration was probably much less realised than expected (and called upon through official diaspora outreach) in the early transition period. The effectiveness and sustainability of return and related policies, however, seem not to have been under scrutiny ever since, and the voices of those engaged in re-migration (let alone those who tried but gave up after a while and returned to their previous places of residence again) have been rarely heard. Even though a target group in more recent diaspora outreach policies tertiary educated, skilled re-migrants as a group and category of its own right were neither taken notice of nor particularly considered, in spite of growing concerns already back in the 1990s

---

[17] Barbić 2008: 7.

about the brain drain. Returning guest workers and also the engagement of returning political *emigreés* in the transition process have received some scholarly attention. This is less the case with respect to re-migrating members of the diaspora business community or for experts and scientists. The same holds true for the offspring of former emigrants who moved to Croatia after independence but also at later stages of the transition process.[18] Some of these perspectives shall now be looked at.

Re-migration experiences

The diverse re-migration experiences are not only shaped by gender, socio-economic, educational, status group and generational belonging, but also by initial reasons and circumstances of (individual, parental or ancestral) emigration, by collective migration itineraries and memories, which set the tone of daily life in any residence environment - be it *home* or *host* (to be treated as fluid and preliminary categories). What holds true for voluntary migration in general, also re-migration, is driven by wishes to create better, more satisfying future lives. However, as individual as migration is, there are similarities regarding motivations, responses to chance structures and timing of migration, integration strategies, role projections and views on identity - across generational, gender and status lines.

The following observations are based on statements made in loosely structured, narrative interviews which I conducted between 2010 and 2013 with re-migrants from Germany, Austria and overseas (Canada and the United States). Some of my interview partners were representatives of the 1st migrant generation, but the majority was born or at least raised abroad and they were thus members of the 2nd generation, holding also another citizenship next to the Croatian. I conducted fifteen interviews during that period in total. In the following I will present quotes from three selected interviews with 2nd generation re-migrants from Germany and Canada. The interviews were conducted in German and English. Quotes from interviews conducted in German were translated into English for this article.

Motivations for coming to Croatia

Even if it is not a return in the straight sense of the word moving children from former emigrants who grew up abroad back to Croatia is perceived of as a re-

[18] After Croatia's accession to the EU the media, however, increasingly have primarily given attention to return success stories in order to counterbalance the reporting about increasing outflows of young and highly skilled Croatian citizens.

turn nevertheless. It may be that the „return myth" characteristically cherished in diaspora is eventually turned into a reality[19] by a child on behalf of the parents. Ivana, a language teacher, who moved back to Croatia from Canada in the course of the 1990s as the only member of her family - not directly, but via the United Kingdom, where she did her studies and then worked for a while - tells the following:

> The idea always was that one day, when Croatia was free, we would go back. My father was politically active in organisations in Canada; he used to drag us ... I say drag us ... (laughing) ... we all used to go, my family, me and my sister used to sit in the back while my father would be in different meetings and things like that. So there was always this idea that one day we could go back. But it wasn't actually real, I mean it wasn't real until 1990. It was an abstract thing.

Being raised by parents who used to socialise within diaspora networks - some of them even engaged in homeland-directed politics, as in Ivana's case - and who would nurture a sense of "home" related to the homeland left behind is emphasised as influential experience for creating an understanding that "home" was elsewhere, a place where one would once move back to. A sense of "being torn" between "here" and "there" is what Nina remembers who, back then in her thirties, moved to Croatia from Germany in 2006 and later established a consultancy firm.

> ... that we would sit down and concretely talk about plans to return: this never happened. But what I extremely felt was this feeling of being torn. The way my parents spoke about Croatia and what they gave me along the way ... this is nostalgia, also homesickness in a way. At the beginning I did not understand the idealisation, which was part of it. Only in the course of time I understood how much they idealised the homeland.

"Returning home" is described by both women as a dream nurtured in families, based on an idealised construct of "home", and their return subsequently is the fulfilment of a longing projected from parents onto their children. The driving force of nostalgia provides meaning to a homeland orientation taken over as urging to search for one's "roots" - hence "roots migration". Unlike interpreting in a rather essentialising manner a "homing desire" (Brah 1996)[20] as a "defensive and nostalgic reaction to the hardships of displacement and the stigma of ethnic minority status" (Stefansson 2004: 3) one might alternatively understand it as what Stefansson himself calls in reference to Appadurai a potential "charter of new social projects" (Appadurai 1996).[21] This interpretation seems more ad-

---

[19] Some of the findings presented in this paragraph have been taken up in a recent publication in the Croatian language (Hornstein Tomić 2014).

[20] Brah 1996: 193, quoted in Stefansson 2004: 3.

[21] Appadurai 1996: 2, quoted in Stefansson 2004: 3.

equate especially when taking into account that what was left behind were often well established, successful and economically affluent family lives (outside Croatia).

A new social project may be to contribute to establishing a young democratic state and market economy and to support such development processes with the necessary knowledge and experience – a motive expressed by quite a few, who were driven by curiosity, openness and enthusiasm for the transition from socialist Yugoslavia to something new and unknown, and by a generally optimistic image of the Croatian society and its future within an independent state (emphasising change, opportunities and potentials). Most interview partners had, one way or another, been drawn intensely into lobbying for Croatia's quest for independence (through demonstrations, public speaking, humanitarian aid etc.). Contributing to, profiling in and experiencing a situation as exciting, undefined and amorph as the early period of transition from socialism is reported to often go hand in hand. Davor, today a diplomat who came to Croatia to study in the early 1990s, explains:

> Really decisive was the phase before the war, actually the democratisation. Well, that was the time when I took a strong interest in Croatia. It was also the time, when the wall came down in Germany, 1989, Eastern Europe in general (...). And that was when you as a young person had the possibility to experience democracy in Croatia. And then the feeling developed that one could participate; to make your contribution – let's say in quotation marks "development aid". As a Croat with the background I had at the time I could make a bigger contribution in Croatia than as someone in Germany. That was my idea at the time.

The extent to which re-migrations have actually been motivated by patriotism and pioneership seems to have slowly diminished with the transformations progressing. However, emotional, life-stage, career or life-style reasons[22] spin that web of motives out of which migration decisions are made – in interaction with times of passage, as Davor continues to describe:

> When I was getting closer to finishing high school I started to think more or less independently and to make decisions for myself (I had to decide; CHT) whether I would go now, directly after finishing high school, and that I would try to study in Croatia. Croatia for me would continue to be a country for vacation, but not a country in which I would ever really touch ground.

Times of passage, but also a personal crisis, difficulties on the educational or labour market, professional stagnation or status blockages could trigger to realise

---

[22] For similar observations see King and Christou's study on second generation returnees from America to Greece (2010: 178).

pending migration decisions thus underlining the relatedness of individual career and life plan considerations and idealistic motives, integrated into the project of exploring what a Croatian identity might mean to oneself. How motivations, plans and real actions interact and actually stretch over long periods of time reveals Nina's following statement, pointing furthermore to the structural openness of the migration cycle:

> I said I really want to live in this country where I actively contributed to building it up (through political commitment in Germany in the 1990s; CHT). I spoke to so many people and often read the newspapers: there are so many options, there are German firms! Hey, that's a perfect moment – in Germany everything stagnates (in 2006; CHT) – to do something new, to create something new. (...) And I realised that the reason for my studies, why I had started to study: I wanted to help people! I have to admit it was very idealistic. There were people dying and fighting for something what belonged to them, and I wanted to contribute. This actually was a running thread through different phases of my life, and then I said, there are so many options in Croatia, that I really have to try it now, otherwise I will always reproach myself for not having tried it.

Identity constructions in integration processes

Migrant mobility is intertwined with identity constructions already in pre-migratory phases of planning, as Davor revealed in the previous quote when stating the urge to prove himself "as a Croat" in Croatia. An advantageous position imagined due to a German socialisation, which would enable him to provide what Davor with slight irony calls "development aid", however, is deconstructed once integration takes off in daily interaction. When faced with limited cultural competences and a lack of language musicality, imagined transferable knowledge proofs less relevant than what needs to be learned anew. Davor remembers clashes with behavioural routines and unfamiliarity with frames of references, crucial for example regarding the understanding of humour:

> The beginning was very exciting but also very difficult. Without a Croatian school education it was difficult to find my way around at university, especially in my law studies, which are very much based on language. It was not easy. But I had to connect to the society here and to the mentality (...) – I had developed mine in Germany. You behave differently, think differently and therefore it was not easy at the beginning. I was never really negatively received, I cannot not say that. I was interesting, but from my point of view I had problems to behave as people behaved here. And also to understand jokes, which were told and vice versa, my humour at the beginning was a bit different, as well.

When a presupposed belonging is put into question through behavioural frictions and difficulties of cultural understanding, identities get unsettled, awareness of difference appears. Unlike Davor who stresses that his different background appeared to others as interesting, Ivana remembers that a sense of non-belonging was gradually created in local encounters. She remembers „cool welcomes“:[23]

> There are a few people who went back (to Croatia; CHT), gave it a try. It is different to live here than being here on holidays. On holidays it's great ... everybody wants you to be with them. You have enough money because you still have money from Canada. You don't have to try to find work, you don't have to try to earn a living here, you don't have to go through all of the bureaucratic things to ... whatever ... find a place to live, get the documents that you need and so on and so forth. And some of the cases that I knew that came to Croatia ... went back (to Canada; CHT). My cousin (...) it was all nice when he came as a tourist to visit his relatives. When he came to stay here, he was staying at his fathers' house. He wasn't staying with someone that he was ... I don't know ... bothering someone in their home or anything like that. "Why did you come, why are you here? You don't belong here." And my cousin, when he went back to Canada, he never came back (to Croatia; CHT), and he probably never will.

Ivana describes the collision of two perspectives: on the one hand the re-migrant who feels entitled to stay and claims to belong by settling in "his fathers' house"; on the other hand the resident who questions the motives and the legitimacy of the re-migrants' claim by stating "you don't belong here". If belonging is hence denied the idea of "returning home" turns out to be an illusion – and consequently a shared identity of those living in diaspora and those in the "homeland" is profoundly shattered.

The dynamics of settling in, of integrating into every-day-life routines, of finding one´s own place in society (work, school, health care, residence, social networks etc.) furthermore reveal hidden social imperatives unknown to someone who comes from diaspora, from "outside". Clashes with what is often called "the system", be it with its formal or informal sides, with bureaucratic procedures and with officials are mentioned as typical moments in which boundaries are constructed, when stereotyping takes place, when differences become apparent and subsequently "otherness" is brought to the front. Nina mentions such clashes:

> I had to go 48 times to clarify something. "We are doing this here differently. You have to come to terms with this and to accept it." It is stubbornness. And because I came from outside, everybody thinks, that I be-

[23] Such „cool welcomes“ are mentioned also by Stefansson (2004: 9), Winland (2005), Scholl-Schneider (2011), Povrzanović Frykman (2011) and others.

> lieve that I know everything better. (...) I always felt that I was a Croat, but this is when I realised and when I felt for the first time that I was a foreigner.

And also Davor recalls:

> The university system was quite difficult for me. I could not understand properly how it was structured. (...) The law school was very much orientated on encyclopaedic learning, on learning things by heart – an approach, which was completely unknown to me from Germany. We were always orientated towards critical thinking and much less towards reproducing knowledge. We were much more personally committed, found compromises, searched for original solutions. Here, this was not the case at all. You were a good student when you knew the footnote on page 345 in the book. This for me was on the one hand something I could not understand. And on the other hand it appeared backwards to me, and I was openly in opposition to it. But it actually did not help me; I had to come to terms with it. I could not change the system.

Ivana likewise comments:

> In Croatia, I think a lot of it ... you really have to know people ... know people in the right places. Often it doesn't matter, I think, what you know, or what you do. I also felt that this was a disadvantage, a downside of Croatia.

Concluding remarks

Nostalgic sentiments, idealisations and role projections are all part of re-migration particularly when it is imagined as a "homeland return". Re-migration to a country of origin which is in transition particularly holds ample space for disillusionment. If "homecomers" expect to be welcomed as those who bring along knowledge needed for developing a democratic and prosperous society based on fairness and shared values, they perceive political, economic and social transformations mostly as processes of positive change. Such imaginary is doomed to fall apart once structural continuities, stagnations and backslashes become visible, when old networks deny access to the one who comes from abroad, when the rules of the game for participating competently in fierce competition are different to those learned elsewhere (Hornstein Tomić and Scholl-Schneider 2015); when economic decline, growing social disparities and disregard, clientelism and corruption show their face. Ivana, Davor and Nina, like other re-migrants, imagined a role as change agent. However, they all experienced what it meant to be held at bay, to simply having to adjust and learn, rather than to initiate and support changes.

More than anything else integration processes seem to be struggles for recognition. That foreign work and cultural experience are approached with curiosity and openness, that knowledge transferred from elsewhere is embraced or that degrees are notified without problems cannot be expected. In re-migrant accounts integration efforts reappear as difficult, painful and sometimes deeply unsettling experiences, and reactions to those who undertake such efforts even as offence. The ones who decided to keep on staying often question their move and hold in limbo whether they might leave again.

If re-migration is meant to be a "homeland return" and may as such be considered an exploration of origins as elements of one's identity, of re-affirming a sense of belonging, daily life interactions rather provoke awareness of difference and, last but not least, of multiple attachments. Alfred Schuetz (1945) once described "home" as a temporal place which changes over times of absence of the one who returns. His "homecomer" misfits, needs to make himself belong again by creating a „home" through engaging with those who stayed and with their way of life. His effort of integrating and adjusting is detrimental to them for opening up to what he brings along: "difference". What Schütz wrote about is reciprocal dynamics, which leaves traces on both sides. The re-migrant who imagines to "return home" might thus introduce a diversification process – as (wanted or unwanted) agent of change.

References

Balalovska, Kristina and Francesco Ragazzi 2011: Diaspora Politics and Post-Territorial Citizenship in Croatia, Serbia and Macedonia (Working Paper, 2011/18). CITSEE Working Paper Series, University of Edinburgh School of Law. URL: http://www.law.ed.ac.uk/citsee, accessed 10. 8. 2015.

Barbić, Branko 2008: Useljeničke politike Republike Hrvatske [Immigration Policies of the Republic of Croatia]. In: Croatian Chamber of Commerce (ed.): Useljenička politika u funkciji razvoja hrvatskoga gospodarstva [Immigration Policy in the Service of the Development of the Croatian Economy]. Zagreb: 7–12.

Barbić, Branko 2009: Croatian Migration Laws, Policies and Institutions. URL: http://www.osce.org/eea/40846, accessed 10. 8. 2015.

Barišić, Petar 2011: Ministry of Foreign Affairs and European Integration, Republic of Croatia: Country Presentation Croatia, at the "Workshop on Emigration Issues in the Western Balkans – Joint Approach to Linking Migration and Development of the Countries of Origin" organized by TAIEX, Sarajevo, October 13, 2011.

Božić, Saša 2005: From Diaspora to Transnation and Back: Croatian Migrant Institutions and the Re(making) of Croatia. In: Henriette Riegler (ed.): Beyond the Territory, within the Nation. Diasporic Nation Building in South Eastern Europe. Baden-Baden: Nomos Verlagsgesellschaft, 33–57.

Brubaker, Rogers 2005: The "Diaspora" Diaspora. In: Ethnic and Racial Studies, Vol. 28, No. 1: 1–19.

Brunnbauer, Ulf 2013: Balkans, Migration, mid-19th Century to Present. In: Immanuel Ness (ed.): The Encyclopedia of Global Human Migration. Oxford: Blackwell Publishing, 1–8.

Čapo Žmegač, Jasna 2005: Ethnically Privileged Migrants in Their New Homeland. In: Journal of Refugee Studies, 18, 2: 199–215.

Čapo-Žmegač, Jasna 2010a: Return Migration: The Changing Faces and Challenging Facets of a Field of Study. In: Klaus Roth and Jutta Lauth Bacas (eds.): Migration in, from, and to Southeastern Europe, Part 2: Ways and Strategies of Migrating. In: Ethnologia Balkanica, 14/2010: 227–245.

Čapo Žmegač, Jasna 2010b: Različiti pristupi povratnim migracijama: primjer Hrvatske [Different Approaches to Return Migration: the Croatian Example]. In: Studia ethnologica Croatica: 11–38.

Čapo, Jasna 2012: Zweidaheimlichkeit. Kroatische Gastarbeiter - Migration - eine zwischenräumliche Erfahrung [Zweidaheimlichkeit/Double Homes. Croatian Guestworkers - Migration - Experience between Spaces]. In: Angelika Welebil and Jörn Nuber (eds.): Gastarbeit [Guestwork]. Wien/St. Wolfgang: Edition Art Science, 129–157.

Crnković-Pozaić, Sanja 2008: Buduće potrebe na tržištu rada - možemo li bez imigracije [Future Needs on the Labour Market: Can We Make Do without Immigration]? In: Croatian Chamber of Commerce (ed.): Useljenička politika u funkciji razvoja hrvatskog gospodarstva [Immigration Policy in Service of the Development of the Croatian Economy]. Zagreb: 21–28.

Croatian Bureau of Statistics 2012a: Stanovništvo prema starosti i spolu, popisi 1953–2011 [Population According to Age and Sex, Censuses 1953–2011]. URL: http://www.dzs.hr/Hrv/censuses/census2011/results/graphs/usp_G1_HR.pdf, accessed 10. 8. 2015.

Croatian Bureau of Statistics 2012b: Migration of Population of Republic of Croatia. URL: http://www.dzs.hr/Hrv_Eng/publication/2012/07-01-02_01_2012.htm, accessed 10. 8. 2015.

Government of the Republic of Croatia 2013: Nacrt prijedloga migracijske politike Republike Hrvatske za razdoblje 2013.–2015. [Outline of the Migration Policy Proposal for the Period 2013–2015]. URL: http://www.vlada.hr/hr/content/download/242728/3559216/file/74.%20-%2010.pdf, accessed 10. 8. 2015.

Hockenos, Paul 2003: Homeland Calling: Exile Patriotism and the Balkan Wars. Ithaca, London: Cornell University Press.

Hornstein Tomić, Caroline 2011: Das Deutschlandbild von Zuwanderern aus Kroatien [The Image of Germany by Croatian Immigrants]. In: Helmut Reifeld (ed.): Das Deutschlandbild in Herkunftsländern [The Image of Germany in Countries of Origin]. Sankt Augustin: Konrad Adenauer Foundation.

Hornstein Tomić, Caroline 2014: "Ovdje sam vječno Švabica": o izgradnji identiteta u kontekstu migracijskih procesa ["Here I am mainly the Svabian": about the Construction of Identity in the Context of Migration Processes]. In: Jasna Čapo, Caroline Hornstein Tomić and Katica Jurčević (eds.): Didov san. Transgranična iskustva hrvatskih iseljenika [Grandfathers' Dream. Cross-border Experiences of Croatian Emigrants]. Zagreb: Institute of Social Sciences Ivo Pilar/Institute for Ethnology and Folklore Studies, 103–131.

Hornstein Tomić, Caroline and Katica Ivanda Jurčević 2012: Gäste auf Zeit - Grenzgänger - transkulturelle Vermittler: Identitätsbildungsprozesse in der Migration [Temporary Guests - Border-Crossers - Transcultural Mediators: Processes of Identity Construction in Migration]. In: Angelika Welebil and Jörn Nuber (eds.): Gastarbeit (Guestwork). Wien/St. Wolfgang: Edition Art Science, 173–222.

Hornstein Tomić, Caroline and Borna Pleše 2013: Skilled Mobility as a Challenge for Croatian Diaspora and Migration Policies. In: Vitalie Varzari, Gabriela Tejada, Sergiu Porcescu et al. (eds.): Skilled Migration and Development Practices: Republic of Moldova and the Countries of South East Europe. Chisinau: Acad. De Stiinte a Moldovei and École Polytechnique Fédérale de Lausanne, 80–95.

Hornstein Tomić, Caroline and Sarah Scholl-Schneider 2015: Ein leichtes Spiel? Erfahrungen der Rückkehr im postsozialistischen Kontext Kroatiens und Tschechiens [An Easy Game? Experiences of "Homecoming" in the Post-Socialist Context of Croatia and the Czech Republic]. In: Markus Kaiser and Michael Schönhuth (eds.): Zuhause? Fremd? Migrations- und Beheimatungsstrategien zwischen Deutschland und Eurasien. Bielefeld: transcript, 205–237.

Horvat, Dražen 2008: Tko nam dolazi u Hrvatsku [Who Is Coming to Us in Croatia]. In: Croatian Chamber of Commerce (ed.): Useljenička politika u funkciji razvoja hrvatskog gospodarstva [Immigration Politics in Function of Development of the Croatian Economy]. Zagreb: 29–34.

International Organization of Migration (IOM)/Slovenia Ministry of the Interior 2007: Migration Profile Croatia, 10: 31–32.

King, Russell 2000: Generalizations from the History of Return Migration. In: Bimal Gosh (ed.): Return Migration: Journey of Hope or Despair? Geneva: IOM and UN, 7–55.

King, Russell and Anastasia Christou 2010: Diaspora, Migration and Transnationalism: Insights from the Study of Second-Generation "Returnees". In: Rainer Bauböck and Thomas Faist (eds.): Diaspora and Transnationalism. Amsterdam: Amsterdam University Press, 167–183.

Koska, Viktor 2011: The Evolution of the Croatian Citizenship Regime: from Independence to EU Integration. Edinburgh: University of Edinburgh Law School. URL: http://www.lse.ac.uk/europeanInstitute/research/LSEE/ECPR_Standing_Group_on_SEE/PDFs/Citizenship_Croatia.pdf, accessed 10. 8. 2015.

Krauss, Marita 2001: Heimkehr in ein fremdes Land: Geschichte der Remigration nach 1945 [Return to a Foreign Country: History of Remigration after 1945]. München: Beck.

Lajić, Ivan 2004: Noviji razvoj stanovništva Hrvatske – regularno i neregularno kretanje stanovništva [Latest Developments in the Population of Croatia – Regular and Irregular Population Moves]. In: Migracijske i etničke teme, 20, 2–3: 171–185.

Mesić, Milan and Dragan Bagić 2011: Manjinski povratak u Hrvatsku – Studija otvorenog povratka [Minority Return in Croatia – a Study of Open Return]. Zagreb: UNHCR.

Perica, Vjekoslav 2011: Mit o dijaspori u konstrukciji novog hrvatstva i srpstva [The Diaspora Myth in the Construction of New Croatianhood and Serbianhood]. In: Politička misao, 48, 4: 113–132.

Povrzanović Frykman, Maja: Why is the Transnational Paradigm Useful? Considerations Based on Ethnographic Research among the Croats in Sweden. URL: http://www.formig.net/index.php?option=com_content&view=article&id=194%3Aworkshop-paper-von-maja-povrzanovi-frykman-why-is-the-transnational-paradigm-useful&catid=43%3Apublikationen&Itemid=96&lang=DE, accessed 10. 8. 2015.

Ragazzi, Francesco 2009: The Croatian "Diaspora Politics" of the 1990s: Nationalism Unbound? In: Ulf Brunnbauer (ed.): Transnational Societies, Transterritorial Politics: Migrations in the (Post-) Yugoslav Region, 19th–21st Century. München: Oldenbourg Verlag, 145–167.

Ratha, Dilip, Sanket Mohapatra and Ani Silwal 2011: The Migration and Remittances Factbook. Washington: The World Bank.

Rogić, Ivan and Ivan Čizmić 2011: Modernizacija u Hrvatskoj i hrvatska odselidba [Modernization in Croatia and Croatian Migration]. Zagreb: Institut društvenih znanosti Ivo Pilar, 164–170.

Scholl-Schneider, Sarah 2011: Mittler zwischen Kulturen. Biographische Erfahrungen tschechischer Remigranten nach 1989 [Mediators between Cultures. Biographical Experiences of Czech Re-Migrants after 1989]. Münster: Waxmann.

Schuetz, Alfred 1945: The Homecomer. In: American Journal of Sociology, Vol. 50, No. 5: 369–376.

Sopta, Marin 2003: Return to the Homeland: the Building of a State. In: Vlado Šakić, Howard Duncan and Marin Sopta (eds.): Immigrants and Homeland. Zagreb: Institute of Social Sciences Ivo Pilar, 23–28.

Stefansson, Anders H. 2004: Homcomings to the Future: From Diasporic Mythographies to Social Projects of Return. In: Fran Markowitz and Anders Stefansson (eds.): Homecomings: Unsettling Paths of Return. Lanham et al.: Lexington Books, 2–20.

Vidak, Nick 1998: The Policy of Immigration in Croatia. In: Politička misao, Vol. XXXV/5: 57–75.

Winland, Daphne 2005: Nation-Building, Nation-Bonding: Croatian Diaspora and the Homeland. In: Henriette Riegler (ed.): Beyond the Territory, within the Nation. Diasporic Nation Building in South Eastern Europe. Baden-Baden: Nomos Verlagsgesellschaft, 59–68.

Transforming Traditions of Bulgarian Rudari Migrating to Greece

Magdalena Slavkova

Introduction

The contemporary labour migration of Romanian-speaking Rudari from Bulgaria to Greece has different economic, social and cultural dimensions. A much neglected field in the scholarly literature related to migrations in Southeast Europe is the community's own perspectives towards "journey". This article, which uses an ethnological approach, will contribute to the understanding of the specificity of Rudari mobility through the analysis of the following question: How does the "journey" affect their understanding of social and cultural traditions?

In the text, I deal with empirical material collected in Bulgaria and Greece. Ethnographic field research in Bulgaria was carried out between 2006 and 2010. In Greece, the study was conducted in 2011.[1] The field trips were related to my postdoctoral project of Gypsy/Romani mobility to the Mediterranean countries. There have been interviews with representatives of different Gypsy/Romani communities who migrated to various destinations such as Spain, Italy, and Greece. Part of the ethnographic materials is related to Rudari travelling to Greece as one of the most important factors in post-socialist labour mobility. Interlocutors identify Greece as the most desirable destination for working abroad, followed by Spain, Italy, France and Cyprus. Methods of detailed field observation, participant observation and ethnographic interviews were employed during the fieldwork.

Conceptually, the Rudari are defined as a small community with specific ethno-cultural features. They live dispersed throughout Bulgaria numbering some dozens of thousands people (as an unofficial count). They maintain various kinship ties with their representatives living in different places and are, in effect, an endogamous group. They are also linked with the representatives of the people surrounding them by various social relations. The Rudari are vernaculars of the Romanian language, which is their mother tongue. They are traditionally Orthodox Christians; however, some of their representatives have converted to Evangelical Christianity (Slavkova 2005: 277–294). Because of their nomadic way of life in the near past and certain cultural characteristics, the Rudari are per-

---

[1] This study was carried out under the project "Moving People, Changing Perspectives: Bulgarian Migrations and Economic Crises", supported by ERSTE Foundation, Austria.

ceived as 'Gypsies' by the Bulgarian citizens and sometimes they, too, identify themselves as Romanian Gypsies, but usually emphasize the difference between their group and the population generally labelled as "Roma". Its members have a multi-layered identity and, depending on the situation, their self-presentation ranges from identifying themselves as Romanians, Vlachs, Gypsies (Romanian Gypsies), Rudari or Bulgarians, with the consciousness of belonging to completely different communities. The term "Rudari" is not only a construct used by academics to refer to them but it is their own appellation which has gained much popularity recently in Bulgaria thanks to the increased scholarly and society's interest in them (Еролова и Славкова 2013: 127–154). Ethnographically speaking, we have a community with the common name "Rudari" which in the past included two separate subgroups practising different occupations, *Lingurari* ("spoon makers"; also called *Kopanari*, "trough makers", the more popular name among Bulgarians) and *Ursari* ("beartrainers"). Lingurari have another level of group division (regional), for example *Intreni, Monteni, Kamchieni, Zagoryani, Dobrudzheni, Trakieni* and others. These names derive from certain regions people have inhabited. Their regional groups may be compared to ethnographic groups of Bulgarians who have inhabited different regions and who could differ from each other in certain cultural and dialect features.

Bulgaria's post-socialist migrations

Since the end of the socialist regime in Bulgaria in 1989 major political and economic changes have taken place. The transition from a government-run economy to a market economy, transformation of economic structures and the reorganisation of social life has affected the entire population. The changes have caused a social and economic crisis, as a result of which a new phenomenon has appeared among various ethnic communities: labour migration (seasonal or longer-term) abroad. It has involved different ethnic communities such as Bulgarians, Turks, Roma, Vlachs, Karakachans and others. All of them, although they might have different general or individual motivations for leaving the country, have equally been challenged to take cross-border travelling as a result of the high inflation and unemployment rates, and the significant lowering of the living standard. The common crisis has severely affected all communities but the ethnic minorities in particular. Many Roma, for example, remained without jobs when the industrial giants of the past closed production and the agricultural cooperatives went bankrupt. For them migration was one way out of the difficult economic situation and, along with the desire of finding a job, to improve the living standards of their families.

Western European countries like Austria, Germany, the UK, some central European countries of the former Socialist bloc, like the Czech Republic and the Benelux countries, such as Belgium and the Netherlands have become attractive destinations for migrants from Bulgaria. Along with this, a new model of labour migration, namely the movements from Bulgaria to the European Mediterranean countries, such as Italy, Spain, France, Cyprus and Greece has emerged. Although the Mediterranean countries became preferred destinations at the end of the 1990s, when the economic situation in Bulgaria complicated and travels abroad intensified, Greece began to attract Bulgarian citizens immediately after 1989 due to its geographical proximity and the possibility of fewer costs in reaching it. It became suitable for both short-term migration as well as for settlement for longer periods of time. Migration has often been short-term due to the fact that part of the work available for migrants is seasonal. There is another fact that makes migration not long-term: return travels as a result of the recent economic crisis in Greece, which has an impact on the local population but mostly on the migrants. Some of the well-established families have decided to return back home because they remained jobless.

Over the years, the Bulgarian community in Greece has become one of the biggest. According to the Greek statistical institute in 2001, there are 37,230 Bulgarian citizens, and they are the second largest community after the Albanians (National Greek Statistical Service 2001). To this date, the unofficial number of migrants from Bulgaria to Greece is at about 200,000–250,000 people (Филевска 2010).

Why they travel abroad

The conception that the Rudari as former nomads, who travelled through Bulgaria until the 1960s of the twentieth century, selling their homemade wood products or showed playing bears and monkeys at village festivals and fairs, have been motivated to migrate because of their nomadic past, does not appear to be true. Most of them give economic reasons and the desire to seek for a job as motivation to migrate. The travellers expected to solve their material problems through transnational movement. In the words of the interlocutors themselves, they went abroad because they had lost their jobs and had no other alternative apart from seeking work in Greece, which is geographically and culturally the closest EU member state. People assumed that they would be close to their families and would not completely have to change their lifestyle. However, they actually had a lot of worries and problems in looking for a job and in their social adaption. In the past, as well as today, the Rudari's big pride has been that they are hard-working and change their way of life and the place where they live because of the demand for livelihood. In fact, one of the first ethnographic data on the Rudari comes from the travel writings of British researchers and state officials who described them as honest people and workers of wood articles: "The most honest tribe in Bulgaria, and perhaps the most numerous. Of very pure blood, and exceedingly dark" (Gilliat-Smith 1915–1916: 6) and "Makers of spindles, wooden spoons, large wooden ladles, troughs" (Macfie 1916: 64–65).

According to the interlocutors' narratives, Greece appears to be equally attractive to Bulgarians, the Rudari and other ethnic communities such as Karakachans with Greek identity. A very important reason for choosing Greece is the possibility of finding a job relatively quickly, although at first it is hard. Another reason is that there are enough jobs even in the informal sector, which the Greeks do not want to work in, such as jobs in the agricultural and livestock production, nursing of elderly and sick people, domestic work and unskilled jobs in the tourism industry. In terms of non-economic motives, the interlocutors have also emphasised that the Greeks often do not distinguish Bulgarians and the Rudari and thus stereotypical attitudes on the basis of ethnic origin is missing. In Greece they present themselves as Bulgarians, trying to adapt as Bulgarian citizens by developing similar migration strategies, such as the kind of work practiced. Motives connected with religion which are indicated by the Bulgarians, have not been mentioned to me by the Rudari, although most of them are Orthodox Christians. The Greeks have the same Orthodox religious affiliation as the Bulgarians and for my Bulgarian interlocutors that has turned out to be important. Another fact that is mentioned by the Bulgarians but is not placed in the foreground by the Rudari is that social life at the place of destination is similar to that in the homeland.

Concerning the initial representations about Greece before travelling there, many interlocutors remark that they had very few images; Aliki Angelidou found the same for Bulgarians who left for Greece. The images they had were constructed by the narratives of relatives, colleagues and other villagers who had migrated to Greece. Images also arose through Greek movies and soap operas that are displayed on Bulgarian television. The very first impressions after arrival in the host country were mostly positive. However, for many of them these positive impressions were followed by some disappointment (Angelidou 2008: 215–218). The same applies for the Rudari who were disappointed by the low payment for hard work and the negative attitude of the employers towards foreign employees.

Creation and functioning of migration channels

The ethnic communities have managed to sustain some kind of distinctive identity within the migration flow, mostly by forming groups of people from the same group and place of origin when they settle abroad. Each of the ethnic groups can be seen both as a participant in the common Bulgarian migration waves and as creator of their own migration channels.

Most of the interlocutors' narratives indicate that channels were created relatively fast after 1989. They were formed on the level of subgroup belonging and regional basis. The Ursari who numbered less than the Lingurari joined the common Rudari flows or formed their migration networks. The members of regional communities were likely to choose different countries for emigration. For example, the Intreni of the Veliko Tarnovo region, North Bulgaria, emigrated to Italy and Spain, and those of Bourgas, Southeast Bulgaria (Trakieni or identifying themselves as Kopanari), to Greece. In cases where they travelled to the same country of destination, representatives from different regional groups settled in different villages. In Rethymno in Crete, for example, the newcomers are mainly from the region of Strazhitsa and Letnitsa, Veliko Tarnovo region (Intreni); in Heraklion in Crete the settlers are Kopanari from Rouse, Northeast Bulgaria; and the Kamchieni from the town of Beloslav (Varna region, Northeast Bulgaria) have settled in the region of Athens. There is no official information about the number of Rudari people in Greece, but according to field data a large number of them has chosen this country for emigration.

The job factor has been the most important one for the Rudari leaving for Greece. Initially only one member of the family or a pair (spouses, two brothers, two sisters-in law, etc.) went abroad, in order to be able to find a job more quickly. Quite often the pioneers are men but also women because they consider finding work easy and fast in the field of domestic service. This is a completely different pattern from that of their nomadic past when the whole family travelled together around Bulgaria. Although this pattern leaves only one or two relatives together, it is a family strategy for mobility rather than for individual migrations. The families of those who previously went abroad to East Germany, the USSR, Libya during the Socialist times, were among the pioneers who went to Germany, the Czech Republic (as construction workers, drivers or service staff), and then to the Mediterranean countries.

For the pioneers in the early 1990s it was most difficult. They were enthusiastic to work abroad but only had a small amount of money and vague information on where and what kind of work was available. Some of the interlocutors explained that they just waited for the border to be opened in 1989 to go there and seek for a job. They also lacked knowledge of the local language, legal documents or acquaintances to rely on. Later arrivals were able to more rely on their relatives. It was a trustworthy source of information in so far as would-be migrants tended to trust the practical information from members of their networks more than they trusted information coming from other channels and sources. Information about reaching the host country, possible destinations, and the availability of jobs and the value of payment were exchanged mainly between relatives and were rarely shared with Bulgarians or Roma. The Rudari have not expected to get information from them anyway.

In the 1990s, it seems that the Rudari who went to Greece quickly figured out a way to reach the destination, as the clandestine border crossing through small paths appeared to popular. For example, there has been a practice where men who successfully passed the Greek border become guides and lead other migrants through paths by payment. Another popular way of travelling prior to 2001 was the tourist visa to Greece that guaranteed a legal passage of the border checkpoints. People who went with legal tourist visas in most cases remained "illegally" in the country after their expiry. They travelled with one of the specialised Greek-Bulgarian tourist companies that organise the trip to Greece. A less common way, although it was also used, is entering the country by sea route through Italy. For example, a young woman and her husband came to Greece in 1997. Before that "they went to visit relatives" in Italy, stayed a week there and then went to Greece on a ferry.

In the late 1990s and especially after 2001 the Rudari travels to Greece intensified; this process was the same among Bulgarians and was influenced because of the worsening of living conditions in the homeland. The legalisation programmes conducted in 1998 and 2001, through which illegal migrants were given the opportunity to legalise their status, attracted new migrants (Fakiolas 2003: 535–548, Markova 1999). The mass migration was also provoked by the fact that in 2001 Bulgarian citizens obtained the right to travel without visas. According to Tanya Dimitrova, from that year on family chain migration became particularly prominent. Regarding chain migration, the author indicates that the first representative of the family who started the migration was a woman (Dimitrova 2012: 331–332). Indeed, other authors also state that women prevail over men (Rangelova 2006).

The multiple stage migrations are characteristic for both the Bulgarian population and for the Rudari. Settling by means of grouping together provides quicker adaptation to the new living conditions. During the development of channels, the most popular model is that the parents live abroad with their children in working age, while the elderly, looking after the grandchildren, are left behind. The final stage in the migration process from Bulgaria to Greece is that all family members leave, with the elderly who continue to look after the grandchildren, but this time abroad. Regardless of the fact that the family members may gather to live together for a long time, they perceive their stay abroad as temporary and because of this save the money to improve their living standard back home, which is typical not only for migrants in Greece but also for settlers in other countries. George Gmelch found the same for Barbadians who left Barbados after World War II and migrated to Britain and North America. Most of them left with the expectations to find better opportunities for themselves abroad and only planned to stay away just long enough to save money to buy a house and perhaps a car and then to return home, but it seldom turned out the way they had expected (Gmelch 2004: 206–223).

The very first destinations in Greece were Thessaloniki, Patras, Athens and Crete but later the number of people who settled or moved to other areas (e. g. other islands) increased. The workers have usually directed their migratory projects to two types of settlements – big cities where they expect work to be most available. The second mode is oriented to small towns and villages, which are situated, however, in developed tourist regions or in fruitful agricultural regions. Speaking about patterns of different communities from Bulgaria, they all settle in the same regions within Greece, unlike the Albanians, for example, who might group in other regions. Specifically, the representatives of certain ethnic communities choose the same towns and villages within a certain area, related to each other with various family, friends' and neighbour contacts. In the process of mass migration, however, the channels of ethnic groups have mixed and in one area representatives of various communities originating from Bulgaria or migrants from other countries have settled. The Rudari headed for various settlements throughout Greece in the regions of Thessaloniki, Katerini, Kavala, Komotini, Volos, Larisa, Lamia, Gastuni, Kalamata, Filiatra, Kyparissia, Messini, Patras, Gargaliani, Sparta, Athens; various villages on the islands of Crete, Rhodes, Lesvos, Mykonos, Zakynthos, which could also be attractive for Bulgarians and other migrants.

Following the development of the migration process, regional networks progressively differentiate. In some regions the migration has acquired such dimensions that the Rudari from the same neighbourhood go to the same city or village abroad, whereas people from another neighbourhood from the same place of origin in Bulgaria leave for a totally different part of Greece. Furthermore, information about possible destinations or job vacancies can be passed on to Bulgarian or Roma neighbours and acquaintances. For example, as a female interlocutor of Northeast Bulgaria mentioned, the first one to leave for Greece among the family was her husband who trusted native Bulgarians villagers to go abroad. They went by car but when they arrived in Greece they left the interlocutor's husband alone. He slept wherever he found a place to stay because he had no acquaintances. Another result of the development of channels is the involvement of relatives in different networks. Participating in a channel for migration might be relatives to the third grade cousins but it is also likely for relatives from the father's line of relatives to migrate to one settlement, and for those from the mother's line to a completely different area. For example, the first ones settled in North Greece, others to live and work on the islands of the South.

Transforming social and cultural traditions

Maintaining social ties between relatives away from the motherland and reproduction of cultural practices abroad, but also the creation of new relationships demonstrates group flexibility and the ability to adapt in a milieu different from where the travels started. Migration has significant influence on the group's perception of traditions.

The working process, which is the most important daily practice, involves all family members, except those children who attend school. In some cases relatives work together. For example, in agriculture more than one family member works in the field. Employment in agriculture is quite common among the Rudari because it is accessible to foreigners, even undocumented, and there is no need for any pre-qualification. However, because the work is seasonal it is possible for the family to move to various regions of Greece in search for a job. This work, which is hard, is an option for newcomers to be included in the local labour market. In the early 1990s some families began seasonal work in agriculture, such as picking olives, peppers, strawberries, peaches, oranges and more. They usually adhere to a mobile lifestyle. During the warmer months they live in tents and in the winter they rent houses. This mobile way of life is similar to their nomadic past, but it is not a "revival" of the previous mobility pattern because they ceased to travel as soon as they found a good job and settled permanently in one place. There are cases where people remain in agriculture for a long time or return again to this employment when they remained jobless otherwise. A good example of employment in the agricultural sector is that of the relatives of a young married woman who has lived with her husband's family in Crete, and her parents have lived in the town of Argos in Peloponnese. In the time of my fieldwork in Greece in 2011, they worked as pickers of oranges and olives, although arrived at the destination in the mid-1990s. More often the employment is gender and age profiled and women and men do different kinds of work. Job in animal breeding is an option for men. For example, a man arrived in Kavala in North Greece in 1991 and began working as a shepherd, although in Bulgaria he used to be a musician of traditional folklore music. But without acquaintances and support from locals he was not able to find another job. After a while he found a job in a stonemason's factory. Employment in the sphere of tourism is also seasonal. People are usually engaged for 6–7 months on temporary contracts and during the rest of the year they receive unemployment benefits and do not work or they find another job which does without contract.

Following the initial settlement, there is a number of internal migrations within the various regions of Greece. The main reason is job searching. For example, a Rudari family settled initially in Lamia, then moved to Volos and finally went to live in Chania in Crete. Finding a permanent employment is a way to successfully adapt to the new life abroad. The Rudari have mostly trusted their relatives' contacts regarding job search, unlike the Bulgarians who also rely on their friends. In the case of Greece, the Bulgarians can find work at the private employment agencies called *grafia;* however, this does not apply for the Rudari. As Nikolay Gabărski notes, the Rudari in Greece have relatives all over the country with whom they have close social ties and through whom they receive regular information on where and what type of job is available and how much is paid. Therefore, they are much more mobile than the Bulgarians and rarely use the services of the employment agencies (Gabărski 2008).

Some of the families who used to work in Greece go to other countries such as Spain or Italy, for example, as they failed to adapt or because they did not find a well-paid job. A good example of this is that of an interlocutor from North Bulgaria who went to Greece by bus in 1992 with his uncle and cousin and arrived in the town of Kalamata in Peloponnese. They found a place to stay close to the bus station and the local Greeks promised to provide them with work with good payment. They began to pick oranges and olives. They returned home not long after that because they did not obtain their payment and were very disappointed. Later, the families of these men migrated to Spain. The interlocutor said that in Spain he and his relatives have a better life because the local people are nicer and accept foreigners as people while the Greeks only accept them as workers. It is also possible for the families to combine work in more than one country abroad. For example, the families of two married sisters live in North Spain during the agricultural season and work on farms. In the cold season, they move to Greece, where the men work in the construction sector and the women in sweet factories.

Life abroad leaves its imprint on various cultural and social life of the group. For the first time money holds a different value in the life of the Rudari. They start showing signs of prestige that were not typical of the group's mentality. The Rudari have never been rich in Bulgaria and there has been no way ostentatiousness could be part of their behaviour. Now the money they have made abroad gives them reason to feel self-confident and they invest in the construction or purchase of a house in their home town, as well as in new "fancy" cars. They spend a fortune on lavish weddings and other family celebrations. Recently they have started investing a great deal in the education of their children. For example, a Rudari parent went to Greece in order to earn money to sustain the family and support the children's education. Meanwhile, the grandparents took care of them. The biggest sister married before completing her pedagogical education. The middle-aged sister became a nurse and the youngest graduated in Ecology.

Changing the workplace is also associated with the desire to earn more money. For example, women seek job in taverns and hotels while men usually hold second jobs in construction and transportation or become garage mechanics. Some Rudari have found jobs in different carpentry warehouses, which is associated with their traditional skills making various articles out of wood. The Rudari have been more entrepreneurial, more than they had been at home, although the men continued to be afraid of "big business enterprises", as one interlocutor said. Like other Bulgarians they established family businesses and opened disco clubs or shops for Bulgarian staple foods. Although settlers in Greece began to earn more money, some of the older interlocutors regarded the way of life under Socialism as better and they perceived their lifestyle abroad as harder: "Before 1989 we lived better, we were not rich, but there was no split between people, everyone was equally rich, there were no luxury cars, but we had the money to sustain our families." That is why they perceived the money earned abroad as "blood money" because the "life abroad brought us only sorrow".

Rudari initiatives, no matter of their backgrounds and regardless of the social milieu, take place within the circle of families and kin unit. The relatives usually settle together in one town or village and even in one neighbourhood where they rent cheap old houses or apartments because of the lower costs. Settling by grouping together, means they try to recreate their social life from Bulgaria. What they see as the difference between the way of life in Bulgaria and the one in Greece is that in Greece they do not have much time for maintaining social contacts, unlike in Bulgaria, where they worked in a more moderate way and where they had more time to communicate with their relatives. In the circumstances of migration, the Rudari have new social contacts outside the circle of relatives. They start to communicate more frequently with members of other regional groups, with Roma, Bulgarians, etc. The latter groups continue to be perceived as "others" but the mutual contacts in their daily life can make them neighbours, friends and even relatives.

By tradition, marriages among the Rudari have been concluded within the regional group and mixed ones have not been considered to be successful. In the recent past, however, there have also been mixed marriages with members of other regional groups, such as the Ursari, with Bulgarians or with Roma. So, the boy who lives in Greece "returns to Bulgaria to marry". However, mixed marriages abroad are one of the results of the influence of migration on the group's culture. The intermarriages with members of other regional groups who live in the same or in neighbouring villages, and also with foreigners have become more frequent. The intermarriages can also be seen as a strategy for integration into the new society. They are still perceived negatively, but the ideas have begun to change. In Greece, several examples of co-habitation between Greeks and the Rudari can be found as well as of intermarriages. Examples of co-habitation with Greeks are more common, especially if both spouses had already been divorced.

Social contacts between the Bulgarian and Greek Rudari or Vlachs, with whom they feel closely related to in terms of language and culture, are rather exceptional. For Bulgarian Rudari it does not make sense to communicate with the local Rudari or Vlachs, and they even have a negative attitude towards them. In some cases Bulgarian Rudari often do not know much about them and think they have nothing in common because in comparison with them they feel more Bulgarian. For example, some men from Bulgaria arrived in Greece in the early 1990s in order to look for a job, and, in their words, they met some local Vlachs/Rudari (which for them is one and the same group) who promised them a well-paid job in agriculture. They bargained without a problem, because they "spoke the same language", but the Bulgarian Rudari were cheated on and did not receive their payment. So, those interlocutors have an opinion that local Rudari are not as honest as themselves.

Another interesting point is mutual relationships between Bulgarian Rudari and Romanian migrants from Romania. While living in Bulgaria interlocutors demonstrate an identity of Romanians, but during their stay in Greece they always present themselves as Bulgarians in front of Greeks. This does not happen in the meaning of changing their ethnic identity. However, through comparison with the Romanians from Romania they realize that they are totally different from them. The Rudari avoid speaking Romanian in front of the Greeks in order to not being recognised as Romanians. Their worst fear is to be identified as "Gypsies" because they do not want to be excluded. According to the interlocutors' stories the Romanians from Romania are bad workers and thieves and that is why nobody wants to be identified as one of them. For example, my interlocutors from Crete were the neighbours of a Romanian family. They did not maintain any contacts with them and to my question why they did not communicate with them, they told me that they "felt Bulgarians and there was no need to communicate with Romanians". However, there are other cases in which Bulgarian

Rudari have or had close contacts with Romanians and have perceived them in a positive way. For example, a returnee who is now retired said that he worked for a Romanian owner and was pleased to work for him. His wife also had a friend from Romania, who helped her a lot and who taught her the Greek language.

Contacts between Evangelical Christians present us another type of social relations. Although the Rudari are Orthodox Christians by tradition, some of them, in most cases women, converted to Protestant Christianity in Bulgaria, and under the terms of migration, some of the converts have not continued to attend Evangelical Churches. Others, however, have preserved their faith and have attended religious practices. Concerning the social contacts of Evangelical migrants there are two different trends. In the first case, Evangelists maintain contacts mostly between their relatives. They gather for worship in home churches, which are attended by relatives or visit Protestant churches on their returns to Bulgaria. They also have opportunities to do conversations about faith with their relatives via Skype or Facebook. Furthermore, non-ethnic forms of gathering connect migrants in social ties built on factors other than kin or ethnicity. In Evangelical services migrants form social relationships with the local Greeks and migrants who bear different ethnicity. Nina Glick Schiller, Ayşe Çağlar and Thaddeus Guldbrandsen found the same in analysing their ethnographic cases of African Christian migrants in Halle in Germany and Manchester in the US. They argue that most of the migrants' Evangelical Pentecostal social relationships are built on non-ethnic links (2006: 612–633). In the case of the Rudari, some of them are involved in local Greek Protestant communities. Women visit local churches and have opportunities for expanding their social contacts beyond traditional family circles. Female interlocutors in Crete, for example, visit a Church of Jehovah's Witnesses lead by the Rudari pastor from Bulgaria and a Greek Pentecostal Church. They drink coffee together, chat, share information about job availability after the end of religious services or on other free days. By attending Greek Pentecostal societies they find their integration into local life by religious pathways. Men rarely attend Evangelical services and maintain their social life by, for example, fishing together or by organising weekly football or volleyball matches with relatives, or by drinking coffee with their Greek colleagues after work.

Although the Rudari live abroad, they intend to adhere to their traditional festivals and rituals, which are of greater importance to them in "being Rudari" and which keep them attached to their homeland. However, the Greek sociocultural environment impacts their cultural practices. The most important family gathering, for which cross-border travelling is initiated in order for relatives to be together, is the wedding. It is held both at home and abroad. Engagement is made usually in Bulgaria and after that, a civil ceremony is concluded, and a modern wedding takes place in a restaurant in Greece. For example, an elderly retired couple lives in a village in Northwest Bulgaria, while the families of their two children live in Athens. The wedding parties took place in Greece and the parents travelled to attend these special occasions.

There have been some changes in organising the Rudari wedding in Greece. The celebration is organised a long time beforehand and a great number of guests gather. For them it is a "revival" of the 'traditional' big weddings because during the last years in Bulgaria they were not able to invite many people due to economic reasons. Besides the traditional gifts such as blankets or carpets, they give different household appliances, as well as money in an envelope. They invite popular Roma musicians from Bulgaria to play. Next to traditional Bulgarian folklore music more contemporary Bulgarian and Greek pop-folk music is played at the celebrations. An important part of the repertoire are the so called "migrant" songs in which different new motives have appeared – enrichment of the Rudari, difficulty in living abroad, problems appearing as a result of the economic crisis in Greece. Greeks are also invited as guests, which is a new cultural modification.

Maintenance of community life abroad is facilitated by the use of modern communication (Skype, Facebook, YouTube), which is as a new tendency in terms of weddings. The content of amateur video materials that are displayed on YouTube is mainly weddings. The materials and the comments on them are usually in Bulgarian rather than in Romanian. The most popular name, Kopanari, by which they are known among Bulgarians, is more often used on the internet than the term "Rudari", as, for example, the following titles of uploaded videos show – "Kopanari at wedding"; "Kopanari in Athens" etc. According to Elena Marushiakova and Vesselin Popov, Bulgarian Rudari create dense networks of relatives living in different countries, visible in the virtual space. By sharing everyday and festive video materials their group's identity is strengthened, but still they continue to feel attached to Bulgaria as their motherland and identify themselves as Bulgarian citizens (2013: 266–267).

Conclusion

The transition from nomadic times when certain families or groups of relatives travelled together from one village to another to migration to Greece has brought about a number of dramatic changes in social and cultural life. The 'journey' to Greece has changed their understanding of social ties' creation and cultural traditions. By travelling, the communities have been able to sustain their families. One of the important consequences is that they have been able to increase not only their economic but also their social status. For them, migration has also been a form of cultural adaptation because it strengthens the links between relatives.

Some of the migrants who left have been temporary migrants travelling between the two countries or returning to Bulgaria sooner or later, while others have turned into emigrants settling permanently in the host country and adjusting to the "Greek way of life". Migration has placed them in a position where they are able to use various strategies for keeping social contacts between their relatives, but they also have opportunities for establishing new contacts with Greeks. There are different possibilities of keeping the links between relatives, such as gathering at festive events, attending the home church's services or by maintaining contacts on the internet with those living in other countries. By preserving their cultural practices abroad, although in a modified version, they continue their "tradition" and feel attached to Bulgaria. However, the Rudari do not form a closed community because there have been examples of the creation of ties outside their ethnic group, based on shared religion or neighbourhood, collegiality and also of mixed marriages, which are an extension of the ties beyond the boundaries of the traditional community. One possible strategy for successful integration in the country of destination is the religious pathway through which they adapt to local life.

References

Angelidou, Aliki 2008: Re-Imagining "Europe" through Daily Life in Greece: Representations of Greece and the EU among Bulgarian Immigrants in Athens. In: Elena Marushiakova (ed.): Dynamics of National Identity and Transnational Identities in the Process of European Integration. Cambridge: Cambridge Scholars Publishing, 214–222.

Dimitrova, Tanya 2012: Migrant Networks and Social Chains between Bulgaria and Greece. The Case of Bulgarian Migrants in Greece. In: Petko Hristov (ed.): Migration and Identity. Historical, Cultural and Linguistic Dimensions of Mobility in the Balkans. Sofia: Paradigma, 326–341.

Еролова, Йелис и Магдалена Славкова 2013: Етничност, религия и миграции на циганите в България [Ethnicity, Religion and Migrations of the Gypsies in Bulgaria]. София: Парадигма.

Fakiolas, Rossetos 2003: Regularising Undocumented Immigrants in Greece: Procedures and Effects. In: Journal of Ethnic and Migration Studies, 29, 3: 535–548.

Филевска, Благородна 2010: През последните години в Гърция пристигат все повече млади емигранти от България [The Number of Young Emigrants Arriving in Greece from Bulgaria Has Increased in the Recent Years]. In: Focus News. URL: http://www.focus-news.net/?id=f14625, accessed 15. 4. 2012.

Gabărski, Nikolay 2008: Les expériences migratoires bulgares en Grèce depuis 1989. In: Balkanologie, XI, 1–2. URL: http://balkanologie.revues.org/index 1142.html, accessed 15. 4. 2012.

Gilliat-Smith, Bernard (Petulengro) 1915–1916: Report on the Gypsy Tribes of North-East Bulgaria. In: Journal of the Gypsy Lore Society (new series), 9, 1: 1–109.

Glick Schiller, Nina, Ayşe Çağlar and Thaddeus Guldbrandsen 2006: Beyond the Ethnic Lens: Locality, Globality, and Born-again Incorporation. In: American Ethnologist, 33, 4: 612–633.

Gmelch, George 2004: West Indian Migrants and Their Rediscovery of Barbados. In: Ellen Oxfeld and Lynellyn D. Long (eds.): Coming Home? Refugees, Migrants, and Those Who Stayed Behind. Philadelphia: University of Pennsylvania Press, 206–225.

Macfie, Andreas (Mui Shuko) 1916: With Gypsies in Bulgaria. Liverpool: Henry Young and Sons.

Markova, Eugenia 1999: Changes in Social and Economic Status of the Legalized Bulgarian Immigrants in Greece a Year Following Legalization. URL: http://www.cgdev.org/doc/event%20docs/10.23.03%20GDN%20Conf/Markova%20-%20Changes%20in%20Social%20and%20Economic%20Status%20of%20the%20Legalized%20Bulgarian%20Immigrants%20in%20Greece.pdf, accessed 16. 6. 2014.

Марушиакова, Елена и Веселин Попов 2013: Миграции на циганите от Югоизточна Европа (история и съвременност) [Migrations of Gypsies from Southeast Europe (History and Contemporaneity)]. In: Мила Маева и София Захова (съст.): Етнография на миграциите. Българите в Средиземноморието. София: Парадигма, 237–296.

National Greek Statistical Service 2001: Data on Immigrants in Greece from Census 2001. URL: http://www.statistics.gr/portal/page/portal/ESYE, accessed 16. 6. 2014.

Rangelova, Rossitsa 2006: Gender Dimension of the New Bulgaria's Migration: Comments on Empirical Data. In: Migration Online. URL: http://www.migrationonline.cz, accessed 16. 6. 2014.

Славкова, Магдалена 2005: Рудари у источноі бугарскоі и јеванђоски покрет [Rudari in East Bulgaria and the Evangelical Movement]. In: Биљана Сикимић (уредн.): Бањаши на Балкану. Идентитет етничке заједнице. Београд: Српска Академија Наука и Уметности, Балканолошки Институт "САНУ", 277–294.

After-Life Politics and Religious Governmentalisation: a Critique of the Post-Structuralist Theory of Secularisation

Sorin Gog

Introduction: The secular and the ontologisation of power

The debate between Talal Asad and Jose Casanova regarding the issue of secularisation sheds light on the epistemological usage of the concept of 'secularism' in contemporary religious studies (Casanova 2006, Asad 2003, David and Hirschkind 2006). Casanova attempts to reframe the issue of secularisation and purge it from the implicit positivist presuppositions in which it has been embedded since the Enlightenment (Casanova 2006). He distinguishes between three main axioms of the classical formulations of the secularisation theories: the social differentiation between sub-systems, religion losing is legitimising functions and becoming one system among others where each functions according to its autonomous logic; the erosion of individual religious behaviour; and privatisation of religious views and decoupling from structuring the public sphere (Casanova 1994). Casanova claims that only the first thesis can be rigorously maintained and that the remaining two are either not consistent with empirical evidence or are positivist normative assumptions that regard secularisation as a necessary consequence of social modernisation (Casanova 2006: 14). Casanova is mainly interested in showing how the process of de-privatisation of religion is compatible with the structural differentiation of modern societies (the core of the secularisation theory which he thinks is still valid). Focusing on public religions Casanova aims at analysing how religion can contribute to the democratisation of society and advancement of human rights (Casanova 2006: 27–30).

Talal Asad's criticism shows how the thesis of societal differentiation which Casanova still holds as a valid component of the secularisation theory is not defendable (Asad 2003). Asad argues that when religious people and organisations are mobilising themselves as actors in the public sphere they aim at modifying how each of these spheres (economy, law, art, etc.) functions by embedding their logic in a religious mode of existence (Asad 2003: 182–183). In doing this Asad does not want to completely discard the secularisation theory and he emphasises the role that the category of the secular has to play in drawing analytical frameworks for understanding the erosion of religious practices in Western Europe. Asad shows how the idea of a public sphere guided by communicative rationality, in the way Habermas conceives it, misses out the way this modern spaces are constituted by power (Asad 2003: 184). Being capable to employ discursive competences when participating in the deliberations of the public sphere requires being part of power structures and privileged networks of decision making. This power is secular in its very nature and codifies any religious attempt to transform the public debates as an inauthentic and non-modern conduct (Asad 2006). While religion is understood as an external breach of human rationality, the secular subjectivity portrays itself as an authentic expression of enlightened humanity. But this is always achieved through violent forms of power that embed secularism in how law is articulated or in how power hierarchies are instituted; and it does this by excluding non-secular subjects from the public sphere. The secular subjectivities and practices are not neuter forms of existence or the result of an emancipating process. They rather have to be understood as highly ideologically charged projects that aim at producing new forms of sovereignties and exertion of control over populations (Asad 2003: 192).

Secularism as a sovereign mode of power has its genealogy in Hegel's philosophy of the teleology of the Spirit and the explicit codification of the secular existence as the implacable development of history (Asad 2003: 192). This is consistent with the ideals of the Enlightenment and with the societal reforms advanced by the French Revolution (Asad 2003: 192). The main device through which the secular ideology has spread in Western Europe is the nation state and the widespread forms of secular nationalism. Referring to Benedict Anderson's work on "Imagined communities" Asad shows the role nationalism has played in producing a specific mode of how modern states have represented themselves to its subjects and the secular ideology it required to produce a homogeneous time through which it could rationally administer people. This secular power is also responsible for constantly defining how religion has to reinvent itself and redefine its proper boundaries in order to be allowed to function in modern secular societies. For Asad secularism is the force that generates secularisation, and as such it is an ideological practice that is part of what Foucault has labelled as biopolitical governmentality (Asad 2003: 187–194, Asad et al. 2013). Secularisation is not a descriptive-empirical concept but one that is a function of political (secular) power (Asad 2003: 200).

Casanova seems to agree with the epistemological frame of the "power of the secular" and argues that the ideology of secularism is actually responsible for Europe's secularisation. He shows how societal secularisation (differentiation of spheres) does not necessary lead to individual secularisation and this has roots in the specific way in which the modernisation process was advanced (Casanova 2006: 22). In the US, where religion played an important role in the formation of modern society, the separation of state and church has not implied the secularisation of everyday life as was the case with continental reforms marked by the French Revolution and its secular ideology (Casanova 2006: 22–23). By pointing out that the US remains a religious country in spite of the advanced modernisation of its society, he wants to emphasise that secularisation is a culturally and historically specific process that can be traced back to the European Enlightenment. It is not social modernisation that triggers secularisation, but:

"[...] the secularization of Western European societies can be explained better in terms of the triumph of the knowledge regime of secularism than in terms of structural processes of socio-economic development, such as urbanization, education, rationalization, and so on" (Casanova 2006: 17). The political force of secularism not only structures the every-day life of the Europeans, but according to Casanova it forms as well the attempt of social scientists to explain religious identities and practices. The theoretical devices they elaborate are biased and are implicitly advancing secularism by linking a normative way of modernity with secularism.

Talal Asad's concept of secularism instantiates the same Foucauldian epistemology he articulated in his work on the genealogy of religion, which focused on the production of religious subjectivities and the power technologies that enabled distinct practices of the self (Asad 1993, 2006). In both his work on religion and secularism Asad shows how the authoritative discourses and governmentalising dispositives have precedence over meaning-formation and life-world when explaining (religious) social action. For Foucault the contemporary bio-political form of power that aims at enhancing the well-being of a population through specific governmentalisation polices has its roots in the Christian pastoral power which had the same type of structure and employed the same mechanisms of controlling the flock (Foucault 2009, 2010). Likewise for Asad the secularism embedded in the nation-state has its roots in a specific Christian ontology of salvation and both the secular and the religious parts are constituted through specific disciplinary processes and power practices (Asad 2003: 100). In what follows I would like to explore the limits of this post-structuralist epistemological model which analyses on the one side religiosities in terms of the power technologies that enable them, and on the other side secularisation in terms of governmental policies which are articulated through hegemonic bureaucratic networks of the nation-state.

Old Believers and the embodiment of religious identities

My fieldwork site is an Old-Believers town (Sch.)[1] in South-East Romania in the vicinity of the Danube Delta. I discussed the painful history of this religious community and the complex reasons for its migration from Russia during the 18th century all over the world (Gog 2008). Here I would like to point out just some relevant contextual information. Towards the middle of the 17th century the Russian Orthodox Church, led by Patriarch Nikon, was undergoing an important religious reform that sought the standardisation of liturgical practice. The explicit motives for this were the wide disparities existing across the Russian Em-

[1] In order to protect the persons I interviewed during my fieldwork the name of the town where the research was conducted is not mentioned by its real name.

pire in terms of religious rituals and the divine service and the differences between the Russian Orthodox Church and the Greek Orthodox Church, the latter being perceived as the genuine preserver of the Byzantine tradition. But at the same time this reform was also a direct consequence of a centralisation of state and church power and its expansionist tendencies. The reforms were minimal in terms of religious dogma and theological doctrines, the aim being rather the regularisation of the religious practice. The main changes were related to those elements that were perceived as departures from the Greek tradition where the sign of the cross had to be performed with three fingers instead of two; the painting style of icons had to be changed in accordance with the Greek style, the direction of priestly processions had to be clockwise and not counter-clockwise and some minor spelling corrections in the creed and liturgy had to be made (Gog 2008: 7). Later scholarship would reveal that most of these differences did not come up due to syncretism and heterodox practices but due to the inheritance of a different Greek lineage of tradition, the Russian one drawing in fact on a much older Greek tradition than the existing modernised Greek tradition. Considered in terms of religious cultural systems and symbolic meanings these changes are rather insignificant, but in terms of religious practices, ritual prescriptions and rules of action all these changes were of great significance.

This is why the reforms were strongly resisted both by regular believers and by minor clerics and received occasional support from members of the aristocracy. The people who did not accept these changes were called pejoratively "raskol'niki" – schismatics, and the event Raskol – the Schism. The reasons for resisting the reforms were multiple, ranging from early forms of religious nationalism that did not accept Greek influence, attachment to a century-old tradition which the reforms portrayed as heterodox, the fear that the institution of the church was corrupt etc. At the level of popular culture, these innovations were perceived as something dangerous and the fear that straying from God's ancient ways could have severe consequences was spreading among the believers. Narratives of Antichrist ruling the official church were increasingly heard in various corners of the Empire.

An important aspect of this reform, which makes the widespread resistance much more intelligible, is related to the sacralisation of state power and to the embedding of the ecclesiastical pastoral mission within administrative structures. In pointing this out, we do not need to understand state and church, the political sphere and the religious sphere as something distinct from each other that the reform wanted to unite. Religion was already embedded in power-structures and temporal authority was codified as part of God's providence and will on earth. Nikon's reform has to be rather understood as an important transformation of pastoral power and religious governmentalisation and its attempt to produce a standardised religious community which would have enabled better religious care for individual believers. The interpretation of this reform as the personal ambition of patriarch Nikon and a circumstantial result of his friendship with Tsar Alexis completely misses the fact that it continued even after the deposition of Patriarch Nikon and the death of Tsar Aleksis. We are dealing with an Orthodox instance of early formation of sovereign pastoral power and the consolidation of church authority.

The resistance to this reform was eventually crushed brutally by massive killings, public executions and a ban on religious gatherings. Because of this, a lot of the Old Believers migrated to various places of the world where they were able to escape the persecution led by the Russian authorities. One of these destinations was Dobrogea (nowadays located in Romania), close to the Danube Delta where the Ottoman Empire granted them the freedom to have their own church in exchange for military alliance with the Turkish authorities. Here they managed to keep their faith, their Russian language and their traditions intact. They had their own church and their own cemetery, which they could organise according to their religious rules.

An important strategy of the Russian authorities in wiping the Old Believers out as a religious community was to exterminate the bishops and priests who led them. Within the Orthodox faith, the apostolic succession is a vital element that ensures the transmission of grace: the religious hierarchy is important not only because it mediates the sacred liturgy in the present time but it also connects it with the lineage established by Christ himself. This meant that the Old Believers were soon confronted with a lack of priests and religious leaders and this shortage was resolved in two different ways. Some religious communities thought that because of the ongoing persecution the apocalyptic ending was in sight and this allowed regular members of the church to perform the religious sacraments and the liturgy themselves. They were called *Bezopopovtsi* ("those without priests") and were split into several other smaller groups mainly because of weak institutionalisation and lack of organising structures. Other religious communities did not want to take such a radical position and adopted fugitive or excommunicated priests and gradually established their own episcopates. They were called *Popovtsi* ("those with priests"). The majority of the Old Believers belonged to this group.

The issues stemming from the precariousness of the religious hierarchy followed the Old Believers everywhere, including Dobrogea. Several decades after their settlement in this area the religious community split into two because some did not want to adhere to the Belokrinitskaya hierarchy, which was led by a controversial bishop figure. Because of this, the town was separated into two different religious communities – *Bezopopovtsi* and *Popovtsi* – and the settlement became antagonised by this division. This was followed by numerous struggles, a ban on establishing kinship with the other religious group through marriage, sometimes even the requirement of rebaptism, in case a person from the other group decided for various reasons to join the other religious community. In spite of the facts that both groups had a similar history, that they preserved the old traditions together, that they spoke the same language and maintained the same liturgical practice, this did not prevent them from despising each other and creating two radical separate communities. What has been important for my research is that this division of the Old Believers was followed by the establishment of two separate churches (after the problematic attempts to share the same church) and, what is even more important, by the creation of two distinct cemeteries. It is important to notice that the creation of new cemetery borders has little to do with different narratives of afterlife and cosmologies. It can rather be related to the way pastoral powers function: by articulating a distinct form of politics of after-life it attempts to delineate the religious community in order to governmentalise it better and more efficiently.

By politics of after-life I understand the articulation by the pastoral powers of a specific type of social management of death through a specific type of narrative that wants to organise the cemeteries as earthly images of after-life. The politics of after-life are not simple cosmologies that stipulate what happens to people after they die, but are every-day strategies that integrate the deceased persons into a meaningful structure: the specific spaces within cemeteries to which they are assigned and the rituals that the priest performs together with the religious community for the soul of the departed. By doing this, they regulate not so much the after-life of the dead but the life of the living (Gog 2007: 5). The pastoral powers require not only separate churches but also separate cemetery spaces in order to exert their sovereign authority.

At the end of the 19th century when Dobrogea was integrated into the Romanian Kingdom this area was increasingly colonialised with Romanian ethnics. This was part of a wider strategy of exerting influence over a region that was once controlled by the Ottoman Empire and inhabited by a mix of ethnic populations: Turks, Tatars, Bulgarians, Lipovenians (Russians), Romanians and others. By the beginning of the 20th century a small community of Romanians appeared in the town where I have done my research. They belonged to the Romanian Orthodox Church and they built their own church close to the area of the town where they received land from the Romanian government. This was not very far from the *Popovtsi* cemetery but, because the settlers felt closer religiously to the *Bezopopovtsi* group, they established their cemetery close to the *Bezopopovtsi* cemetery at the other end of the village. The Romanians I interviewed reproduce the same type of narrative today and consider this religious community to be closer to them. I believe this is partly because they are a minority compared to the Popovtsi religious community and partly because they did not have strong institutional structures and their religious ethno-nationalism was weak. Nevertheless, this third cemetery space functioned autonomously, according to the rules of the Romanian Orthodox Church. Each of the ethno-religious institutions exerted control over their religious members and there were no major problems in accommodating this new religion. From the outset, they were supported by a strong state with colonial interests over the whole of Dobrogea but this did not require a religious assimilation of the Old Believers. Because of the ethnic and cultural differences the two religions (Old Believers and Romanian Orthodox) could have little impact in attracting members from the other religious group. The three distinct cemeteries and different cultural practices were thus gradually naturalised and the burial of the dead was registered as a function of ethno-religious traditions to which everyone gradually got accustomed.

In spite of the fact that the Romanians were a minority they occupied a dominant political position in this area throughout the 20th century. The whole of Dobrogea gradually became populated by a majority of Romanians, but in some of the towns and villages they still remained a small community. The communist period enabled new types of nationalist policy and the Russian language and traditions of the Old Believers were subject to state regulations with the intention of gradually assimilating them. After the fall of communism most ethnic minorities from Romania mobilised themselves to regain their cultural and linguistic rights and control through democratic elections and the local political structures. The usage of the mother tongue in state schools and the emergence of ethnic associations with the aim of preserving their cultural heritage were part of the post-communist transformations in most areas of Romania. In the town where I have done my research this meant that the Romanians were increasingly aware of their minority status and of the gradual erosion of their dominant position. As a result of this, a new cemetery space appeared in the town, in the precinct of the Romanian Orthodox Church. The Romanian believers that I interviewed insisted (in spite of the reservations expressed by the priest in charge of the area) on having their cemetery much closer to them. This was a bit unusual since the churchyard was located very closely to the centre of the town and in the vicinity of the main administrative institutions. The locals did not think that this would be an appropriate place for burial grounds, but the Romanian community argued that their cemetery was located too far from their area (this signals an important mutation in their social representations regarding the usage of space) and so they managed to create a new cemetery and to project the new emerging ethnic boundaries that were functioning in every-day life during the post-communist period through it.

The appearance of this fourth cemetery was also gradually incorporated by the social imaginary of the community, and its 'natural' existence was acknowledged by most of the inhabitants as something normal. The emergence of a fifth cemetery space, that of the Adventist religious community was more problematic and created quite some tension within the community. By analysing the formation of this distinct cemetery space I would like to point out the relationship between pastoral power and social control and focus on death as a technology of power that is employed for producing docile religious subjectivities.

Post-socialism in Romania produced various structural transformations in every sphere of life, the religious one included. New religious movements emerged and the already existing ones (Pentecostal, Baptist, Adventist, Christian Brethren and other Evangelical movements) started to intensify their activities. Eventually some of the Old Believers converted to Adventism and renounced the faith of their ancestors. There are several characteristics that made Adventism a radically different religion from the one they practiced previously. An important aspect was an ethical rationalisation of the way of life, the emphasis on a radical personal change and the claim of an unmediated religious experience. This meant that technically there was no need for clerics to interpret and mediate the liturgy, since each individual believer could do that. The Old Believers still use Church Slavonic as a liturgical language but this is hardly understood by the wider community. The religious text and interpretation of the Bible is done by the priests and it is considered a vocational activity. By contrast, the Adventists insist that each believer should read the Bible in a language they can understand (Russian or Romanian) and all religious services are held in these languages. Most of their church activities are related to reading and interpreting the Bible and this produces several important institutional devices that mediate a strong religious socialisation. The Adventists are known by their neighbours as very knowledgeable when it comes to the Bible and to a leading a puritan life centred on strong ethical requirements. This has produced a full confrontation with the Old Believers' way of life. Their traditions, their customs, holidays, saints and leaders were all critically scrutinized by the Adventists and everything that did not have Biblical precedent was given up (Gog 2007: 12–16).

This has resulted in a violent clash with the clerics who were very concerned regarding the emergence of this "heresy" among them that was questioning their core religious traditions and thus the very reason why their forefathers had migrated from Russia. Preserving their religious identity was one of the most important aspects of their ethnic group. Adventists consider religious icons as false worship and as a form of idolatry, for example. The icons play a very important role in the religious life of the Old Believers. First, it is an important marker for a tradition of a community that refused to be assimilated by Patriarch Nikon's reforms and endured great persecutions throughout the centuries. The distinct painting style is still preserved today and the importance of the icons is transmitted from generation to generation. Each house has to have an icon from the moment of its construction on. Each child receives an icon at birth from his godparents and has to take care of it for his or her entire life and has to respect all sacred rules regarding handling it. Icons have to be painted on material that does not break and if damage is done to it the priests have to be notified immediately. When the wood on which the icon is painted starts to decay the icon has to be buried in the cemetery together with the deceased believers and it cannot be disposed of without the consent of the priests. This shows how revered these objects are and the sacred aura that surrounds them according to the Old Believers (Gog 2007: 12–16).

The Adventists have not only renounced their icons but have also taught others that according to the Bible it is sinful to worship these objects. As a result of all these tensions Adventists were considered impure people who had given up the faith and traditions of their ancestors and because of this a great deal of symbolic violence followed and so the Old Believers were encouraged to avoid interacting with them. The codification of this new religious movement as a source of spiritual pollution became most apparent whenever one of the Adventists died. The family wanted to bury him next to his parents and relatives in the cemetery belonging to the Popovtsi group of the Old Believers, but this was met with great resistance by the entire community. The priests I interviewed recalled organising a watch around the cemetery so that the dead Adventist would not be buried there secretly (Gog 2007: 16). If this had happened it would have spiritually defiled the entire cemetery. What was important for the Adventists was registering the corpse as part of a kinship structure and they wanted to place the deceased next to his parents and relatives. The cemetery also had an ethno-cultural meaning for them and not a religious one. They wanted to signal that in spite of the fact that they had adopted a new religion they remained Russian speaking Lipovenians. But this was precisely what was problematic not only for the Popovtsi group but for all Old Believers. The Bezopopvtsi group also refused to allow such a burial to take place in their cemetery and soon this message was sent to other Old Believers in the surrounding area in order to prevent them from accepting such a burial as well. The issue would be resolved only after the legal term for burying the dead expired and high-ranking government authorities had to intervene and create a fifth cemetery in the town of Sch. This space appeared not because the Adventists wanted to have a cemetery of their own, but because there was no conceivable place for them at the Old Believers' cemetery.

Old Believers articulate a distinct cosmology regarding the organisation of cemeteries. It is common knowledge to most of the people that not all the burial spaces are ontologically homogenous within the cemetery. Everyone makes a distinction between burial plots that are in the shadow and burial plots that are in the light. In order to tell the difference between the two you have to notice those places that have shade on them around noon – and so are almost constantly under it. They are located close to the fence of the cemetery or to a natural elevation. The church decides where each person has to be buried in accordance with the life he or she led while still alive. If a person did not attend the church services during his or her lifetime, lived with his/her life-partner without being married, committed suicide or died under mysterious circumstances that could even hint at suicide (as for example dying in the steam sauna), the person is buried in the shade. No religious service is held and none of the priests take part in the funeral. In the case of a suicide, to dramatise and signal even more clearly the after-life trajectory of the deceased person and his/her lack of communion with the church and its believers (dead or alive), the dead body has to be brought into the cemetery by passing it over the fence of the graveyard, not through the entrance gates. To be buried in the shadow is one of the most shameful ways to end one's life and this is strongly embedded in the local culture. "For the person that has no fear of God, it would've been much better for him not to be born at all" a priest says, and the cemetery objectifies this ontology (Gog 2007: 18).

In the case of less grievous sins, such as the refusal to participate in the sacrament of confession for more than seven years, there is an intermediate category in which the deceased is allowed to be buried in the light, but no religious service is held and the priests are not present. This type of death is not a grey zone (the after-life trajectory is clear to everyone); the deceased has the same fate as the persons buried in the shadow. His/her name will not be written in the church registers and no religious service will be held in his/her memory either in church or in the cemetery where priests come recurrently to pray for the after-life of the believers. As one of the priests puts it: "if no religious service is held, he remains forever like that, so everyone forgets him, and it appears that he had never existed" (M. R.). The reason why such an intermediate category exists has to do with humanitarian considerations. People try to negotiate with the priests in order to avoid a shameful burial in the shadow and sometimes they succeed in saving the appearances (Gog 2007: 13). But this only reinforces the traditional religious power's right to evaluate and decide on the after-life trajectories of the people who have died. The aim of this pastoral governmentality is ultimately to exert social control over the living and ensure that they die as good believers. Those that manage to do so are buried in the sun and this is signalled to everyone by a public religious service and a public procession. Specific church flags and the official church stretchers for carrying the coffin are used to mark a good death and a good burial. The names of these people will be remembered in prayers by the priests and they will benefit from the religious rituals that are performed recurrently in the cemetery when priests intercede for their after-lives.

It should come as no surprise that Adventists do not have a place in this religious cosmology: "It is much worse to become an Adventist than to commit suicide. They have left our church and gave up our faith" (M. F., Popovtsi priest), which is why they cannot not be buried in the cemetery. Their sinfulness was considered so great that no place could be assigned for them in this ontological scheme that organises the cemetery as an earthly image of the after-life. This is why the cemetery space that was assigned to the Adventist by local authorities is widely considered to be an impure ground, a "forsaken garden" full of weeds. Many of the people I talked to referred to this cemetery as existing outside the borders of the cemetery, as being a non-place where the lowest of lowest are buried in the most shameful way possible (Gog 2007: 18).

For the Adventists, this cosmology does not hold any meaning; in a sense they secularise these religious representations that are embodied in rituals and cemeteries through spiritualising death and transforming the burial into a non-religious category. What matters is how you lived and it is this living that establishes your after-life trajectory. Death in itself and the burial practices are a matter of grief and loss and the cemetery should provide a space for the family to deal emotionally with this. Since it has no religious significance whatsoever, the Adventist pastors would be ready to hold a religious service and open the cemetery to everyone that wanted to be buried there (Gog 2007: 19). We should not understand this to mean that within the Adventist religion there are no power struggles; what differentiates it from the traditional forms of pastoral powers, articulated by the Old Believers, is the focus and emphasis on the cultural production of a religious subjectivity and not on the ritual control of social and symbolic spaces.

I have encountered many instances in my fieldwork in which this cosmology of after-life has strongly structured the every-day life. Some of the Old Believers were deeply impressed how this Evangelical group manages to produce such knowledgeable religious people (reading and interpreting the Scriptures) and to live in accordance to moral principles. But their curiosity to visit the local Adventist local church is kept at bay because they are afraid that their own religious leader might find out and refuses to assign a proper place in the cemetery later on. Others talked about how non-religious people are persuaded by their relatives to go to church towards the end of their lives so that they are able to receive a proper burial and would not be put to shame by an undignified death. People who have not lived according to the religious requirements of the church are advised to repent and thus try to obtain permission to be buried properly in the light. This shows the extent of influence that the pastoral powers have on the religious community and the way the religious governmentalisation of the after-life is connected with the social control of every-day life. The cemeteries in Sch. are important spaces where these power structures are articulated and where the traditional religious authorities manage to materialise specific forms of after-life politics that structure not only social relations but also have an influence on how people think of their own death and burial.

Cemetery borders and religious segregation between villagers are encountered in other parts of Romania as well. For example, the Roma, Hungarians and Romanians from the Transylvanian region are all buried in their own separate sections of the cemetery or have distinct cemeteries. But apart from that nothing is similar. The strong social ontology that we have encountered in the case of the Old Believers is exceptional: the pastoral power operates at its full strength here. In the next section I will pay attention to what extent this strong religious governmentalisation manages to produce religious subjectivities. Does pastoral power have a value-added effect on generating more religiosity as the post-structuralist Foucauldian model of Talal Asad suggests?

Conclusion: A critique of the post-structuralist model of secularisation

There are several issues I find problematic regarding this post-structuralist model of analysing religious and secular practices. This approach subordinates subjectivities to practices and analyses secular and religious identities in terms of the authorising discourses and governmentalising dispositives that enable such identities. Religious and cultural life-worlds are a function of the modes of power and of the productive forces that structure the social spaces. Subjectivities and the life-world in which these are embedded are conceptualised in this tradition as power effects and as products of quasi-mechanical coercive forces. Although this narrative avoids what Charles Taylor (2007) calls a "subtraction story" of secularisation it has a too simplistic view on how the secular 'immanent frame' emerged. The secular life-world that we see today in most of the Western European societies has not come about through a humanist ideology forced upon societies through governmentalising technologies. To explain the major cultural shift and the secular formation of the "buffered self" (Taylor 2007: 26–27) in terms of unilateral power structures that are imposed on people through bureaucratic networks, it is to miss out the gradual cultural formation (in which the religious movements have played an important role) of instrumental rationalisation of time and society, the mundane forms of authenticity and vocational self-development that have played a major role in establishing an immanent self-understanding and a secular culture (Taylor 2007: 539–593). In the production of a secular imaginary power disciplinarian practices have played an important role, but we cannot assume a direct structuring force that produces these secular subjectivities. These were rather the product of century-long transformations that generated "closed world structures" and were gradually naturalised in a differentiated life-world (Taylor 2007: 559). Religious nominalism, deism, the protestant reformation etc. have played an important role in generating these transformations and the immanent frame and the production of a secular culture has rather been an unintentional consequence.

It is true that structural modernisation (industrialisation, education, urbanisation, etc.) does not intrinsically produce secularisation as Casanova points out (this would also imply a positivistic understanding of secularisation) but nevertheless these transformations have produced structural social effects and reconfiguration of life-worlds. An immanent framework is much harder to embed in traditional rural societies where the religious plausibility structures still provide the main socialisation mechanisms; modern societies that have undergone a process of societal rationalisation are able to accommodate an immanent frame much easier, given the internal capitalist production and consumption requirements. When Casanova acknowledges the societal differentiation between the religious sphere and the economic, educational, political etc. spheres as the core valid axiom of the secularisation theory and rejects all other aspects (Casanova 2006), he leaves this open to an interpretation that makes this differentiation a supra-temporal process. This structural differentiation cannot subsist outside the every-day life; it is reproduced by social actors and structures and has an important effect on the value orientations within the life-world, and this implies a structural change in how religious identities and practices are reproduced.

Religion is not a homogeneous category nor is it a tradition that invariably reproduces itself as a transcendent world-view. Religions are embedded historically in cultural and social settings and because of this they always require a hermeneutic grounding. In pluralist societies where religion is not imposed on people and where people can choose between alternative life-worlds the specific capacity to couple its relevance structures to the immanent secular culture in order to meaningfully address the native horizons of authenticity is critical. What a lot of analysts miss out when referring to the religious American life and how this contradicts the idea of a secular modern society is how much the religious field has been transformed in order to adapt to the requirements of a contemporary society. From "praise and worship" to religious rock music, from the production of religious techniques for appropriating religious competences to highly developed organisational church structures, from the creation of popular devotional literature to the diversification of religious media – all these are various ways in which the religious field is being structurally transformed in order to embed its religious worldview and transform the modern structures of self-understanding.

Asad's post-structuralist model of analysing religious and secular practices asserts the continuity between the two in terms of their governmentalising capacities and their force of producing intimate social identities, and so methodologically neglects the important role that culture plays in the formation of subjectivities. Most of all his post-structuralist epistemology does not explain why there is a transition from religious to secular modes of power in the first place. The two might have the same structure, employ the same type of coercive mechanisms, share the same form of productive action and embodiment of subjectivities – but what is it that enables a switch from one to the other? Are there any social conditions that enable the abandonment of a religious finite province of meaning and the attempt to integrate social reality from a secular finite province of meaning, to put it in "Schutzian" terms (Schutz 1990)? What enables such transformation and how can we explain the gradual erosion of religious representations or religious practices of the self in Western European countries? The emphasis on power and the post-structuralist insistence that actions are embodied in hegemonic structures or that intentionalities and cultural formations need to give way to dispositions and productive practices do not answer this important question. It only hints to a paradigmatic shift in terms of the epistemological framework used to analyse social and cultural action.

Above I outlined an instance of how pastoral power operates among the Old Believers and the way the religious governmentality attempts to regulate the everyday-life of believers through cemeteries. I called this after-life politics and I tried to show how this is connected with the institutionalisation of a strong religious ontology. Within a post-structuralist framework this is supposed to produce religious subjectivities, since religious power is present in this community in its full force. What we see among this Old Believers community is to a great extent exceptional to the Romanian religious landscape and this strong religious pastoral power should produce more intensive religious lives and practices than elsewhere in the country. But it does not. Generally speaking, we can see the same trend of secularisation of the after-life representations here as in the rest of the country. In spite of the strong mechanisms of religious control this does not produce a more religious culture. In Sch. we can see the same levels of religiosity as in the other regions of the country. There are several reasons for this and I would like to outline them briefly.

The specific religious practices of the Old Believers are interconnected with their ethnic identity, and the religious radicalism should also be understood as an indirect way through which this is preserved and reproduced. International migration erodes this cultural model of imagining an ethnic community. In 2006 over 53.1 % of the persons interviewed stated that since 1990 someone from their household had worked abroad and 41.6 % had some of their family members living abroad.[2] Working abroad and experiencing different styles of living makes them question the existing religious order of things and adopt more liberal values. This does not necessarily mean that they cease to be religious or that they stop believing – but it often generates a social criticism regarding the strict religious rules the priests impose on the community. International migration plays a role in eroding this religious model of ethnicity. But this would give us a wrong impression regarding the sources of secularisation among the Lipovenians from Sch. as being something imported from the West through diffusion of a worldview that apparently is alien to the Old Believers. The younger generations increasingly depart from a religious mode of life and I argue that the post-socialist structural transformations have played an important role in this. The pluralisation of life-worlds, the transition to a free market economy, the institutionalisation of a new logic of self-authenticity and freedom have generated narratives that often collide with the traditional religious view on life.

The younger generations are critical of the austere religious codes the church requires them to internalise (fasting, church attendance, practicing of specific rituals) and of the way it attempts to regulate their sexuality. Pre-marital sexual experiences, although strongly condemned by the Old Believers' Church, are increasingly encountered among young people. Sometimes this is taken further and young couples decide to live together. The church tries to control this by sanctioning the parents that allow this to happen and either imposes on them a ban to attend church or other religious interdictions. But this only reveals the limited impact the pastoral power has on emerging social identities. Another important aspect that young people are critical of is the Slavonic language in which the religious services are held and which makes church activities incomprehensible. It is not only the liturgy that is officiated in Slavonic, but also the sermons, so even for a Russian-speaking community the religious socialisation takes place with great efforts. The younger generations like to think of themselves as having mingled with Romanians and having "modernised" themselves. Learning Romanian is considered much more important than learning Russian because this guarantees them the possibility for social mobility and access to structures of opportunities in the large neighbouring cities. Mastering the Romanian language is an instrument for this. Identifying themselves as Old Believers the younger generations do not necessarily imply a conservative religious practice or the religious beliefs we have seen so strongly articulated by the priests when dealing with "heretic" Adventists. It rather implies a local form of belonging and a way of articulating an ethnic identity. But even this ethno-cultural mode of belonging is increasingly questioned along the religious one.

---

[2] The data stems from a research carried out in Sch. in 2006 on a random statistical sample of 392 interviewed subjects using a standardised questionnaire.

I pointed out earlier that to a great extent the politics of after-life articulated through the cemetery is exceptional in the Romanian society. The important question we have to ask is what degree this pastoral governmentalisation produces corresponding to religious subjectivities. Do believers appropriate the religious representations and the eschatological views that the church presents as the reason for safe-guarding the cemeteries from Adventist "heretics"? Although religion still plays a very important role in this community, we can notice a secularisation of death and the rejection of a religious interpretation of after-life. Only 49.7 % of the population from Sch. do believe in life after death and approximately 67 % believe in the religious categories of heaven and hell.

	Yes	No	DK
Belief in life after death	49.7 %	24.7 %	24.7 %
Belief in heaven	67.9 %	14.3 %	17.3 %
Belief in hell	66.8 %	16.1 %	16.6 %

Table 1: Religious belief regarding the after-life in Sch.

This is consistent with what happens on a macro-level in the entire Romanian society. This data includes both rural an urban spaces, the latter being more secular than the former; even the rural areas from Romania are far from such strong religious control as we encounter in Sch.[3] As we can see, the levels of unbelief and uncertainty in Sch. are similar to the ones existing on the level of the entire society. Generally speaking, the Romanian society is still a very religious one compared to other Central and Eastern Europe countries; nevertheless what I would like to point out is that the strong religious governmentalisation among the Old Believers does not produce more religiosity and stronger religious beliefs than in the rest of the country where such governmentalisation is absent.

	Yes	No	DK
Belief in life after death	58.6 %	20.6 %	19.2 %
Belief in heaven	70.2 %	12.1 %	15.9%
Belief in hell	67.2 %	15.0%	15.0%

Table 2: Religious belief regarding the post-mortem trajectory in Romania

The level of education also leads to an erosion of the traditional religious worldviews and Christian eschatology. This takes place in the Old Believers' community, as well. It would be wrong to interpret education as being incompatible with religion and this association would imply a positivist understanding of reli-

[3] The data has been provided by European Values Survey Romania, 2008. The comparison between the two samples is based on the idea that these religious values do not fluctuate strongly within short amount of periods (in this case two years).

gion. The level of education here acts as a proxy (among other) for the degree to which people are exposed to alternative world-views and ideas, to different social fields and habitus and to social settings that are not regulated by church authorities. This process is usually accompanied by a de-legitimation of the institution of the church and its involvement in political, economic and social issues, and it registers it as a social institution with competences for strictly spiritual issues.

What is important for my argument is to show that the religious governmentalisation does not produce direct and unmediated effects. Religious power cannot produce corresponding religious subjectivities through its hegemonic mechanisms. Religious agents can resist such forms of domination and mobilise alternative representations and practices in accordance with the cultural resources they have available. To presuppose a lineal post-structuralist model that connects religious power with religious subjectivities or secular governmentality with secularisation does not allow for a more complex epistemological model of social action that accounts for how social actors creatively react and indigenise the logic of the cultural fields in which they are embedded.

	Primary Education	Secoudary Education	Tertiary Education
Belief in life after death	52.1 %	47.4 %	50 %
Belief in heaven	75.5 %	59.9 %	54.5 %
Belief in hell	74.5 %	58.6 %	54.5 %

Table 3: Religious belief regarding the post-mortem trajectory in Sch.

Comparing these data with the entire Romanian society we can again see that the values in the Old Believers' community are not very different from the ones existing at the entire level of the Romanian society. In spite of the fact that the religious culture existing in Sch. strongly regulates the every-day life and most of all, as we have seen above, the cemeteries, this does not manage to halt the gradual erosions of these religious beliefs.

	Primary Education	Secoudary Education	Tertiary Education
Belief in life after death	57.3 %	60.8 %	52.0 %
Behef in heaven	74.9 %	72.0 %	60.6%
Belief in hell	71.1 %	69.0 %	58.0 %

Table 4: Religious belief regarding the post-mortem trajectory in Romania

Although what happens in Sch. is to a great extend exceptional, I argue that this case represents a specific instance of how pastoral powers imagine and institutionalise a religious meaning of death and give insight into the symbolic mechanisms used to embody these meanings in cemeteries. My argument is that in spite of the strong religious regulations this does not translate into religious identities and representation among the believers. The secularisation of death among the Old-Believers has comparative levels as to rest of the Romanian society. This can especially be seen in urban cemeteries where these secular representations are embodied in the way mortuary space is organised. The religious meanings are secondary in relation to class and social prestige or political and civic distinctions. The after-life politics do not structure the spaces of cemetery anymore and this is doubled by growing scepticism regarding the Christian eschatology. These processes are instantiated among the Old Believers as well in spite of the strong pastoral governmentality that wants to protect their religious and ethnic identity.

Asad's post-structuralist model that defines religious or secular subjectivities as the direct effect of specific technologies of power and authorising discourses constitutes an reductionist epistemology that overlooks the important impact cultural ontologies and the intentional agency of social actors have on the formation of religious and secular life-worlds.

References

Asad, Talal 1993: Genealogies of Religion. Discipline and Reasons of Power in Christianity and Islam. Baltimore: Johns Hopkins University Press.

Asad, Talal 2003: Formations of the Secular: Christianity, Islam, Modernity. Stanford: Stanford University Press.

Asad, Talal 2006: French Secularism and the “Islamic Veil Affair”. In: Hedgehog Review, 8.1/2: 93–106.

Asad, Talal, Wendy Brown, Judith Butler and Saba Mahmood 2013: Is Critique Secular? Blasphemy, Injury, and Free Speech. Oxford University Press.

Casanova, José 1994: Public Religions in the Modern World. Chicago: University of Chicago Press.

Casanova, José 2006: Secularization Revisited: A Reply to Talal Asad. In: David Scott and Charles Hirschkind (eds.): Powers of the Secular Modern: Talal Asad and His Interlocutors. Stanford: Stanford University Press, 12–30.

Foucault, Michel 2008: The Birth of Biopolitics: Lectures at the Collège de France, 1978–1979. Edited by Michel Senellart. Translated by Graham Burchell. New York: Palgrave MacMillan.

Foucault, Michel et al. (eds.) 2009: Security, Territory, Population: Lectures at the Collège de France 1977–1978. Vol. 4. New York: Palgrave MacMillan.

Gog, Sorin 2009: Cemeteries and Dying in a Multi-Religious and Multi-Ethnic Village of the Danube Delta. Working Papers in Romanian Minority Studies No. 14. Cluj-Napoca: Institutul pentru Studierea Problemelor Minorităților, 1–20.

Schutz, Alfred 1990: On Multiple Realities. In: M. Natanson (ed.): Alfred Schutz Collected Papers I. The Problem of Social Reality. Dordrecht, Boston, London: Kluwer Academic Publishers, 207–259.

Scott, David and Charles Hirschkind (eds.) 2006: Powers of the Secular Modern: Talal Asad and His Interlocutors. Stanford: Stanford University Press.
Taylor, Charles 2007: A Secular Age. Cambridge, MA: Belknap Press of Harvard University Press.

The Fifth EU Enlargement: Reuniting Europe or Reinventing Eastern Europe?

Antoinette Primatarova

Introduction

Back in the Cold War days, defining Western Europe and Eastern Europe was easy. There was a clear demarcation line: the Iron Curtain that divided the democratic part of Europe from the totalitarian communist Soviet sphere of influence.

In the wake of the fall of the Berlin wall successive waves of EU and NATO enlargement dramatically changed the geopolitical map of Europe and blurred the clear-cut West-East divide. The 2004 "big bang" EU enlargement, widely proclaimed as a reunification of Europe, created expectations that the whole continent would be covered by a post-modern European security system based on increased mutual dependence and that any further usage of "Eastern Europe" and "Western Europe" would make sense only in terms of geography. Ten years on, the enlarged EU is challenged by an increasingly assertive and aggressive Russian foreign policy and the fifth EU enlargement looks more like a process of shifting the dividing line between Western Europe and Eastern Europe further to the East.

The borders of "Eastern Europe" as a concept and as part of the European continent have been oscillating wildly, not only in recent years, but also historically and so have the borders of the very concept and continent of "Europe".

Part I of this article deals with the oscillations of "Europe's" borders that have had an impact on the oscillations of "Eastern Europe's" borders.

Part II discusses the oscillations of "Eastern Europe's" borders in the process of preparing the fifth enlargement and the prospective enlargement to the Western Balkans.

Part III is about the reinvention of "Eastern Europe", defined with regard to the current European Neighbourhood Policy (ENP) and its Eastern dimension, the Eastern Partnership Initiative (EaP).

The article is a modest attempt to give an overview concerning the process of reinventing Eastern Europe, mainly with regard to the role of the European Union. From the perspective of 2015 an assessment of NATO's and Russia's role in the shaping of the post-Cold War geopolitical map of Europe seems indispensable, but has to remain outside the scope of this article.[1]

---

[1] The article is based on the author's paper which was prepared as an introductory lecture to the 2012 International Conference "Issues of Cultural Diversity in Post-Social-

Part I: What is Europe?

Both pre- and post-1989 Europe have often been used as interchangeable terms with the European Union and vice versa. But "How convincingly can we really define what we mean by 'Europe'? Or is that a concept that is constantly being revised and reconceived, through centuries, right up to the present moment, as the European Union decides whom to admit to Europe and whom to keep waiting?" (Wolff in Wolff and Yanov 2002).

The question raised by Wolff has several implications: when Europeans define themselves as Europeans, is this a question about whom to include or about whom to exclude, about resemblances or about divergences? Last but not least, is Europe an issue of self-perception, the result of inward constructivism, the attempt to understand Europe from inside Europe or rather an attempt to imagine Europe, to try to understand it from the outside?

The inclusion/exclusion dimension of different concepts of Europe can be best illustrated by the different attitudes towards Iceland, Norway and Switzerland, that are not members of the EU but well part of the European Economic Area and of the Schengen area, on the one hand, and towards the Ukraine and the other five countries included in the EU's "Eastern Partnership" initiative on the other hand. Iceland, Norway and Switzerland are not members of the EU because of the will of their own people, but their European identity is not debated at all. For the countries included in the "Eastern partnership" EU membership is not an issue on the agenda and might never become one; but some of the "Eastern partners" have clear aspirations for EU membership and their people tend to perceive the reluctance of being granted such a perspective as putting in question their European identity.

A more complex answer to the question "What is Europe?" with reference to the EU has been offered by the British historian Timothy Garton Ash:

> "It's a place. It's a history. It's an ideal, a vision. And, it's a set of institutions, a complex set of institutions. You have the OSCE and the Council of Europe, but central to those institutions is the European Union, which is sui generis; it cannot simply be defined. In the terms of conventional political science, it's an unidentified flying object" (Garton Ash 2009).

In terms of geographical borders there is a substantial difference between Europe and the European Union. This can be best demonstrated by comparing the number of EU members (28 since 1st July 2013) and the Council of Europe members (47 at present, with Belarus and Kosovo not being members yet). In the wake of the fifth enlargement and of the EU institutional crisis triggered by the 2005 referenda in France and the Netherlands several politicians raised ques-

---

ist Europe" at the University of Fribourg and was broadly overtaken by the events of 2013–2015. Only minor updates have been included.

tions linked to the limits concerning further EU enlargement and to the borders of Europe.

Regardless of heated debates about these issues Article 49 of the Treaty on the European Union continues to provide EU eligibility for any European State which respects the EU's values and is committed to promote them.

However, it is more than evident that the mental map of Europe of quite many EU citizens is not stretching as far as the European continent of the Council of Europe, Turkey being by far not the only difficult case.

The limits of the prevailing European mental map have become quite evident on several occasions with regard to the European aspirations of countries like the Ukraine, not to talk about the other countries included in the EU's "Eastern Partnership" initiative. In 1999, on the eve of the fifth enlargement process, Enlargement Commissioner Verheugen told the European Parliament's Foreign Affairs Committee that "I think that anybody who thinks that the Ukraine should be taken in the EU ... should perhaps come along with the argument that Mexico should be taken into the US", thus rebutting the idea that being part of the same continent can per se be a sufficient eligibility criterion for becoming part of a political club. Furthermore, during his term as the Commission's President Romano Prodi made statements that the Ukraine "has as much reason to be in the EU as New Zealand", implicitly putting into question that the Ukraine is part of the European continent. Few years later Enlargement Commissioner Olli Rehn had a more flexible view on the limits to EU enlargement. He viewed the issue of defining the borders of Europe as a generational project, meaning that each successive generation must make up its own mind about Europe. In the context of the "new European disorder" (Krastev and Leonard 2015), as a result of the 2014 annexation of the Crimea, the question about further enlargement to the East seems to be off the agenda for the present generation for clear geopolitical reasons.

Against the backdrop of a geographical border not clearly drawn between Europe and Asia, changing geopolitical circumstances and interests have played a role in defining Europe on several occasions in the past, too.

In 1959 General De Gaulle as President of the Fifth French Republic had a vision of a Europe stretching from the Atlantic to the Urals and thus including Soviet Russia. In 2005 his fellow countryman Valéry Giscard d'Estaing, Chairman of the Convention on the Future of Europe (2002–2003), insisted that Europe should be seen as defined by the Atlantic Ocean being the border in the west, Russia being the border in the east, Turkey being the border in the southeast and the African shore of the Mediterranean Sea being the border in the south, thus excluding both Russia and Turkey from Europe. Giscard d'Estaing's Europe was defined on the basis of his own understanding of history, religion and culture as the main building blocks of the European identity (including its roots in the Greco-Roman civilisation and the 18th and 19th century's humanist inheritance).

The different concepts of "Europe" are closely related to identity issues and the different possible dimensions or levels of identity – regional, cultural, linguistic, religious, ethnic, political etc.

After 1989, depending on geopolitical circumstances, there have been attempts to define the political dimension of European identity both as distinct from and as identical with the American one. On the one hand, there was Jürgen Habermas' and Jacques Derrida's vision. In 2003 they regarded the mass demonstrations against the Iraq war as a new chance for developing a European identity, an identity expressed through defending and promoting a cosmopolitan order on the basis of international law against the competing American vision. On the other hand, there was former French Prime Minister Edouard Balladur's vision. In 2008 he made a plea for a Union of the West, arguing that the United States and Europe ought to form an *"organic"* alliance in order to avert the risk of being overtaken by the rest of the world (Vinocur 2003). Interestingly, while for Habermas and Derrida public reactions to the 2003 Iraq debate raised hope for a rebirth of Europe, the official reactions of governments in Central and Eastern Europe made former U.S. Secretary of Defence Donald Rumsfeld refer to European countries that did not support the U.S., especially France and Germany, as "Old Europe". Thus he referred to a new dividing line between "Old Europe" and "New Europe".

Putting "Old Europe" (mainly Germany and France) in stark contrast to "New Europe" (new NATO members and prospective EU members from Central and Eastern Europe) was a clear instance of applying an outward perspective. Habermas and Derrida's vision of an Anti-American European identity, on the other hand, was an instance of applying an inward perspective to the complex European identity issue. While politicians and philosophers were debating in terms of Americanism and Anti-Americanism, British historian Timothy Garton Ash made his own observations on the ground:

> "In the past few weeks, I've divided my time between five European cities: Madrid, Warsaw, Berlin, London, and Oxford. In real life, they have so much in common. One of the things they have in common – and this is where Europhiles may start getting uncomfortable – is a huge dose of America and the Anglosphere" (Garton Ash 2003).

The few examples provided above could easily be extended by many others – both from the past and from the present – confirming that "the determination of what is essentially 'European' can be very individual, subjective, arbitrary, and strategic" (Wolff and Yanov 2002).

> "'European' is clearly not a neutral term and it's a very, as it were, value-loaded notion, saying, 'We're a European country', with a lot of ideas and a lot of implications. And that's a good thing, as long as it doesn't imply – which it tends to – that if you're not European, you can't be those things. So we have a difficult double act. We have to keep this sense of our val-

> ues and standards without falling back into what are essentially colonial, imperial stereotypes of superiority" (Garton Ash 2009).

Part II: What is Eastern Europe?

The legacy-thinking

The division of Western Europe/Eastern Europe is not a product of the Cold War. It goes back to the 18th century when a conceptual re-orientation from the previously accepted northern/southern division was triggered by the philosophers of the Enlightenment. They viewed the continent from the perspective of Paris and deliberately cultivated an idea of the backwardness of "Eastern Europe" to affirm the importance of "Western Europe", as argued by Larry Wolff in "Inventing Eastern Europe: The Map of Civilization on the Mind of the Enlightenment", a book not so much about Eastern Europe as about Western Europe. It is a book about the 18th century West/East divide but it also touches the issue that this divide greatly facilitated the acceptance of the West/East divide at the end of World War II.

There are of course also other explanations for the acceptance of the West/East divide during the Cold War and after the collapse of communism. Davis talks about the "Allied Scheme of History", one of its elements being "The unspoken acceptance of the division of Europe into Western and Eastern spheres. Whereas 'Atlantic values' are expected to predominate in the West, the East is considered as Russia's legitimate sphere of influence" (Davis 1996).

That the West/East divide of the Cold War era was not about geography and culture but about geopolitical spheres of interest is illustrated by the inconsistency of considering Prague Eastern Europe and Vienna and Athens "the West", even though Prague geographically lies further west than Vienna and Athens.

Both in the West and in the East there were, on the one hand, people who felt comfortable with the geopolitical West/East divide of the Cold War and, on the other hand, people hoping one day it would be overcome.

> "For 50 years since the Atlantic Charter, those of us East and West who didn't believe it was all okay instead believed the rhetoric that we would all be one were it not for the evil Soviet Union and its lack of democracy, and that we could redeem ourselves from the graceless half century by working hard, speaking freely, following the rules, and doing our homework. We believed that Western Europe yearned for us as we yearned for it, as Aristophanes described in Plato's *Symposium*, two halves of a whole split by the gods, perpetually seeking our other half, to live in a Europe *whole and free*" (Ilves 2013).

For many people the "Return to Europe" was therefore the catchword for the democratic transition in post-communist Europe. Expectations on how fast and how far this process could go turned out to be overoptimistic on the part of the Eastern Europeans.

In 1996, seven years after the fall of the Berlin wall, Czech President Vaclav Havel's disappointment and concerns about the slow pace of a "Return to Europe" were shared by many in post-communist Europe.

> "In the long run, we simply cannot imagine a Europe that, though no longer cut in two by the Iron Curtain, would be divided into a stable, prosperous and increasingly united Europe and a less stable and less prosperous Europe that would not unite. Just as it is impossible that one half of a room be forever warm and the other half cold it is equally unthinkable that two different Europes could for ever exist next to each other without detriment to both, and it is the more stable and more prosperous one that would pay the higher price. It is not that the uniting part of Europe would come to harm if it expanded. Just the opposite: in the long run, it would come to harm only if it failed to expand" (Havel 1996).

After the enlargement waves of the NATO (in 1999 enlarged by the Czech Republic, Hungary and Poland; in 2004 by Bulgaria, Estonia, Latvia, Lithuania, Romania, Slovakia and Slovenia; and in 2009 by Albania and Croatia) and of the EU (in 2004 enlarged by the Czech Republic, Estonia, Hungary, Latvia, Lithuania, Poland, Slovakia, Slovenia; in 2007 by Bulgaria and Romania; and in 2013 by Croatia) the West/East divide unfortunately persists even within the enlarged NATO and EU space, a situation captured with ironic bitterness by incumbent Estonian President Toomas Ilves:

> "We discovered that to Western Europe the liberation of enserfed and silenced Easterners turned out instead to mean 'social dumping' by Polish plumbers in France, and 'lazy Latvian' construction workers in Sweden, and in our case – to believe some Finnish newspapers from as late as Spring 2011, 'criminals from Tallinn' disembarking each night in Helsinki harbour by the hundreds ..." (Ilves 2013).

In the "old West", people from the new EU member states are wrongly perceived as the culprit of many of the EU's difficulties, including developments in the wake of the 2008 worldwide financial and economic crisis and the crisis within the Eurozone. Thus, for some pre-2004 EU citizens and politicians "Eastern Europe" continues to include post-communist states that joined the EU in 2004 and 2007.

The inward perspective of people and politicians in this part of post-communist Europe is a different one. Drawing a parallel to the linguistic disappearance of "East Germany", Estonian President Ilves strongly argues that post-communist countries that joined the NATO and the EU should no longer be considered "Eastern Europe":

> "Similarly we can get rid of 'Eastern Europe' insofar as it is not a geographical but geopolitical notion. We do not talk about 'Post-Habsburg' or 'Post-Ottoman' European states today, so how long should we be talking about 'Post-Soviet' states, meaning countries that share a certain tragic episode in their history but come from different cultural backgrounds and have developed in very different directions after the breakup of the Soviet empire? We cannot keep defining the world or our place in it by referring to what once was, it just makes no sense. Now it makes sense to talk about the EU, NATO, the Nordic-Baltic area or the Baltic Sea region – political and cultural spaces that have something in common; alliances, shared values, goals and interests" (Ilves 2013).

The strategic dimension

Every time the EU was shaken to recognise that it has to expand its mental map of Europe and to enlarge, there was reluctance. Reluctance has quite often been linked to debates on *deepening* (development towards an ever closer Union) versus *widening* (enlargement). Proponents of the view that *widening* contradicts *deepening* have always been afraid of "diluting" and "overstretching" the EU. Decisions on enlargement have always been *ad hoc* rather than part of an overall strategy towards a continent-wide European Union.

Whereas for post-communist Eastern Europeans the EU enlargement was framed as liberation, "return to Europe" and an identity issue EU expansion was primarily driven by pragmatic economic and security concerns, in the West.

The pre-accession strategy (first, the Essen pre-accession strategy from 1994 and, later on, the more elaborate Agenda 2000 from 1997) was developed relatively slowly; given the lack of an overall strategic vision from member states it focused on technical and *ad hoc* solutions suggested by the Commission.

"Central Europe" and the eventual division between "ins" and "outs"

The "Reunification of Europe" as the main result of the fifth enlargement is enshrined in the information on the 2004 enlargement on the EUR-lex website:

> "This historic enlargement of the EU from 15 to 25 members is the culmination of a long accession process leading to the reunification of a Europe that had been divided for half a century by the Iron Curtain and the Cold War."

But the reunification of Europe as the moral dimension of the fifth enlargement played by far a less important role than the political and economic interests of the EU15.

There was a clear difference between the overall policy stances on enlargement of the two big players – Germany and France. Throughout the whole process candidate countries perceived Germany as the real driving force for enlargement and France as the country eager to put on the brakes to it.

The French lack of enthusiasm for enlargement was demonstrated immediately after the fall of the Berlin wall. On 31st December 1989, French President François Mitterrand called for the creation of "a European confederation" designed to "associate all states of [the] continent in a common and permanent organisation for exchanges, peace and security". For the next one and a half year the confederation plan continued to be in the air as a strong French passion but it was vehemently rejected by the expected benefactors, the Eastern Europeans. They were interested in nothing less than EU membership.

Views on which candidate countries were most important and should thus join earlier than others were affected by particular geo-political and economic interests and strongly influenced by geographical proximity. Scandinavian countries were particularly concerned about stabilising their Baltic neighbours. Germany was more focused on Poland, the Czech Republic and Hungary. Greece had an interest in its Southeast European vicinity. Austria had a special interest in Croatia.

As argued by Grabbe and Hughes in 1998 at the start of the implementation of Agenda 2000:

> "[...] although historical experience may lead some member states to recognize the moral dimension of enlargement – [...] this is unlikely to override political and economic interests" (Grabbe and Hughes 1998: 5/6).

Back in 1997/1998 the general expectation was that only three countries might join the EU in 2002 – the Czech Republic, Hungary and Poland. They themselves were ambitious to join even earlier than that and very active in promoting their image as "Central Europe", historically and culturally an integral part of Europe. An important role in this respect played the Visegrad Group, a format for cooperation established on 15th February 1991 at a meeting of the presidents of Czechoslovakia, Poland and Hungary. After Czechoslovakia's peaceful divorce both the Czech Republic and Slovakia remained part of the cooperation, so the group got four members and is also known as the V4.

The perception that EU enlargement might be designed to integrate Central Europe, but not necessarily Eastern Europe, resulted in an interesting tendency.

> "There is even a growing tendency for all of the applicants, even those farthest east, south and north, to claim to be 'central European countries' (Grabbe and Hughes 1998: 7).

The attractiveness of claiming a Central European identity is illustrated by the development of the Central European Initiative. The forum developed from an initiative of four countries, back in 1989, when Austria, Hungary, Italy and the Socialist Federal Republic of Yugoslavia on 11 November 1989 started cooperation at a meeting in Budapest. In 1990, Czechoslovakia was admitted and the Central European Initiative was renamed Pentagonale. In 1991, with the admission of Poland, it became Hexagonale. Further countries joined in 1992, and back then it was decided to rename the organisation to Central European Initiative. The expansion of the Initiative continued with Montenegro becoming the last member in 2006. At present the Central European Initiative has 18 members: Albania, Austria, Belarus, Bosnia and Herzegovina, Bulgaria, Croatia, Czech Republic, Hungary, Italy, Macedonia, Moldova, Montenegro, Poland, Romania, Serbia, Slovakia, Slovenia, Ukraine (thus, ten EU members, five countries from the Western Balkans and three countries from the EU's Eastern Partnership initiative).

The intentions to limit the enlargement to the three Central European frontrunners Czech Republic, Hungary and Poland were modified in two steps. Firstly, at the Luxemburg European Council; in December 1997 a decision was taken to start negotiations not only with these three countries but also with Slovenia (as a positive signal towards Southeast Europe) and Estonia (as a positive signal towards the other two Baltic States). Secondly, at the Helsinki European Council; in December 1999 a decision was taken to also involve Bulgaria, Latvia, Lithuania, Slovakia and Romania in the negotiations. In both cases it were security considerations rather than moral arguments that made member states add a more outspoken strategic dimension to the technical Agenda 2000.

For the countries that joined in 2004 and 2007 it is no longer an issue whether they joined as Central Europeans or as Eastern Europeans. What they have in common is that they do not like to be perceived as a "second class" Europeans. "Because the world had such a low opinion on Eastern Europe, nowadays nobody wants to admit that they live there. [...] If you were to believe everyone you talked to, you would conclude that Eastern Europe just doesn't exist! When pressed, Eastern Europeans admit that Eastern Europe exists, but they all believe that the region starts just east of whatever country they happen to live in" (Tapon 2012: 14).

Southeast Europe and the Western Balkans

Interestingly, one of the four founders of the Central European Initiative in late 1989 was the Socialist Federal Republic of Yugoslavia (SFRY). In the second half of the 1980s former Yugoslavia was much closer to the West than to the East in economic terms; there have been even considerations in the former European Community about prospects for a potential SFRY membership.

The dissolution of SFRY and the wars and ethnic cleansing on its former territory revived the old negative image of the Balkan Powder Keg and the use of "Balkanisation", a term coined at the beginning of the twentieth century "to denote the parcelization of large and viable political units" but also as "a synonym for a reversion to the tribal, the backward, the primitive, the barbarian" (Todorova 1997: 3). Whereas the West and the Orient have usually been presented as "incompatible entities, antiworlds, but completed antiworlds", the Balkans "have always evoked the image of a bridge or a crossroads [...]", "a bridge between East and West, between Europe and Asia" (Todorova 1997: 15). This "transitionary status" of the Balkans did not fit neatly into the "return to Europe" paradigm of the fifth enlargement.

In an effort to avoid the negative connotations of "Balkan" and "Balkans" after the 1995 Dayton peace accord there was a tendency to talk about Southeast Europe instead and to use this designation in the name of different political initiatives for cooperation in the region, in particular the 1996 Southeast European Cooperative Initiative (SECI) or the 1999 Stability Pact for South-Eastern Europe. Whenever the term Southeast Europe has been used, it has always been difficult to delineate the region on the basis of clear and universally accepted geographical or historical divisions. This does easily allow for uploading different geopolitical implications to the Southeast Europe concept.

In 1999, on the eve of the launch of the Stability Pact for South-Eastern Europe, German diplomats involved in the process were about to give in to Russian demands for the inclusion of a sentence that the region is part of Russia's traditional sphere of interests. The Southeast European countries had the feeling that they succeeded in preventing a second "Yalta" when – upon their joint insistence – the sentence was deleted in the very last minute. Russia's intention was to prevent further expansion of NATO rather than further EU enlargement in the region, but this raised serious concerns in Bulgaria and in Romania. In the initial months of the Stability Pact the two countries considered Southeast Europe a geopolitical concept that might keep them out from the EU beyond the 2007 accession date they had set themselves as a target date. The evolvement of the "Western Balkans" concept in 2000 and the 2000 Nice European Council lingered these concerns and opened the way for Bulgaria's and Romania's accession to the EU in 2007 as part of the fifth enlargement.

In the year 2000 "Western Balkans" was introduced as a designation for the so called "potential" candidates that were given EU membership perspective, but would not be part of the fifth enlargement. Regardless of strong political support on behalf of Austria and Germany Croatia did not succeed to be excluded from the "Western Balkans" and to become part of the fifth enlargement together with Bulgaria and Romania. Still, in 2013 Croatia joined the EU as the first of the so called "Western Balkan" countries. Moldova, however, regardless of its participation in the Stability Pact for South-Eastern Europe, was excluded from the group of the "potential candidates". Instead, it was included in the "Eastern Partnership". The "Eastern" label implied for Moldova the exclusion from the perspective of joining the European Union, whereas the "Western" label artificially attached to the Balkans implied a promise to become part of the enlarging "West". The new demarcation line between the West and the East turned into a demarcation line between the EU (including prospective members) and states with no realistic perspective to join the EU.

Regardless of the European perspective of the Western Balkans, the countries in the region remain "the soft underbelly of Europe" and put into question the claim that 2004 was the year of Europe's unification; in 2014 and 2015 there have been several alarming indications that Russian President Putin might be tempted to challenge European unity through making the Balkans his "next playground" (Krastev 2015).

Part III: Reinventing Eastern Europe: The Eastern Partnership

The year 2004, the "big bang" enlargement with ten new Member States, eight of them post-communist countries, definitely marked the division of the former East bloc into two groups of states: the ones that already joined the EU or were on the way to join it (Bulgaria and Romania in 2007, and at a later stage the Western Balkans) and the countries affiliated in the Commonwealth of Independent States, which were pursuing strategies of reform and development in a way clearly different from the strategy of the countries of Central and Eastern Europe.

Ahead of the enlargement, in 2003 the European Neighbourhood Policy was presented as a new framework for the EU's relations both with its eastern and southern partners with the main objective to avoid new dividing lines.

> "The objective of the ENP is to share the benefits of the EU's 2004 enlargement with neighbouring countries in strengthening stability, security and wellbeing for all concerned. It is designed to prevent the emergence of new dividing lines between the enlarged EU and its neighbours and to offer them the chance to participate in various EU activities, through greater political, security, economic and cultural cooperation" (COM 2004).

How to avoid a new Iron Curtain falling between the new members of the EU and European countries remaining outside the EU was a real concern that was reflected in new metaphors: "Fortress Europe", "Raising the Drawbridge", the "Great Wall of Europe", "Schengen Wall" etc.

The real concerns beyond the design of the ENP in 2003/2004 were, however, not the concerns of the neighbouring countries in the East but how to avoid a commitment of those with strong aspirations for EU membership. Commission President Romano Prodi induced the early discussions on the ENP with statements like "We cannot go on enlarging forever", "Accession is not the only game in town", "more than partnership and less than membership", "sharing everything with the Union but the institutions". The EU addressed its relations with the European post-Soviet countries in stages and grouped and re-grouped them on several occasions.

Considerations started with talking about a new "Eastern scope" of the EU's Neighbourhood Policy and in parallel introducing for Belarus, Moldova, Russia and Ukraine the label "Western" CIS states (maybe to avoid the implication of a new clash between East and West?). However, the Western CIS concept did not survive long. On the one hand, Russia insisted on being a strategic partner and not simply a neighbour among others. On the other hand, the 2003 Georgian "Rose Revolution" prompted the extension of the Neighbourhood Policy to the three South Caucasian republics Armenia, Georgia and Azerbaijan. So, the "Eastern Neighbourhood" was born.

In 2004 the EU merged its Eastern European and Southern non-European neighbours in the framework of the European Neighbourhood Policy, a complicated South-East balancing act that resulted in a policy devoid of a comprehensive vision for a regional approach with regard to the "Eastern countries".

A common ENP for both the Eastern and Southern neighbours was a way to avoid stronger commitments to the post-Soviet countries. On the one hand, there was no appetite for a further enlargement of the EU. On the other hand, the relations with Russia started to deteriorate. The EU's attempt to introduce the "common neighbourhood" as a key concept for the strategic partnership with Russia failed because of the clash between the EU's "neighbourhood" and Russia's "near abroad" concept. The 2003 Rose Revolution in Georgia and the 2004/2005 Orange Revolution in the Ukraine resulted in a situation in which many believed that Russia returned to its Cold War position.

> "Russia wants to know where the European Union will stop. Does it plan to swallow up Ukraine, Belarus and the Caucasus too? Brussels sees this as an open question unlikely to be resolved in the foreseeable future, but Moscow may see a smokescreen hiding our true intentions" (Bot 2004).

In hindsight, there can be no doubt that "The Orange Revolution in Ukraine was Putin's 9/11" (Krastev and Leonard 2015). The Orange Revolution marked the beginning of the crisis of the post-Cold War European order that in the EU's perception was to be an order of a post-modern shared sovereignty. With Russia getting more and more suspicious of any post-national constellations and subscribing to a classical nineteenth-century concept of sovereignty, the 2004/2005 crisis went through several stages and culminated in the Kremlin's violation of the territorial integrity of the Ukraine in 2014.

In 2008, in the wake of the Russian-Georgian war, concerns about Russia's reaction were the backdrop for postponing NATO's decision to offer Georgia and Ukraine the chance to join the alliance's Membership Action Plan (MAP) as a decisive step towards NATO membership.

But regardless of the internal and external challenges there was no lack of a vision for the future of the EU's Eastern neighbours. As early as 2003, ahead of joining the EU, the Polish government in a non-paper proposed an "Eastern dimension" of the EU as a complementary one to the "Northern dimension" (institutionalised by Finland at the end of 1999 and further promoted during the Swedish and the Danish Presidencies in 2001, and 2002 respectively). The 2003 Polish proposal envisaged a future for the Ukraine, Belarus and Moldova in the European Union. This vision was shared by several Swedish politicians. In 2004 Carl Bildt argued that after the 2004 and 2007 enlargement the EU must think big and design a comprehensive strategy for the Western Balkans and Turkey and indicated that afterwards there might be one more final enlargement that would cover the countries between the present Union and Russia.

This more visionary approach towards Eastern Europe was reflected in the launch of the "Eastern Partnership" in 2009 for Armenia, Azerbaijan, Belarus, Georgia, Moldova, and the Ukraine – an attempt to remedy some of the deficiencies of the ENP, but also a strategic response to the Union for the Mediterranean driven by France in 2008.

The 2009 the Prague Eastern Summit Joint Declaration made no commitment to a further Eastern enlargement but did not exclude it either:

> "It (the EaP) will be developed without prejudice to individual partner countries' aspirations for their future relationship with the European Union" (Council of the European Union 2009).

Two years later at the 2011 Warsaw Summit the EU agreed to a stronger wording:

> "The participants of the Warsaw Summit acknowledge the European aspirations and the European choice of some partners and their commitment to build deep and sustainable democracy. They highlighted the particular role for the Eastern Partnership to support those who seek an ever closer relationship with the EU" (Council of the European Union 2011).

In the framework of the fifth EU enlargement Russia did not oppose the Baltic States' EU membership. Moreover, in late 2004, at the peak of the Ukrainian crisis, President Putin surprisingly expressed a relaxed attitude towards a possible Ukrainian EU membership. In response to a question during a press conference together with Spanish Prime Minister Zapatero on 10th December 2004 in Moscow he said he considered that if the Ukraine were to join the EU this would be a positive factor that, unlike NATO expansion, would help strengthening the system of international relations.

In recent years the situation has changed. "The EU's presence in the post-Soviet space is now viewed by Moscow as a menace as powerful as NATO's enlargement" (Krastev and Leonard 2015). The Lithuanian EU Presidency in the second half of 2013 was intended to move the Eastern Partnership into a higher gear and to mark the start of a new era in the EU's relations with Eastern Europe at the Third Eastern Partnership Summit on 28th and 29th November 2013. This turned out to be at odds with Russia's intentions. Throughout 2013 Russia used all kinds of financial, economic and political blackmailing in an attempt to sway the countries involved from their European path. In early autumn 2013 Armenia gave up on its association and free trade deal with the EU just a few weeks after the negotiations had been finalised. The Russian and Armenian presidents jointly declared that Armenia was to join the Customs Union of Belarus, Kazakhstan, and Russia instead. (The Customs Union itself is supposed to grow at a next stage in 2015 into a Eurasian Union.)

The Armenian move was followed by an even more surprising U-turn of the Ukraine. On 21st November 2013, just a few days before the summit, Ukrainian President Viktor Yanukovych announced he would not sign an EU association and free trade treaty, citing Russian threats to cut off trade. Yanukovych's U-turn provoked mass protests in the streets of Kiev (the Euromaidan) and other Ukrainian cities. In what was perceived as a battle between the EU and Russia ordinary citizens insisted that the Ukraine should stay on the European path.

The 2013 Vilnius Eastern Partnership Summit rejected Russia's policy of blackmailing the countries in its neighbourhood and attempts to force them to join its own integration project – the Eurasian Union.

> "In the framework of the European Neighbourhood Policy and the Eastern Partnership, the Summit participants reaffirm the sovereign right of each partner freely to choose the level of ambition and the goals to which it aspires in its relations with the European Union" (Council of the European Union 2013).

Russia's unlawful annexation of Crimea in March 2014 made the context for the further implementation of EU's Eastern Partnership even more complex and difficult. As stressed by German Chancellor Angela Merkel on the eve of the 2015 Riga EaP Summit, "in the given situation, the idea of the Eastern Partnership is more important than ever".

In the two years between the 2013 Vilnius Summit and the 2015 Riga Summit there was some progress in the EU's relations with the Ukraine, Moldova and Georgia. Still, the big question remains whether the EU could and should have been more ambitious.

Taking stock of what has been achieved with the 2015 Riga summit allows for two interpretations. On the one hand, the EU diplomats' view "that they went as far as they could in Riga to reassure the union's Eastern neighbors", and, on the other hand, the critical view that EU politicians "went as far as they could to reassure Russia that the EU's relationship with Eastern Europe would not be taken to its logical conclusion" (Dempsey 2015).

The Eastern Partnership is not an instrument of EU enlargement policy and *The Eastern Partnership is not directed against anyone, and particularly not against Russia,* were two of the main reassurances Chancellor Angela Merkel gave the German Bundestag on the eve of the Riga Summit. Both of them sounded in fact more as reassurances addressing Russia's concerns rather than the concerns of the countries falling under the Eastern partnership, especially their pro-European civil societies and individuals that were hoping to hear that joining the EU, however far down the road, was a perspective.

Conclusion

Throughout history, "the East" and "Eastern Europe" have been relational concepts, depending on normative values and the observation point of the speaker/researcher. Thus, without a reference to the respective normative values and observation points in time, any use of the two concepts will be ambiguous and vague.

The Cold War and the end of the Cold War did imply a big difference both in terms of normative values and observation points. "The Cold War ended without a peace treaty or a victory parade. It was heralded as a common victory of the West and the Russian people" (Krastev and Leonard 2015). Interpreted in this way, the late 1989 developments facilitated the belief that what were previously perceived as "Western" values, as opposed to the "Eastern" ones, will turn if not into universal, so at least into Pan-European ones. When in December 1989 Soviet President Gorbachev and US President Bush were discussing the terms of the end of the Cold War, US Secretary of State James Baker had to respect Gorbachev's reaction against labelling democracy, openness and the market as "Western" values and to suggest talking instead of "democratic" values as the basis for a prospective German re-unification (according to a Russian transcript referred to in Garton Ash 2004).

In the late 1990s and early years of the new century, EU's enlargement and neighbourhood policy towards the "Eastern neighbours" were shaped on the basis of a belief in a new European order based on these common democratic values. This approach was in line with the European Security Strategy adopted in 2003 and the assessment of the European and global environment at that point of time:

> "Europe has never been so prosperous, so secure or so free. The violence of the first half of the 20th century has given way to a period of peace and stability unprecedented in European history. The creation of the European Union has been central to this development. (...) European countries are committed to dealing peacefully with disputes and to co-operating through common institutions. Over this period, the progressive spread of the rule of law and democracy has seen authoritarian regimes change into secure, stable and dynamic democracies. Successive enlargements are making a reality of the vision of a united and peaceful continent" (Council of the European Union 2003).

As long as the belief in "co-operation through common institutions" had not been challenged by Russia, presenting EU's enlargement and neighbourhood policy as elements of a process of European reunification had full credibility. However, at the time of the 2004 big bang enlargement the basic premises of the 2003 European Security Strategy were already overtaken by events; serious signs that Russia and the European Union did not necessarily share common values emerged. Putin's reaction to the 2003 Ukrainian Orange Revolution should not allow for any further illusions in this respect. However, the EU continued to develop and to frame its foreign policy in general and enlargement and neighbourhood policies in particular on the basis of a firm belief in common values and the feasibility of common spaces for the cooperation with Russia. In the EU-centric vision, "Eastern Europe" was imagined to follow in the steps of Central Europe in virtually everything but just short of membership; the "Eastern Partnership" was the instrument supposed to facilitate the democratic transformation processes in the Eastern neighbourhood.

The 2003–2013 decade and the 2013 tussle over whether Ukraine would join the EU's Eastern Partnership or Russia's Eurasian Economic Union (EEU) and the divergences between the six countries covered by the EP initiative made it evident that the EU's 2003 vision was not recognised as the only game in town and that Russia was a stakeholder with strong ambitions to be part of the imagining Eastern Europe exercise. By way of simplification, in Russia's vision, there is a new dividing line in Europe – a line between the EU's "liberal democracy" and the Russian type "sovereign democracy". It remains difficult to predict whether Russia will be successful with the EEU as an integration process of its own. At present, ideas for cooperation between the EU and the EEU as a way out of the new confrontation mode in Europe sound more like wishful thinking and too good to become true:

> "If the EU offers the prospect of engaging with the EEU, it would send a clear signal to Moscow that the EU recognises Russia's right to have an integration process of its own. It would show that a new European order will not be built around the promise of a never-ending enlargement of the EU and NATO. Instead, it would be conceptualised as a cooperation and competition between two integration projects, based on different philosophies, but with openness to dual membership and various forms of overlap or collaboration" (Krastev and Leonard 2015).

The EU has embarked on a process of reviewing both its Security Strategy and its European Neighbourhood Policy. The European External Action Service will prepare an EU Global Strategy for foreign and security policy by June 2016. This Strategy will also be the basis for EU's involvement in the further shaping of Europe's future. The strategic review, released in July 2015, offers three catchwords that are in stark contrast to the main premises of the 2003 European Security Strategy (unprecedented peace and stability; prosperity, security, freedom): it will consider EU's role in a *more connected, contested and complex* world. The strategic review is aware of the fact that *In Europe and beyond, new narratives challenge the open society model.*

The narrative of the fifth EU enlargement as the reunification of Europe on the basis of the open society model was a driving force for essential democratic, economic and social transformations in many countries divided from the liberal West through the Iron Curtain. This narrative has been seriously challenged in our more connected, contested and complex world. In the 2016 Security Strategy the EU will have to take into account the visions of Russia and the six countries covered by the Eastern Partnership initiative in its imagining Eastern Europe exercise. A reunification of Europe on the basis of same values and standards is definitely not on the agenda at present. Nonetheless, reinventing Eastern Europe through giving up the hope for anchoring the open society model in Eastern Partnership countries should remain a red line for ever.

References

Bildt, Carl 2004: If Europe Is to Keep Growing, It Must Think Big. In: Financial Times, October 24, 2004.

Bot, Bernard 2004: Great Game or European Fair Play? The European Union and the World in the 21th Century. Speech at the European Studies Centre, St Antony's College, University of Oxford. December 1, 2004.

COM (2004) 373 final. Communication from the Commission. European Neighbourhood Policy. Strategy Paper. URL: http://ec.europa.eu/world/enp/pdf/strategy/strategy_paper_en.pdf.

Council of the European Union 2003: A Secure Europe in a Better World. European Security Strategy. 12 December 2002, Brussels. URL: http://www.consilium.europa.eu/uedocs/cmsUpload/78367.pdf.

Council of the European Union 2009: Joint Declaration of the Prague Eastern Partnership Summit, Prague, 7 May 2009. URL: http://www.consilium.eu ropa.eu/uedocs/cms_data/docs/pressdata/en/er/107589.pdf.

Council of the European Union 2011: Joint Declaration of the Warsaw Eastern Partnership Summit, Warsaw, 30 September 2011. URL: http://eap-csf.eu/en/news-events/news/joint-declaration-of-the-warsaw-eastern-partnership-summit/.

Council of the European Union 2013: Joint Declaration of the Eastern Partnership Summit, Vilnius, 28–29 November 2013. URL: http://www.consilium.europa.eu/uedocs/cms_Data/docs/pressdata/EN/foraff/139765.pdf.

Council of the European Union 2015: Joint Declaration of the Eastern Partnership Summit,Riga, 21–22 May 2015. URL: http://www.consilium.europa.eu/en/meetings/international-summit/2015/05/21-22/.

Davies, Norman 1996: Europe: A History. Oxford University Press.

Dempsey, Judy 2015: The EU's Blindness about Eastern Europe. Carnegie Europe. URL: http://carnegieeurope.eu/strategiceurope/?fa=60229.

EUR-lex 2007: The 2004 Enlargement: the Challenge of a 25-Member EU. URL: http://eur-lex.europa.eu/legal-content/BG/TXT/?uri=URISERV:e50017.

European External Action Service 2015: The European Union in a Changing Global Environment. A more Connected, Contested and Complex World. URL: http://www.eeas.europa.eu/docs/strategic_review/eu-strategic-review_strategic_review_en.pdf.

Garton Ash, Timothy 2003: The Real New Europe. Hoover Digest No. 3. Stanford University. URL: http://www.hoover.org/publications/hoover-digest/article/7900.

Garton Ash, Timothy 2004a: Free World. Why a Crisis in the West Reveals the Opportunity of Our Time. London: Allen Lane.

Garton Ash, Timothy 2004b: Bitter Lemons. Six Questions to the Critics of Ukraine's Orange Revolution. In: The Guardian, December 2, 2004. URL: http://www.theguardian.com/world/2004/dec/02/ukraine.comment.

Garton Ash, Timothy 2009: Interview with Timothy Garton Ash for Radio Free Europe: For Timothy Garton Ash, Europe Means Shared History. URL:

http://www.rferl.org/content/For_Timothy_Garton_Ash_Europe_Means_Shared_History/1748651.html.

Giscard d'Estaing, Valéry 2005: Vu d'Europe – Où sont les frontières? In: Le Figaro, March 5, 2005.

Grabbe, Heather and Kirsty Hughes 1998: Enlarging the EU Eastwards. The Royal Institute of International Affairs. London: Chatham House Papers.

Habermas, Jürgen and Jacques Derrida 2003: Nach dem Krieg: Die Wiedergeburt Europas. In: Frankfurter Allgemeine Zeitung, 31 May 2003. English translation "February 15, or What Binds Europeans Together: A Plea for a Common Foreign Policy, Beginning in the Core of Europe". URL: http://platypus1917.org/wp-content/uploads/archive/rgroups/2006-chicago/habermasderrida_europe.pdf.

Havel, Vaclav 1996: Europe as Task. An Address in Aachen on May 15, 1996. URL: http://www.pro-europa.eu/index.php?option=com_content&view=article&id=27:vaclav-havel-europe-as-task&catid=11:the-struggle-for-the-union-of-europe&Itemid=17.

Ilves, Toomas Hendrik 2012: I'll Gladly Pay You Tuesday. Policy Review No. 172. Hoover. Stanford University. URL: http://www.hoover.org/publications/policy-review/article/111786e.

Ilves, Toomas Hendrik 2013: Removing the Division Lines & Re-Shaping Our Perspective. URL: http://eastbook.eu/en/2013/09/material-en/news-en/estonian-president-toomas-hendrik-ilves-removing-the-division-lines-re-shaping-our-perspective/.

Krastev, Ivan 2015: The Balkans Are the Soft Underbelly of Europe. In: Financial Times, January 14, 2015.

Krastev, Ivan and Mark Leonard 2015: The New European Disorder. European Council on Foreign Relations. URL: http://www.ecfr.eu/page/-/ECFR117_TheNewEuropeanDisorder_ESSAY.pdf.

Merkel, Angela 2015: Regierungserklärung von Bundeskanzlerin Merkel. 21 May 2015. URL: http://www.bundesregierung.de/Content/DE/Regierungserklaerung/2015/2015-05-21-regierungserklaerung.html.

Tapon, Francis 2012: The Hidden Europe. What Eastern Europeans Can Teach Us. WanderLearn Series. URL: http://francistapon.com/images/book/The-Hidden-Europe.pdf.

Todorova, Maria 1997: Imagining the Balkans. New York: Oxford University Press.

Wolff, Larry 1994: Inventing Eastern Europe: The Map of Civilization on the Mind of the Enlightenment. Stanford University Press.

Wolff, Larry and Alexander Yanov 2002: Is Russia a European Country? Correspondence. URL: http://www.eurozine.com/articles/2003-02-26-yanovwolff-en.html.

"I am not so much afraid of the Minister of Culture, but rather of the Minister's Culture"

About the Lack of Political Legitimacy in Bulgaria[1]

Sonja Schüler

Introduction

After the latest Bulgarian parliamentary elections on 5th October 2014 – the second within two years – the country's 43rd national assembly came into office. The elections were won by the so-called "liberal-conservative" party GERB (Citizens for a European Development of Bulgaria) with 32.7 %. The Bulgarian Socialist Party (BSP) which came second after GERB only got 15.4 % of the votes. With a participation of nearly 50 % the voter turnout was rather low. Eight political parties passed the 4 %-hurdle; consequently the new national assembly is a very heterogeneous one.[2]

Due to the lack of an absolute majority GERB currently forms a minority government under Sofia's former mayor, Boiko Borisov. He was the former bodyguard of the communist leader Todor Živkov and owned a security service in the 1990s. After the socialist era Borisov climbed up in the political sphere as a specialist and leader. This is his second mandate as a prime minister, a novelty in Bulgaria's post-socialist history. This novelty is of special interest because Borisov who had been in his first period in office since 2009 resigned in February 2013 after several months of street protests against high energy costs, poverty and perceived political clientelism and corruption. GERB's current coalition partner, the Reformer's Block (RB), also propagates liberal-conservative values and positions. This alliance is based on and shaped by democratically and liberally oriented "historical" opposition forces and emerged from anti-government protest. Initially the block showed a very critical attitude concerning Borisov. Without an absolute majority the coalition has to rely on the support of two further small parties: the nationalistic alliance Patriotic Front (PF), as well as the leftist BSP-splinter-group Alternative for the Bulgarian Rebirth (ABV).

---

[1] The German original version of this article will be published in 2015: Schüler, Sonja 2015: „Ich fürchte mich nicht vor dem Kulturminister – jedoch vor der Kultur des Ministers." Über politische Legitimitätsdefizite in Bulgarien. In: Balint Balla, Wolfgang Dahmen, Anton Sterbling (eds.): Demokratische Entwicklungen in der Krise? Politische und gesellschaftliche Verwerfungen in Rumänien, Ungarn und Bulgarien. Beiträge zur Osteuropaforschung 19. Hamburg: Krämer Verlag.

[2] Centralna izbiratelna komisija (2014).

Due to a continued strong reform pressure the government set out with the promise to deal rigorously with the implementation of pending reforms in the judiciary as well as in the economy, in the health sector and in the sphere of education. However, it is far from sure that the new government will prove readiness for and willingness to reforms, that it will show decisiveness, credibility and legitimacy in the eyes of the people. It is absolutely not obvious that the coalition will be able to remain in office for a full legislative period. The parliament's fragmentation, personal and programmatic differences and conflicts, lasting socioeconomic difficulties and economic insecurity are only some of various reasons. The latest elections were preceded and followed by scandals concerning political corruption and clientelism. The criticism of election observers referring to manipulation and vote buying represents a further continuity that occurred in the course of all elections of the last years. The scandals as well as a gross wage level of only around 420 EUR – the EU's lowest wage level[3] –, an unemployment rate of 11.6 %[4] and comparably high living costs have fostered repeated mass protests since the beginning of 2013. The protesters criticised lacking political problem-solving competences and a widespread abuse of office by the political elites. Under slogans like "mafia" the protesters demanded withdrawals of governments and political leaders, as well as an effective combat of political corruption and nepotism.

Which specific perception patterns of the public and political sphere can be identified in Bulgaria? Which current political and socioeconomic factors, which cultural imprints and historical experiences promote and shape the identified perception patterns? In how far do these factors cause and promote specific, widespread perceptual and also action-related characteristics concerning the political elites' relation to and their understanding of political power? These are the core questions this article deals with. The questions and the first part of the introduction already imply that the analysis of the relationship between the private/personal sphere and the public-political sphere represents the essence of this contribution and that the meaning of corrupt, clientelist networks will be analysed as an aspect of political culture.

Deliberately avoiding questions regarding guilt, lawfulness and system stability the article should illustrate the complexity of the cultural dimension of the political sphere. At the same time the author intends to show the reciprocal relationship between the characteristics of political cultures and imprints of the culture of political stakeholders.

It has to become clear that research which exclusively monitors social opinions and attitudes regarding political models and institutions, stakeholders and decision making processes cannot adequately show the cultural dimension for

---

[3] Of 820 BGN (approx. 417 EUR) in September 2014 according to the National Statistical Institute Sofia.

[4] According to EUROSTAT (2015). See also mediapool.bg (2013).

and in the public and political sphere. Last but not least it also has to become apparent that all kind of research which reflects a model character of political culture that is implicitly or explicitly based on ideals of "Western" influence and history is prone to lead to biased results. Notwithstanding, such a kind of approach leads to a serious risk of a superficial criticism of specific politically relevant attitudes and action patterns, which are observed in different countries and cultural regions.

The basis of this article is an understanding of political culture which indeed includes social attitudes, opinions and judgments regarding political issues, processes and the political system and its institutions as such, as well as regarding the role of the individual within the system in the sense of Almond's and Verba's "traditional" definition (Almond/Verba 1963). In this sense the basic assumption is that these attitudes and opinions do not only occur as reactions and reflexes on current, contemporary political and socioeconomic experiences. At least partly they are results of historically developed sets of value judgments, interpretative patterns, worldviews and guidelines of action which are given and imparted by education and socialisation and which can only by changed in the long run (Pickel and Jacobs 2006: 31 ff.). This is the "depth dimension" of every political culture which is included in the author's understanding of the notion as well. This depth dimension importantly affects the social classifications and evaluations of current political experiences. At the same time it importantly shapes the political interactions. The depth dimension of political culture differs fundamentally in individual societies and also between and even within individual social segments.

This broad understanding of the notion of political culture is important in order to show existing rational reflections, considerations and logics of action "behind" phenomena like political corruption, nepotism and perceived political apathy. Undoubtedly such phenomena occur at any time and in any place or country. Referring to Bulgaria and the Balkans they are sometimes classified very quickly as indicators of a "lack of culture" by Western observers. The author intends to show that such an approach is not only an oversimplification but also reflects a cultural/ethnocentric bias.

Political corruption is defined as the abuse of political power (in the sense of a function/a position in the legislative, the judicial or the executive sphere and/or a leading position in a political party or a position in government bodies, irrespective of their level) for an individual or a group benefit (Center for the Study of Democracy 2009: 33 ff.). The author uses this definition being aware of the fact that it always brings about legal questions and value judgments concerning, for example, the legality, the morality, the guilt or the legitimacy of the abusing actors. Often the answers on these questions vary considerably in different corruption cases, in different countries and regions and in the eyes of different observers. Furthermore, it has to be considered that corruption schemes are *per se* fluid phenomena that cannot be analysed without having in mind their historical and actual socio-cultural, legal and political background and context (Pardo

2004: 1–2). This implies that an approach which superficially defines and implicitly or explicitly criticises corruption phenomena as "function deficiencies" of individual or collective actors or institutions within states and societies cannot be adequate. With this approach it is not possible to analyse political corruption as an element of a political culture and to have a closer look at its socio-cultural context and at its specific logic of action.

Political corruption schemes are developed and maintained by dense informal networks which act at least partly outside legal requirements and/or formalised and institutional mechanisms and codes of action. A personalised network is defined as a specific kind of interaction in the form of a pragmatic alliance among individuals that usually dissolves after a certain time. The interaction aims at the exchange of material, social and or symbolic favours and the partners involved are not necessarily influenced or guided by moral, ethical or ideological principles (Giordano 2007: 27).

About the image of the political stakeholders and institutions

The proverb "I am not so much afraid of the Minister of Culture but rather of the minister's culture" comes from Radoj Ralin (1923–2004), a well-known Bulgarian satirist and regime critic during the era of the socialist ruler Todor Živkov. The proverb has become a dictum for the expression of criticism concerning a perceived lack of closeness of the political elites to the people and concerning the perceived professional incompetence of the political stakeholders. Thus, the dictum symbolises a strongly negative image of the politicians. The lack of social trust in the political stakeholder and the public/political institution as such is revealed by many opinion polls and scientific analyses of the post-socialist time. A poll of the Sofia-based social research institute *Alfa Research,* which claims to be representative and which was carried out in January 2015, shows increasing tendencies of mistrust regarding the judicial sphere. According to the institute's data the level of social trust in Prime Minister Borisov shows an increasing trend with 32 % – although Borisov himself has already come under fire in the past due to accusations of journalists and think tanks that referred to his involvement in corruption and clientelism affairs[5]. However, the confidence value for Borisov's cabinet amounts to only 24 %. The coalition government of Plamen Orešarski which came to office following elections brought forward after the withdrawal of the first Borisov government and which consisted of the Socialist Party (BSP) and the Movement for Rights and Freedoms (DPS) got a comparable confidence value (23 %) in *Alfa Research's* poll of June 2013 (Alfa Research 2013). The anti-government protesters commented on the breakdown of the coalition government and the withdrawal of the government Orešarski with

[5] See Schüler 2012a and Schüler 2013.

victory shouts (Tagesspiegel 2014). The current government that came into office through direct elections got a confidence value of only 11 % in January 2015, according to *Alfa Research*. Thus, the newly elected representatives of the people evidently cannot count on the people's premature praise.

The perceptions mentioned above also become apparent through significant voter fluctuations and visible dynamics of change within the party system. They are also visible in the measurable refusal of party membership and participation. Furthermore, the election results disclose a need of a sweepingly strong hand in the form of charismatic leading figures.

In autumn 2012 the author conducted an anonymous online survey to collect information on political attitudes in Bulgaria without claiming to be representative. A standardised questionnaire was distributed via the social network *facebook*, via Bulgarian political parties and foundations operating in the country. The survey was conducted during Boiko Borisov's first term of office as Bulgaria's Prime Minister – and some months before the beginning of the mass protests which caused the withdrawal of his government. The questionnaire contained an open question: *Politics as a dirty business, young people without political interest. These and similar statements can often be heard in public discussions. Does democracy get lost in Bulgaria* (Schüler 2012b)?

The younger (26–35 years) and the middle (36–50 years) age segments as well as residents of urban regions are disproportionately represented in the survey. The declared political orientations of the nearly 100 respondents differ significantly. Irrespective of socio-structural characteristics the overwhelming majority of the answers does *not* reflect a negative attitude towards democracy as a political model. It rather reflects a widespread perception of the political actors of all parties as self-serving opportunists who have their heads in the clouds, and even as bloodsuckers on the body of people. It becomes clear that a large portion of the respondents does not only question the political incumbents' intention to work for the benefit of the state and the people – they even do not expect such an intention. And even more: The existence of such an idealistic intention of the mandate holders is *a priori* denied by a big part of the responding Bulgarians. The dominating characteristics which are implicitly and explicitly attributed to the Bulgarian politician are careerism, empty phrases and a thirst for power, decadence and self-enrichment through public resources.

The image of the politician also resembles a puppet and an incarnation of influential economic interests. Politics is widely perceived as a staging of self-exposers in a primitive knockout comedy. The political institutions are commonly seen as instruments for the abuse of power at the expense of society. *Per se* they are not perceived as trustworthy institutions. *Ergo* the parliament is not trusted to fulfil its formal task to control the government. In the eyes of many respondents "the state" is an institution and a means of manipulation controlling and imposing "from above" without being controlled transparently and constitutionally.

The following comments of some respondents reflect the perception profile mentioned above:

> Since 1989 the governments in Bulgaria have served the same economic interests. The people know: Things will remain unchanged irrespective of their vote. Intelligent people just feel disgusted with politics.
>
> Democracy is getting lost! The politicians, those who 'govern' just mock the people. How can people get interested in politics when it gives them nothing but hunger, misery and a difficult life?
>
> In Bulgaria the leader of the party in power (Boiko Borisov, S. S.) is known for his criminal past. It is an open secret that he participated in smuggle and blackmail. This man governs extortionately! He spreads fear through the state institutions making them instruments of a mob flocked together. [...] Democracy is only an empty word.
>
> Undoubtedly democracy is getting lost in Bulgaria! Currently we have an authoritarian government being active with violent methods, threats and blackmail in the spheres of the economy and the state. The oppositional forces are not willing to oppose these processes. Police methods are omnipresent. At the same time criminality of all kinds is not combatted. People are spied out via telephone, skype, facebook (the social networks, S. S.) [...].
>
> It is not democracy which gets lost. It is rather the belief that there is someone who is willing and able to govern honestly and loyally for the sake of the state and the people. From 1989 onwards, the governments' corruptive practices have been responsible for the lacking belief.

Although many interviewees declare to have certain political orientations and/or to sympathise with certain political parties the readiness to engage actively and officially in political associations is very limited. Indeed, the big majority of the respondents declares to be unwilling to participate in political associations.

It can be concluded that the widespread image of the Bulgarian politician reflects a pronounced deficit of political legitimacy. In this article political legitimacy is understood as the rightfulness of a political rule or a political order. These rightfulness consists of two dimensions: Firstly the *claim for legitimacy*, which means the claim of rightfulness on the basis of general binding principles and laws, and secondly the *belief in the legitimacy* of a political rule or a political order which means the actual recognition of the liability and the rightfulness of an order/rule by the governed (Braun/Schmitt 2009: 53/54). The surveys and developments referred to above reveal that considerable segments of the Bulgarian population clearly question the legitimacy of the perceived political action patterns and decision-making processes, of the public and political institutions' functioning and of the political office holders *per se* as well. In explicit terms: A lacking belief in the functionality of the representative democratic order's fundaments, in the possibilities and mechanisms of democratic participation and also in the transparency of the decision-making processes in the public and political sphere becomes apparent.

Political corruption as a reason for deficits of political legitimacy

Evidently the trust deficits concerning the public and political sphere and its stakeholders have partly developed due to a strong social *perception* of political corruption. This perception is nurtured by the European Union's criticism regarding pending reforms in the spheres of the judiciary and internal affairs in the framework of the Union's "Co-operation and Verification Mechanism" and mainly by the daily presence of corruption scandals in the national media (Schüler 2012a: 93 ff.). But political corruption is not only perceived through the media, it is also present in concrete personal experiences. The author conducted and collected qualitative expert interviews in Bulgaria in order to be able to analyse the character and the action of informal networks and the characteristics and backgrounds of widespread social perception patterns of the public-political sphere. Between October 2005 and February 2013 Bulgarian social scientists, leaders of the economic sphere, journalists as well as active and former political stakeholders were interviewed partly on an anonymous basis. Several interviewees talked about personal experiences with election manipulation, corrupted interactions and fraud involving the public-political sphere, for example concerning the administration of funds of the EU's PHARE-programme and concerning privatisation procedures. Through the interviews a widespread perception of a failed, exploiting state becomes apparent. "Can you make us an offer we cannot reject?" This was the question a former Bulgarian Minister of the Interior posed to the holder of an economic leadership position according to the latter's own statement. He said the minister posed the question after he himself complained about a big state enterprise's illegal attempt to get hold of the whole business of one of his clients.[6] Obviously, the minister was ready to prevent the takeover against payment of a bribe at an amount adequate for him.

The strategies for the reception and preservation of financial resources, power and key positions are indeed manifold. According to the Sofia-based think tank Center for the Study of Democracy (CSD) they include bribery and fraud, the manipulation of privatisation procedures and the support of the business interests of oligarchic enterprises and of enterprises which are *de facto* led by political actors. Illegal donations to political parties, patronage in public procurement procedures, the buying of political support and of parliamentary and judicial decisions also seem to be common practices. The CSD reports that pub-

[6] See for example anonymous interviews with A. M., manager. Sofia, 13. 1. 2013; interview I. T. with G. P., manager. Kărdžali, 23. 8. 2007; interview I. T. with A., political position holder. Trjavna, 15. 8. 2007; interview I. T. with D. J., political position holder. Sofia, 3. 10. 2005 (the author's archive).

lic resources are sometimes misused to sponsor political campaigns and that politicians sometimes manage to influence the work of the police and buy media. Furthermore the centre mentions "sponsorships" by economic stakeholders financing public projects like community centres and grounds for sports activities in order to exert an influence on the communal governments and administrations. Last but not least it mentions that political stakeholders already "bought" social associations or founded "pseudo NGOs" in order to absorb public funds (Center for the Study of Democracy 2009: 34–35, 38 f.).

A former position holder of the Bulgarian Socialist Party describes his perception of the role of corruption and informal networks for the political parties and the political sphere as follows:

> "Only those who adapt to the system can have political success. [...] Qualified people who invested years of their lives in their educational and political development are not able to break the structures although they have quite a lot of sympathisers. But if you support private economic interests you can indeed make a big political career."[7]

The informal network structures in which the favours and return services are exchanged are always shaped by personal, symbiotic relationships of dependence aiming at the preservation of political and economic power. The involved partners are position holders of political parties or political foundations and representatives of economic interests/interest groups in the form of loyal enterprises (also of the grey economy). Sometimes they are formally state-run, sometimes they are partly or entirely privatised. Personal unions of the spheres of both politics and the economy are key figures of these networks which exist at all political levels. Manolov describes these figures as "bosses being partly political and partly economic" (Manolov 2009: 286). The client relationships entertained by the stakeholders of the informal networks develop and persist on the basis of hierarchies and favouritism, kinship and friendship. Anyway, patterns of loyalty and solidarity within corrupt networks may also develop and flourish on an ethnic basis (Manolov 2009: 290 ff.).

The Bulgarian political scientist Ognjan Minčev comments on the effects of these exchange networks for the functioning of democracy:

> "The democratic processes are mostly devoid of content – thanks to the fact that oligarchical structures directly influence the decision-making processes."[8]

Indeed, influence (through the investment of trust in political and administrative position holders) as well as political and administrative key positions at the

[7] See interview with N. G., position holder, Bulgarian Socialist Party (BSP) Sofia. Sofia, 2. 10. 2012.

[8] See interview with Dr. Ognjan Minčev, director, Institute for Regional and International Studies, Sofia. Sofia, 20. 6. 2012.

national and the regional level represent important "trade products" within the informal networks. Political parties (negotiations on coalition promises already before the elections), votes and specific segments of the electorate – for example social and ethnic minorities – are trade resources as well (Manolov 2009: 290 ff.). Favours, complaisance and services "among friends" and the validness of the proverb "one must not betray one's own friends" are the binding forces of these informal networks. Apart from this they also develop and persist on the basis of extortion. People get involved in corrupt networks because their extorters have delicate information, for example about the blackmailed person's work for the socialist secret service or regarding their illegal economic activities. The blackmailed fear violence and/or the loss of their work and their social status.[9]

The *contemporary* backgrounds which have fostered political corruption since 1989/90 are manifold. Among them are weaknesses of institutions and new power vacuums that are results of the regime change and of the globalisation and Europeanisation processes as well. In this sense it is also important to mention that the stabilisation of the principles and practices of an open market economy remains a challenge to cope with. It should be added that the resources of the EU's funds available to the country – for example for agricultural aid, resources for transport and infrastructure projects, for the promotion of the economy or for regional aid – represent external "incentives" for political corruption. Presumably the low wage level in Bulgaria also triggers corrupt behaviour patterns (Schüler 2012a: 103 ff.).

The "public" and the "private" sphere: Historical and sociocultural imprints and continuities

The schemes of political patronage and privileges reflect a blurring of boundaries between the public and political and the private sphere. This phenomenon is not a product of the regime change of 1989/90 but rather a historical continuity. The perception of the state as an institution of demands and sanctions already developed during the centuries of the Ottoman foreign rule (until the end of the 19th century). The centre of power was far off in a geographical and in a perception-related sense and did not allow the political participation of the Empire's Christians. The experience of the foreign rule already brought about a distanced, sceptical, suspicious attitude regarding the exercise of political power and regarding state institutions *per se*. This attitude seemed to prove to be true in the eyes of the people after Bulgaria's independence and the experiences with the Bulgarian nation state and its institutions modelled on the European example. These historical experiences have contributed to the strengthening of private

9 See interview with G. V., specialist of an international construction company, Sofia. Sofia, 14. 1. 2013.

informal networks of kinship and friendship. In historical continuity the latter have represented the "counterpart" to the apparatus of the state which is widely perceived as an obscure, strange, far off power imposing "from above" (Höpken 2012: 29–30).

In Southeast Europe's societies "of public mistrust" (Giordano 2012: 131) the abuse of the political system of rule for private benefits has a historical background. Already during the Ottoman rule Bulgarians active in the business world negotiated profitable administrative positions with Constantinople's Ottoman viziers. The contacts were established with the help of personal networks. After successful negotiations they got public positions, for example as tax collectors, which allowed them to fetch back their "investments" in the viziers and to take profits.

On the one hand the holders of profitable positions were seen as immoral thieves. On the other hand the profiteers provoked envy. To this day political corruption is not only said to be immoral – it is also perceived as a synonym of social advancement. It becomes apparent that there is a tendency towards a moral tolerance of corruption. It is manifest in the well-known proverb "He (she) may steal but he (she) also has to change something".[10]

In January 2013 a taxi driver from Sofia explained his opinion concerning the political performance of Prime Minister Boiko Borisov as follows:

> "At least Boiko does something people experience in their day-to-day-life. Have a look at the new roads, at the extension of the subway. Sure, everything is made possible with European money. Undoubtedly they (the current political and administrative position holders, S. S.) pick a part of this money for themselves, they all do it. However, if the asphalt is finally one centimetre thinner than predetermined – will you really dwell on the subject? Will you?"

In the Balkans the terms "kelepir" and "dalavera" are in use to this day. They are of Turkish and Greek origin and it is difficult to translate them. The terms refer to bargains, to dubious but profitable trade, to fiddles "under the table". They serve to express the ambivalent perception of politics as a fraudulent and obscure but also quite profitable sphere. And they also indicate that this perception has traceable historical and socio-cultural roots. It contains the implicit claim that the "game behind the scenes of those in power – those "up there" – legitimately has to provide a benefit for the small man in the street – for "us down here". And such a benefit is hardly or not at all perceivable in people's eyes.

The widespread view regarding the public and political sphere described above expresses a deficit of trust and legitimacy which is significantly caused by repeatedly experienced failures of the state. Nowadays, "the state" seems to re-

---

[10] See interview with Dimităr Najdenov, professor, faculty for journalism and mass communication, University of Sofia. Sofia, 16. 1. 2013.

semble a body representing and administrating a "façade democracy" neglecting its legal and moral responsibility concerning the interests and legitimate requirements of the governed. *Ergo* the governing and their institutions appear to be an illegitimate player acting at the expense of the people. It results in people legitimately making use of them for their personal benefit following the slogan "one may betray the cheater and rob the thief" (Giordano 2012: 124). Hence, politics and the political sphere seem to be a dirty, dishonest business which, however, is potentially lucrative. The well-known Bulgarian writer Aleko Konstantinov already picked up the image of the politician and the political sphere in a satirical way in the 19th century. Symbolically he introduced the personality of Baj Ganjo[11], a retailer selling the essence of roses perceiving himself as a "true European" but acting with nationalistic arrogance and corrupt opportunism.

The perception of the political sphere expresses double moral standards because the assessment of the legitimacy/illegitimacy of self-enrichment with public resources is at least partly dependent on the individual position "within or outside the game". Social and client relationships, connections and loyalties have always been important personal resources ensuring access to public resources. The successful appropriation of public goods has often brought about social reputation and status. During socialism the population's political loyalty in the form of an active support of the regime or in the form of silence was "bought" with socioeconomic and medical benefits. Indeed, conformism wrung from the population with "generalised corruption" and the absence of any space to freely develop self-initiative decisively contributed to the protection of the regime's survival (Znepolski 2008: 234 ff.). At the same time corruption ensured the political and the personal loyalty of the nomenclature. The total support of the latter's superiors and of the party leadership's policies was the service they had to render. The loyal cooperation was rewarded with the provision of privileges: financial contributions, status symbols, and a preferred treatment in different spheres of life. These privileges facilitated a parallel reality of life. Towards the general population the official propaganda postulated the principles of equality and social justice (Znepolski 2008: 244 ff.).

The described characteristics have fostered an erosion of the sense of justice and counteracted the development of an appreciation for and a commitment to universalist concepts such as "common welfare" and "public interest".

One segment of the stakeholders who acceded to political and administrative key positions after 1989/90 comes from a privileged urban middle class with rural, patriarchal habits and behaviour patterns. Already during socialism they climbed up the career ladder. As part of personalised networks they took up responsible posts at the middle and higher levels of the political and administrative hierarchy. They were socialised within hierarchical relationships of subordination. Autocratic forms of political leadership as well as a strong person-centred-

---

[11] See Konstantinov, Aleko I. (1929): Baj Ganjo. Sofija: Knigoizdatelstvo T. F. Čipev.

ness are historical constants. They promote self-enrichment and strengthen the social conviction that the intentions of the population do not have any political meaning (Schüler 2012a: 104–105). The elites, which moved into political, administrative and also into economic key positions, often come from the socialist "establishment". Numerous reports of the commission for the examination of the socialist State Security files which reveal the secret service past of holders of public positions are just one of many proofs of this fact (Schüler 2008: 86). To this day a comprehensive elite change in the sense of a fundamental change of the understanding of ministry and positions and fundamentally changed relations among the political elites has not taken place. And in the same way there is no systematic opening of the socialist State Security's archives, no transparent lustration on a corresponding legal basis.

In interviews with the author a former Minister of Economic Affairs and a former deputy of the BSP attested that members of the socialist establishment significantly influenced the political developments and the privatisation processes after 1989. They explain how these "old and new elites" made use of their personalised network structures and of their possibilities to control resources before the regime change. According to the author's interview partners these people often acted beyond existing laws, beyond democratic, constitutional and market-economy-oriented regulations for their own benefit. The former Minister of Economic Affairs describes the privatisation process as a public selling off of the state to old networks and cliques under the corruption scheme of "preliminary talks with potential customers". To his mind it is the selling off of the state together with the daily media presence of corruption scandals that significantly encourage the negative social perception of the politicians and the political sphere.[12]

Indeed the great disappointment regarding the political *status quo* and historical and current experiences with the exert of political power have fostered the perception of political power as a consumable resource. *Ergo* political aspirations are only explainable in one way: with an underlying ambition regarding self-enrichment. This perception is also expressed with the well-known proverb "They all steal!", which is used to describe the politicians. It also reflects a strongly person-centred image of political power. Undoubtedly, the perceptional patterns described do not contribute to the credibility of the hypothesis that it is possible that a politician is not corrupt and they contradict the claim that the state is more than an institution of sanctions, demands and threats.

---

[12] See interview with a former Minister of Economic Affairs. Sofia, 16. 1. 2013 and interview with T., former deputy of the Bulgarian Socialist party, Sofia. Sofia, 17. 1. 2013.

The political parvenu and the čalga-politician

The well-known Bulgarian social psychologist Ivan Hadžijski already described and illustrated the meaning of clientelism and the mixing of private and public interests as characteristics of the political elites' culture in the first half of the 20th century. He introduced the figure of the career-oriented political parvenu. In his book "Authority, Dignity and Disguise", which appeared in 1932, he describes the basic characteristics, the set of values and the interactive characteristics of the political parvenu as a widespread type of politician in Bulgaria. Using an excellent, funny and ironic language style Hadžijski describes the parvenu as a personality type from the lowest social strata rapidly rising to the highest public/political positions without merits. He is morally corrupt, unscrupulous, a low qualified peasant ruffian. The political parvenu constantly tries to respond adequately to the status and the perceived needs of his high position (which is bought and obtained by fraud) using an elaborate disguise of airs and graces, pomposity and loud self-praise. He promotes himself arrogantly with boast and status symbols regarding his appearance and habits. Anyway, his hypocrisy is easy to unmask due to his low skills and educational qualification, his insufficient language skills and his rather low educational level (Hadžijski 2002: 322–323).

In contemporary Bulgaria the ethnologists Klaus Roth and Katherina Gehl identify the čalga-politician as a widespread type of political position holder. According to the ethnologists this modern type of politician embodies specific ways of thinking and forms of action of everyday culture. Roth and Gehl argue that these characteristics of everyday culture are expressed and symbolised by the music genre "čalga" (linguistic borrowing from Turkish, originally meaning music/making music), a kind of pop folk. Since the end of the 1990s it has been systematically marketed and popularised.

Čalga is a mixture of elements of Balkan folk music and traditional Roma music and elements of Rap and Pop. The origins of this music date from the middle of the 1980s in the form of a kind of rural celebration music of marginal, underprivileged social strata that was not officially recognised and supported. The contemporary čalga-music propagates a hierarchic role model and a world view which focuses on material values, on quickly and ruthlessly created wealth, status objects, artificially prettied women that subordinate to successful men – rich, powerful, muscled bosses. Roughness and licentiousness – Western stereotypes about the Balkans – are transmitted in a rather positive way in the sense of vitality and emotionality (Gehl 2010: 45 f.). Long since, čalga and the culture and the set of values it incorporates have become a mass culture in Bulgaria and other countries of the region (there, however, under different labels). According to Roth the čalga culture is a product of the rural population's mass settling in the cities during the socialist industrialisation processes. He describes it as an expression of a village-like atmosphere in the cities in the form of familiar, rural instead of universalistic thinking patterns and behaviours which to some extent still endure today (Roth 2012: 90 f.). Roth and Gehl argue that the čalga culture strongly reflects in the political elites' habits and in their widespread understanding of office. According to the ethnologists a neo-patriarchal, business-oriented male model is implicitly and explicitly incorporated and lived by quite a lot of politicians inviting čalga stars to participate in election meetings and showing rural and clientelist behaviour patterns which are based on informal networks of friends and family members. Roth argues that political personalities coming from educated, bourgeois social strata that defended and promoted universalistic sets of values have often retired from public life (Roth 2012: 92 f.).

It can be concluded that the proto-type of the čalga-politician who himself is often of rural origin/of resettled rural origin appears to be at the same time a symbol, a model, a recipient and an opportunistic user of the čalga culture. The type of politician described by Roth and Gehl does not use a disguise in the sense of Hadžijski. And he does not even need a disguise.

Competing norms and codes of conduct

To this day the historical and socio-cultural imprints traced above have influenced the characteristics of the party landscape and the political elites' understanding of office as well as the patterns of interaction in the political sphere. They foster personalisation, centralisation and deficits concerning the settlement of conflicts. They shape party and power structures, processes of elite recruitment and processes of political decision-making and the implementation of policies. They influence the administrative culture and the form of party political ties in the judicial and in the administrative system. The development of an administrative system acting independently of political loyalties and ties can hardly develop because often the administrative staff is completely changed after a change of government.

After the end of socialism with its political and administrative *status quo* in the sense of the Soviet model the former socialist states and societies are exposed to different, often competing norms and codes of conduct (Lovell 2005: 71–74). The current, valid legal and institutional framework is imported and promoted from outside by supranational institutions. With its strict separation of a private and a professionalised public sector in the Weberian sense it follows a legal and rational form of authority with a "Western" ideal image. According to this ideal model the public sector is the sphere of "public servants", of "representatives of the people" that have to act in favour of the "common good" and "public interest" on the basis of negotiated compromises. The model also implies that individuals as social base units exchange goods and values for private use and advantage within functioning market structures. It is supposed that the individuals act with "civic awareness" and on the basis of a value set based on as broad a consensus as possible. And, last but not least, that they are proactive to redress instances of maladministration and alleged grievances.

The political and administrative code of conduct of the socialist one-party system is based less on the priority of the law and the premise of a compromise-oriented negotiation of decisions than on the production of achievements, results, successes. Under the surface of the propagated ideology and the official norms the social interactions happened through and within informal networks which were *de facto* part of the system. At the same time the public institutions were regarded with deep distrust.[13] And the informal networks of kin and friends were used to recover scarce goods by compromises and "arrangements". Informal networks were a pre-condition for the access to power and influence, they were important for dealing with everyday problems – and they guaranteed the viability of the system. Apart from this the networks served as sources of solidarity between people beyond the official norms and codes of conduct.[14]

Corruption was a means of maintaining the system and an everyday necessity as well, which to this day has contributed to its perception as a part of normal life and not so much as an immoral misconduct and transgression at public expense. Thus, political corruption is not just a phenomenon of the transition period or an expression of a "Balkan lack of culture". It would also be pointless to describe it solely as an actor-related and/or institutional malfunction or as a systemic functional disorder. Political corruption should rather be considered as a complex historically rooted, systemic, sociocultural phenomenon. Under the conditions of rapid change and the Europeanisation and globalisation processes it has taken partly new backgrounds, manifestations and schemes. The corruption phenomenon should also be seen in the light of the fact that critical processes of change and "modernisation" may result in crises concerning a society's moral standards. The political corruption in Bulgaria is an indicator of the incompatibility of the principles and norms of conduct which are legally specified and the informal practices of the exercise of state power. It exists at all levels of the public institutions and of the economic sphere, as well. Undeniably it causes considerable damage to the public budgets. The strong public perception of political corruption seriously damages the social perception of the politicians and the political sphere.

Undoubtedly, the introduction of a new, very different political value system and model of order, of a new administrative system, logic and practice and, last but not least, the necessary change of the relationship between the citizen and the state still remain big challenges. In this regard the Bulgarian literary scholar and social anthropologist Aleksander Kjossev describes the *status quo* as a conglomerate: on the one hand a political and institutional framework of "Western" origin which is not sufficiently internalised in the mass consciousness and which

[13] See interview with Prof. Aleksander Kjossev, director, Center for Cultural Studies, University of Sofia. Sofia, 20. 6. 2012.

[14] The satirical comedy „The Whale“ (Kit) of the Bulgarian director Petăr B. Vasilev which dates from 1967 and which is about fishing quotas, economic plans and individual career ambitions shows all this in an excellent way.

is "imitated on the surface" mainly for the democratic legitimation of the governments and parliaments in dealing with foreign and supranational stakeholders and institutions. And, on the other hand, below the surface and as the frame's content, an everyday culture in which social interaction takes place through informal networks in which people invest trust and loyalty. With a view to the former socialist societies of Southeast Europe Kjossev sums up:

> "The result is that in these societies a factual normativity does not exist. There is an official imitation, and below it there is a vague sphere of negotiation, of pre-treating which undermines the existing norms."[15]

Conclusion

The "democratic change" in its broadest sense is still widely perceived as a process taking place at the very top of the state, far away from the reality of social life, as an obscure process showing high losses which is negotiated and led by position holders and cliques. The everyday presence of affairs of political corruption and clientelist self-enrichment with public resources in the national media considerably influences the social perception of the public/political sphere. The same applies for reports on frozen EU funds which were stopped due to criticism concerning corrupt and clientelist practices in the spheres of politics and the judiciary. Within the framework of the democratisation and Europeanisation processes – the latter described by the former Bulgarian Deputy Minister for Foreign Affairs, Antoinette Primatarova, as a "highway to Bulgaria's modernisation"[16] - the country's political and intellectual elites propagated and promised norms and values that focused on participation, basis rights and freedoms, transparency, the rule of law and market economy principles. Eagerly and full of hope large segments of the population believed them. In the light of far-reaching social and economic change processes, critical living conditions and repeated experiences concerning the abuse of their confidence the propagated norms and values have all too easily appeared as the fragments of a broken utopian dream, as an empty frame in which people currently believe as little as they believed in the propagated leading role of the communist party during socialism. Critical authorities and intellectuals defending universalist concepts have lost much of their social legitimacy and/or they have withdrawn from public life. People compare the perceived political and social *status quo* in their country to the perceived political processes and the living conditions in the "old" EU member states. In respect of this comparing view and the nurtured hopes concerning

[15] See interview with Kjossev, Sofia, 20. 6. 2012.

[16] See interview with Antoinette Primatarova, program director "European Union", Center for Liberal Strategies, Sofia and former Deputy Minister for Foreign Affairs (1997–1999). Sofia, 5. 10. 2012.

a fast improvement of a general level of prosperity in the country the raising of the average living standard in Bulgaria has become an indicator for the performance of the political elites. Especially people of the middle and older age segments who lost their social status after 1989/90 without perspectives concerning a new upward mobility predominantly feel "betrayed" by the change. Among the younger generations the phenomenon of the so-called brain drain, the migration of highly qualified specialists and students to foreign countries mainly in Western Europe and North America, is an unbroken trend. An important potential for change gets lost with this trend.

At the same time political power is generally not perceived as a resource which could serve universalist values. As long as public property is widely perceived as nobody's property which can be used for private interests a sense of responsibility for universalist concepts, such as "public interest", "justice", "equality before the law", "public welfare" or "human rights" can hardly develop. Political stakeholders who publicly push such concepts are hardly seen as credible. They are rather understood as clever agitators and it is assumed that they use the agitation for the "common good" as a trick in order to achieve the voters' support and, once in a political position, to enrich themselves.

Želju Želev, a former dissident who served as the first non-communist president of Bulgaria from 1990 to 1997 summarises in a conversation with the author:

> "In Bulgaria there is the proverb that politics is a dirty business. The truth is, it is a very difficult, ungrateful task which eats away people's spiritual and physical forces. But if politics is pursued by shameless thieves it will really become a dirty business. Here in Bulgaria this element is strongly pronounced."[17]

The entirety of the circumstances described points to a complex interrelationship: Economic developments and everyday culture on the one hand and long-term historical imprints in the form of political and institutional framework conditions, the political *status quo* and value orientations and interpretation patterns on the other hand shape the social perception of the public/political sphere. The same factors shape the characteristics of the political elites' understanding of office and their behaviour patterns, as well. *Vice versa,* the imprints of the political elites' culture act as elements of the political culture of societies and social segments; some of these elements are changeable in the short-term, others are only modifiable in the long-term. Neither this interrelationship nor the emergence and the impact of cultural layers "below" political attitudes/attitudes towards the political sphere can be sufficiently understood through opinion and attitude research relying on quantitative research methods. In the case of Bul-

[17] See interview with Dr. Želju Želev, former President of the Republic of Bulgaria (1990–1997), Sofia. Sofia, 21.6.2012.

garia and other societies of Southeast Europe mere questions regarding political attitudes and corruption perceptions on the basis of ideal-typical ideas concerning a "healthy", functioning state system all too easily lead to a one-sided rejection of observed characteristics relevant for the public/political sphere which are qualified as "uncivilised", "savage" and "backward". Such an approach clouds the view in terms of the behavioural logic behind the observed phenomena. In search of explanations regarding the perception patterns of the public/political sphere and politically relevant behaviour patterns, the political elites' approaches to the job and their understanding of office, superficial evaluations concerning the existence/the non-existence of "culture" and concerning the degree of "civilisation" in politics and societies are completely needless and redundant.

Can the growing middle class bring forth new, more independent political forces in Bulgaria and other countries in the region? Can this growing middle class become the fundamental social layer of political alternatives which can cause a decrease of the lack of political trust and legitimacy?

The enlarged European Union is confronted with significant new challenges in the form of new political decision-making structures, new/changing social problems, disparities and fears and with changing impacts of countries and regions in the world. In what sense do these challenges and their social perception and interpretation influence the political attitudes/the attitudes towards the political sphere in different societies and regions?

The so-called "established Western democracies" and democratically elected international bodies suffer from measurable disenchantment with politics and politicians and from sizeable confidence gaps and trust deficits as well. In what sense is it possible to compare or to contrast political perceptions and perceptions regarding the political sphere as well as specific politically relevant behaviour patterns in "old established" and in "new" democracies? Is it possible to trace and to explain similar phenomena across different countries and regions?

How do deficits concerning the social trust in the legitimacy of political stakeholders and institutions reflect on the functioning and the "stability" of democratic political orders?

These and many other burning questions cannot be answered in the context of this article. However, in search of the cultural dimension in the political sphere their importance for research and practical politics must not be underestimated.

References

Alfa Research 2013: Obštestveni naglasi [Social Attitudes], June. URL: http:// alpharesearch.bg/userfiles/file/Public_opinion_AR_June_2013(2).pdf, accessed 10. 10. 2013.

Alfa Research 2015: Obštestveni naglasi, January. URL: http://alpharesearch.bg/bg/socialni_izsledvania/socialni_publikacii.html, accessed 10. 3. 2015.

Almond, Gabriel A. and Sidney Verba 1963: The Civic Culture. Political Attitudes and Democracy in Five Nations. Princeton: University Press.

Braun, Daniela and Hermann Schmitt 2009: Einleitung: Begriff und Konzept der Legitimität. In: Viktoria Kaina and Andrea Römmele (eds.): Politische Soziologie: Ein Studienbuch. First edition. Wiesbaden: VS-Verlag, 53–81.

Center for the Study of Democracy 2009: Crime without Punishment: Countering Corruption and Organized Crime in Bulgaria. Sofia: CSD.

Centralna izbiratelna komisija [Central Electoral Committee] 2014: Izbori za narodni predstaviteli 2014 – rezultati ot izbori za narodni predstaviteli 05. 10. 2014 g. za stranata [Elections of the People's Representatives 2014 – Results of the Elections of the People's Representatives of 05. 10. 2014 for the Country]. URL: http://results.cik.bg/pi2014/rezultati/, accessed 9. 3. 2015.

European Commission, Eurostat 2015: Unemployment Rate by Sex and Age Groups – Annual Average, %, March. URL: http://appsso.eurostat.ec.europa.eu/nui/show.do?dataset=une_rt_ a&lang=en, accessed 9. 3. 2015.

Gehl, Katerina 2010: Čalga-Kultur als bulgarische Elite-Kultur? Zur nationalen Bedeutsamkeit eines populären Phänomens im heutigen Bulgarien. In: Südosteuropa Mitteilungen, 2, 50: 44–57.

Giordano, Christian 2007: Privates Vertrauen und informelle Netzwerke: Zur Organisationsstruktur in Gesellschaften des öffentlichen Misstrauens. Südosteuropa im Blickpunkt. In: Klaus Roth (ed.): Soziale Netzwerke und soziales Vertrauen in den Transformationsländern. Ethnologische und soziologische Untersuchungen/Social Networks and Social Trust in the Transformation Countries. Ethnological and Sociological Studies. Freiburger Sozialanthropologische Studien, Vol. 15. Zürich: LIT Verlag, 21–49.

Giordano, Christian 2012: Die politische Kultur in Gesellschaften des Öffentlichen Misstrauens: Südosteuropäische und mediterrane Parallelen. In: Sonja Schüler (ed.): Politische Kultur in (Südost)Europa: Charakteristika, Vermittlung, Wandel. München: Sagner, 119–137.

Hadžijski, Ivan 2002: Optimistična teorija za našija narod [Optimistic Theory about Our People]. Sofija: Izdatelstvo Iztok-Zapad.

Höpken, Wolfgang 2012: Gibt es eine "balkanische" politische Kultur? In: Sonja Schüler (ed.): Politische Kultur in (Südost-) Europa: Charakteristika, Vermittlung, Wandel. München: Sagner, 23–43.

Konstantinov, Aleko I. 1929: Baj Ganjo. Sofija: Knigoizdatelstvo T. F. Čipev.

Lovell, David W. 2005: Corruption as a Transitional Phenomenon: Understanding Endemic Corruption in Postcommunist States. In: Dieter Haller and Cris Shore (eds.): Corruption. Anthropological Perspectives. London: Pluto Press, 65–80.

Manolov, Georgi L. 2009: Cenata na izborite, ili kak partiite si kupuvat vlastta [The Price of the Elections or How the Political Parties Buy the Power]. Plovdiv: Universitetsko izdatelstvo Paisij Hilendarski.

Mediapool.bg 2013: I horata săs sredna zaplata u nas sa zastrašeni ot bednost [Here with Us, the People with Medium-Income are Threatened by Poverty as Well], 26 July. URL: http://www.me-diapool.bg/i-horata-sas-sredna-zaplata-u-nas-sa-zastrasheni-ot-bednost-news209385.html, accessed 1. 11. 2013.

Nacionalen statističeski institut [National Statistical Institute] (n. d.): Dohodi i razhodi na domakinstvata [Income and Expenses of the Households]. URL: http://www.nsi.bg/, accessed 9. 3. 2015.

Pardo, Italo 2004: Introduction: Corruption, Morality and the Law. In: Italo Pardo (ed.): Between Morality and the Law. Corruption, Anthropology and Comparative Society. Aldershot: Ashgate Publishing, 1–17.

Pickel, Gert and Jörg Jacobs 2006: Der soziokulturelle Unterbau der neuen Demokratien. In: Gert Pickel et al. (eds.): Osteuropas Bevölkerung auf dem Weg in die Demokratie. Repräsentative Untersuchungen in Ostdeutschland und zehn osteuropäischen Transformationsstaaten. Wiesbaden: VS-Verlag, 31–52.

Roth, Klaus 2012: Politische Kultur, Volkskultur und čalga. Beobachtungen zur politischen Kultur in Bulgarien. In: Sonja Schüler (ed.): Politische Kultur in (Südost)Europa: Charakteristika, Vermittlung, Wandel. München: Sagner, 85–98.

Schüler, Sonja 2008: Zur politischen Kultur im heutigen Bulgarien. In: Südosteuropa Mitteilungen, 6: 82–98.

Schüler, Sonja 2012a: Erscheinungsformen und Hintergründe politischer Korruption im heutigen Bulgarien. In: Balint Balla, Wolfgang Dahmen and Anton Sterbling (eds.): Korruption, soziales Vertrauen und politische Verwerfungen. Unter besonderer Berücksichtigung südosteuropäischer Gesellschaften. Hamburg: Reinhold Krämer Verlag, 93–112.

Schüler, Sonja 2012b: Izsledvane za političeski naglasi [Research on Political Attitudes]. Bălgarija 2012 (archive of the author, contact: sonja.schueler@unifr.ch).

Schüler, Sonja 2013: Abuse of Office, Informal Networks, "Moral Accountability" – Political Corruption in Bulgaria. In: Christian Giordano and Nicolas Hayoz (eds.): Informality in Eastern Europe: Structures, Political Cultures and Social Practices. Bern: Peter Lang Verlag, 223–241.

Spiegel online 2014: Proteste in Sofia: Bulgaren wehren sich gegen die korrupten Eliten, 10 January. URL: http://www.spiegel.de/politik/ausland/wut-in-bulgarien-dauer-proteste-setzen-regierung-unter-druck-a-942843.html, accessed 11. 10. 2014.

Tagesspiegel 2014: Bulgarien: Regierung nach nur 420 Tagen zurückgetreten, 24 July. URL: http://www.tagesspiegel.de/politik/bulgarien-regierung-nach-nur-420-tagen-zurueckgetre-ten/10246418.html, accessed 11. 3. 2015.

Znepolski, Ivan 2010: Bălgarskijat komunizăm. Sociokulturni čerti i vlastova traektorija [Bulgarian Communism. Sociocultural Characteristics and Power Structure]. Sofija: Ciela.

Postface

Reflections on an Abused Concept: (Ethnic) *Minority*

François Ruegg

As it often happens, the excessive use or – better – the abuse of a concept in a variety of settings and contexts brings about confusion and a lot of misunderstandings. This is what Pörksen (1988) called "plastic words"[1] that "hierarchize and colonise language and establish an expert elite for whom they serve as a resource".

The concept of *minority* seems to be one of those. It has been essentially used in two very different contexts: a strictly political one which corresponds to (and is controlled by) the respective political systems and rules, and a social, quasi moral one, which is used as a weapon in advocacy, in the general context of human rights.

In the political context of Western democracies, *minority* primarily defines a less numerous group, compared to a more numerous one, the majority. Minority is commonly linked to a political party or a grouping of parties which collect fewer votes among the population and fewer seats in Parliament.[2]

In a more general context, however, particularly in the context of social movements and social actions, *minorities* are just synonyms for *"discriminated groups"*, called minorities on behalf of their assumed smaller number and henceforth their invisibility. But in fact, their admitted smaller number almost always implies that they are, or have been, victims of *oppression* and *injustice*. The origin of this unbalanced – not to say unjust – situation is habitually linked to some traumatic historical events like war or occupation, deportation and similar. But it can also spring from new social representations or considerations of non-mainstream groups, be it according to religion, age, gender or any other factor.

In the frame of the nation-state, the term *minority* essentially points to *legally recognised differences* within the common majority model. It affects primarily the official languages, religions and political rights. With the development of international legislative bodies, however, entire parts of the population, like women and children, or the disabled, are considered as (social) *minorities* worldwide, whatever their number may be. In this post-modern, transnational and

---

[1] Quoted by Sevasti Trubeta 2006.

[2] On the difficulties of finding a common definition of the concept of minority and more specifically national minority, see Liebich 1997: 16–20.

ethnocentric (Western) conception of minorities, the term *minority* is no more neutral, as well as the term *discrimination*, which originally, i. e. etymologically, means the simple fact of being able to make a difference. For the common sense, a *minority* is, from now on, considered as a group whose members face an *unjust* situation. The latter has to be readjusted by some mechanisms or actions of compensation in the name of the sacred (because never questioned) principle of equality. *Discrimination* similarly means *the unjust treatment* of a smaller group of people, a minority.

Is it appropriate to use the same term of *minority* for groups who are non-dominant politically, mentally or physically disabled or speak a non-national language?

Ethnic minorities

One way of resolving the problem has been to add an adjective to the term minority. Hence, we speak of *religious minorities* and *ethnic minorities*. As for religious minorities, it is easy to define them in relation to the constitution of a particular nation; when it comes to *ethnic minority*, a clear definition becomes more complicated. According to the common social representation in Western Europe, an ethnic minority is forcibly non-national, i. e. *alien* and linked to a post-colonial event of displacement, related to any kind of wars or economic crisis. Hence, the concept of *ethnic minority* in Western Europe has been reserved for post-World War II non-European immigrants who generally have no, or only limited political rights. That is not to say that the concept of minority in this case is not charged with the same moral connotations. On the contrary, the supposed abuse or injustice linked to a particular ethnic minority has been exerted twice. It lies at the origin of the migration and it is now unjustly handled by the majority (deprivation of political and other rights).

These moral feelings linked to ethnic minorities in Western Europe mainly result from the common ethnocentric assumption that all groups, whatever their number is, should be equal, a view broadly inherited from the French Revolution, but not applied equally! It also springs from a general complex of culpability in the West versus its colonial past that has replaced the former complex of superiority (Bruckner 1985) linked to its "mission civilisatrice". However, history has shown that this goal, i.e. equality, is only realised, paradoxically, when cultural or ethnic differences are ignored or negated, as it was the case in France until decolonisation.

Ethnic minorities in Central and Eastern Europe

On the contrary, in the former empires that ruled over Central and Eastern Europe, the unequal status of diverse minorities allowed the cohabitation of what was called "nationalities" in the Russian and Austrian empires, and "raïa" (millet) or non-Muslims in the Ottoman Empire. This is why in Eastern Europe today *ethnic minorities* are *natives*[3] from a different *culture*, mainly from a different language and religious affiliation.

They became *minorities* only by the adoption of a constitution in the new nation-states in the last century. Their rights are much extended in certain countries like Romania where they enjoy, as minorities, broad political rights, whereas in others, like Bulgaria, they still struggle with their past as subjects of the Ottoman Empire[4]. It is also to say that sometimes former *ruling* minorities became simple minorities, like the Russians in the former Soviet empire or Hungarians and Germans in Transylvania.

Yet, the question of what an ethnic group really *is* has been eluded for a long time in social anthropology (Gossiaux 1997). Regarding this debate the contribution of the Russian school of ethnography is well known and I shall not recall it here. Max Weber himself renounced using this concept[5] after having pointed to its fuzziness. Ethnicity remains an ambiguous term as it stays between something that *is* and something that is believed to be something. In his critical view, however, Weber nevertheless anticipated the importance of the symbolic dimension of the ethnic arsenal developed by many scholars in the constructivist period (Barth 1969, Anderson 1983, Amselle 2005, among many others). In particular *imagined communities* play a major role in today's politics and the ethnic factor, although imagined, seems to have driven and to still drive the mapping of the post socialist world by main political actors.

It is surprising, though, that the concept of *ethnic minority* is still used in social sciences, at a time when social scientists, rejecting essentialism and preaching methodological individualism, advocate for a better consideration of multiple identities and individual strategies. In principle, interactionism and constructivism have replaced the older classical (cultural) approaches to ethnicity, particularly in the field of religious and ethnic identities (Brubaker 2002, Frame 2013). However, the question remains, of how we can, as social scientists, combine these two contradictory approaches with the concept of identity, as – on the one hand – individuals are part of a community and on the other hand their identities depend on individual choices.[6]

---

[3] That is to say that they are not of recent immigration but have been living under the rule of the above-mentioned empires for several centuries.

[4] The different campaigns to *bulgarise* Turks under the communist regime are well known, as well as the case of Muslims in Bosnia. For Romania the late acquisition of Dobrudja at once brought new "minorities" in the nation state but also created the opportunity for Romanians to colonise this new "Romanian" province.

[5] Quoted in Gossiaux 1997: 28.

[6] In the above-mentioned article Gossiaux proposes to compare the role of ethnicity with the one of kinship (ibidem).

Ethnic minorities and places in Eastern Europe

While referring to Eastern Europe, Rogers Brubaker uses the terms "ethnicity" and "nationality" interchangeably:

> "In US and much of northern and western Europe, 'nationality' ordinarily means 'citizenship', that is, membership of the state; and 'nation' and 'state' are often used interchangeably. In central and eastern Europe, by contrast, 'nation' and 'nationality' do not refer in the first instance to the state, but ordinarily invoke an ethno-cultural frame of reference independent of – and often cutting across the boundaries of – statehood and citizenship. To identify oneself as Hungarian by nationality in Transylvania is to invoke a state-transcending Hungarian ethno-cultural 'nation'. In the text, following the usage in this setting, I use 'ethnic' and 'national' interchangeably"[7] (Brubaker 2002, 178).

Another theoretical problem arises when using the notion of (ethnic) minorities in Eastern Europe. It mainly concerns their *location*. Politically speaking, a *minority* is related to a territory, a state or a province within this state. This place will normally explain the origin of the minority according to the history of the nation it lives in. It can be the borderland of the new nation state which is situated next to the "mother country" and was part of it in former times, like Transylvania for Romanians versus Hungary, or it can also be an enclave or several enclaves in and out of the national territory. Former nomadic populations that have been forced to stay in a confined area and are separated from their fellow ethnics by new national frontiers, as it is the case for Aromanians or Macedoromanians, also represent a kind of minority. But a minority can also form a separate nation, as a result of the successive exchanges of territories, as it is the case in the Republic of Moldova, or as a result of politics and lobbying following possible civil wars, as in Kosovo, Abkhazia and the other former Yugoslavian provinces which became new nations under the pressure of international politics.

To take just one example of the existing confusion in the minority terminology, it is interesting to observe that in Romania there is a distinction in the public discourses between *national*, *historical* and *ethnic* minorities, but also sometimes confusion. The liberal school, following a European trend, speaks about *national minorities* as the constitution does. A more international trend, following the US model, uses the *ethnic* term for ethnic minorities as well as *inter-ethnic* relations, even when speaking about the relations between Romanians and Hungarians, both members of the EU. However, the confusion is frequent in the

[7] See R. Brubaker 2002, footnote 17, p. 178.

public and also in academic discourses, probably partly due to translations, depending on whether they follow the European or the American dictionary![8]

This underlines that it is not possible, and not even useful, to find a universal definition of the term *minority*. As a matter of fact, there is little in common between a "black minority" in Southern Africa dominated by "a white minority" and a "Hungarian ethnic-national minority" in Transylvania, formerly politically dominant. It is more important to consider the political objectives behind the notion of minority than it is to give it a strict definition. Hence, the distinction between *ethnic minorities* and *national* ones, also called *historic* since they are considered to having contributed to the construction of the nation, makes sense in terms of establishing a hierarchy among them. *Ethnic minorities* in Romania are those who had neither shared or even enjoyed any political power during history, nor had a territory in the national state: Jews, Armenians, Roma/Gypsies. Some have a national territory outside their residential nation, others do not. Obviously their social status is lower than the status of *historical minorities;* meanwhile their political status is the same in principle[9].

Another important aspect regarding *minorities* in Eastern Europe is their historical fate. Indeed history remains crucial to understand the present status of (national) minorities. Yet, we all know that among the many present ethnic minorities in Eastern Europe only a few have been stably settled for more than 60 years. Census and statistics nevertheless make us consider ethnic minorities as if they have existed and been "untouched" for centuries. In the process we forget about their mobility, i. e. their free or forced migrations, an important political tool for controlling minorities, a tool used by Russian emperors as well as by Soviet and other communist commissaries during the 20th century (Grigoriantz 2001). Migrations happened in the framework of the Austrian, Ottoman and Russian Empires and later again, after several wars that ended with a change of national frontiers and the instauration of political nationalistic dictatorships and ethnic cleansing policies.

But many of these "exchanges of populations" were ordered by the political leaders after World War I and II in view of reinforcing the national state, as it was the case for the exchanges of populations between Greece and Turkey. These decisions as well as the horrors perpetrated against the civil populations who had the misfortune of being in the way of the German and the Soviet armies (Snyder 2013) – Ukrainians, Poles, Gypsies and Jews, to mention only the most important groups – completely changed the map of minorities in Central and Eastern

[8] In a conference entitled "The Romanian model of interethnic relations" held in 2000 in Bucharest, Minister Isarescu started by speaking of *nationalities*, according to the Soviet vocabulary. The book in which the speech is published uses *interethnic,* meanwhile the collection in which the book has been published says *Ethnocultural diversity in Romania*! See: "Interethnic relations in post-communist Romania" 2000: 47.

[9] On the history of the political status of Roma/Gypsies in Eastern Europe see Barany 2002.

Europe, and also in Central Asia, where millions of deportees were sent to the Gulags in Siberia or Kazakhstan. Religious conversion campaigns, as well as atheist persecution brought many groups to move, too, either voluntarily or forcibly. Finally sedentarisation policies against the Roma/Gypsies but also against the Aromanians and other nomadic pastoral people were implemented in the 18th century and equally contributed to modify the places of these "minorities". The opening of the borders after the collapse of the communist regimes resulted in blurring the map of minorities, mixing up the categories of migrants and creating new minorities of workers and unemployed, if not beggars.

Contradictory minorities

Minorities have been considered in many different ways in social sciences and theories about multiculturalism reflect these views. In his article on anthropology and multiculturalism (1993), Terence Turner analyses *contradictory multiculturalisms* versus *contradictory anthropologies*. Although we do not share his post-modern, anti-Western and egalitarian views, most of his conceptual frame could be used to discuss *our* "contradictory minorities". He opposes the traditional concept of culture in anthropology to the reshaped concept of culture in cultural studies.

Looking at the way in which minorities are treated by politics and activists, one could easily transfer the opposition between an empiric definition of the minorities, based upon the number, an arithmetical minority, and the moral definition used by social scientists and activists in the discourses about minorities, particularly in Eastern and Central Europe.

The politics of multiculturalism does not point to a simple fact. On the contrary, it happens in a political setting, meant to *empower* so called minority groups. In this blurred semantic context minorities are no longer smaller groups of people in a national society, but like it happened with the concept of culture, they are the expression of diverse groups of interest trying to obtain a better, or a so called *equal* status.

Ethnic minorities therefore are only nominally ethnic, since they are mainly created as such from the outside, i. e. they are ascribed identities. This became particularly visible with the emergence of a Roma transnational *minority* in the late 1990s (Boscoboinik and Ruegg 2009). Whatever the conclusions may be about their origin and history, the Roma were and still are the object of a social and political engineering. Activists aim at their promotion as a transnational European minority; meanwhile some media present them also as a minority, but consider them as globally undesirable. This "positive" or "negative" *ethnogenesis* (Liebich 2007) turns a blind eye to their multiply facetted identities in terms of (ethnic) affiliations, occupations and denominations, as well as to economic status and visibility (Ruegg 2009), and once again falls in the grouping trap. Here politics is in full contradiction with social sciences, at least in theory.

Imagined minorities

It might be is better to adopt another, more classic view in anthropology about minorities, ethnic or not, and to consider them as *imagined*. I prefer to use the term *imagined* to that of *constructed* because imagination is powerful and efficient. Minorities are imagined by the majority and by the state as well as by their (imagined) members themselves. In any case, the illusion of existing minorities can become a powerful political instrument, both at the state level and at the grassroots level. In naming and defining ethnic or other minorities, national or alien, the state also finds a way to control them. In proclaiming itself as a minority, a constructed group, be it political, ethnic or social, can claim and obtain new or more rights.

In conclusion, I think that the term *minority* should be kept in its original cradle: the political arena. This political tool is worth being examined as such by anthropologists, but it has little to do with social sciences as an instrumental concept. It shows, however, the mechanics of the political game.

References

Amselle, Jean-Loup 2005: Au cœur de l'ethnie ethnies, tribalisme et Etat en Afrique. Paris: La Découverte.

Anderson, Benedict 2003: Imagined Communities: Reflections on the Origin and Spread of Nationalism. London, New York: Verso.

Barany, Zoltan 2002: The East European Gypsies, Regime Change, Marginality and Ethnopolitics. Cambridge: Cambridge University Press.

Barth, Frederik 1969: Ethnic Groups and Boundaries: The Social Organization of Culture Difference. Boston: Little, Brown and Co.

Boscoboinik, Andrea and François Ruegg 2009: Nouvelles identités rom en Europe centrale & orientale. Transitions, Vol. XLVIII-2. Bruxelles, Genève: Université de Genève, Institut Européen et ULB, Bruxelles.

Brubaker, Rogers 2002: Ethnicity without Groups. In: European Journal of Sociology, 43, 2, August 2002: 163–189.

Bruckner, Pascal 1983: Le sanglot de l'homme blanc: Tiers monde, culpabilité, haine de soi. Paris: Seuil.

Frame, Alexander 2013: Communication et interculturalité. Cultures et interactions interpersonnelles. Paris: Hermès/Lavoisier, coll. Forme et sens.

Gossiaux, Jean-François 1997: Ethnicité, nationalité, nation. In: Marc Abélès: Anthropologie du politique. Paris: Colin, 27–40.

Grigoriantz, Alexandre 2002: Les damnés de la Russie. Le déplacement de populations comme méthode de gouvernement. Genève: Georg.

Interethnic Relations in Post-Communist Romania 2000: Proceedings of the Conference "The Romanian Model of Ethnic Relations. The Last Ten Years, the Next Ten Years". Lucian Nastasa and Levente Salat (eds.). Cluj: Ethnocultural Diversity Resource Center.

Liebich, André 1997: Les minorités nationales en Europe centrale et orientale. Genève: Georg.

Liebich, André 2007: Roma Nation? Competing Narratives of Nationhood. In: Nationalism and Ethnic Politics, 13, 4: 539–554.

Ruegg, François 2009: Tsiganes en Europe centrale-orientale. La fin du voyage? In: Nouvelles identités rom en Europe centrale & orientale, Transitions, XLVIII, 2: 5–17.

Snyder, Timothy 2013: Terres de sang: l'Europe entre Hitler et Staline. Paris: Gallimard.

Trubeta, Sevasti 2006: Hybridity in Post-Colonial Discourse and in South-East European Studies. In: Dieter Stern and Christian Voss (eds.): Marginal Linguistic Identities, Studies in Slavic Contacts and Borderland Varieties. Wiesbaden: Harrassowitz, 31–43.

Turner, Terence 2013: Anthropology and Multiculturalism. What Is Anthropology that Multiculturalists Should Be Mindful of It? In: Cultural Anthropology, 8, 4: 411–429.

The Authors

Prof. Nebi Bardhoshi, Institute of Cultural Anthropology and Art Studies, University of Tirana, Albania

Prof. Nino Chikovani, Cultural Studies, Ivane Javakhishvili Tbilisi State University, Tbilisi, Georgia

Ingrida Gečienė, Researcher, Lithuanian Social Research Centre, Vilnius, Lithuania

Prof. Christian Giordano, Chair of Social Anthropology, University of Fribourg, Switzerland

Dr. Sorin Gog, Lecturer, Department of Sociology, Babeș-Bolyai University, Cluj-Napoca, Romania

Dr. Caroline Hornstein Tomić, Researcher, Institute of Social Sciences Ivo Pilar, Zagreb, Croatia

Prof. Nino Pirtskhalava, Institute of Comparative Literature, Ilia State University, Tbilisi, Georgia

Antoinette Primatarova, Programme Director European Union, Centre for Liberal Strategies, Sofia, Bulgaria

Prof. François Ruegg, Chair of Social Anthropology, University of Fribourg, Switzerland

Dr. Sonja Schüler, Research and Teaching Assistant, Chair of Social Anthropology, University of Fribourg, Switzerland

Dr. Magdalena Slavkova, Post-Doc, Institute of Ethnology and Folklore Studies with Ethnographic Museum, Balkan Ethnology Department, Bulgarian Academy of Sciences, Sofia, Bulgaria